Build a software development environment with Vim and Neovim

Ruslan Osipov

D1736603

Packt>

BIRMINGHAM - MUMBAI

Mastering Vim

Commissioning Editor: Pavan Ramchandani
Acquisition Editor: Chaitanya Nair
Content Development Editor: Pooja Parvatkar
Technical Editor: Divya Vadhyar
Copy Editor: Safis Editing
Project Coordinator: Ulhas Kambali
Proofreader: Safis Editing
Indexer: Rekha Nair
Graphics: Tom Scaria
Production Coordinator: Deepika Naik

First published: November 2018

Production reference: 2181218

Published by Packt Publishing Ltd.
Livery Place
35 Livery Street
Birmingham
B3 2PB, UK.

ISBN 978-1-78934-109-6

www.packtpub.com

To my mother Lilia and my loving partner Elisabeth, who survived my anxiety over writing this book

– Ruslan Osipov

`mapt.io`

Mapt is an online digital library that gives you full access to over 5,000 books and videos, as well as industry leading tools to help you plan your personal development and advance your career. For more information, please visit our website.

Why subscribe?

- Spend less time learning and more time coding with practical eBooks and Videos from over 4,000 industry professionals

- Improve your learning with Skill Plans built especially for you

- Get a free eBook or video every month

- Mapt is fully searchable

- Copy and paste, print, and bookmark content

Packt.com

Did you know that Packt offers eBook versions of every book published, with PDF and ePub files available? You can upgrade to the eBook version at `www.packt.com` and as a print book customer, you are entitled to a discount on the eBook copy. Get in touch with us at `customercare@packtpub.com` for more details.

At `www.packt.com`, you can also read a collection of free technical articles, sign up for a range of free newsletters, and receive exclusive discounts and offers on Packt books and eBooks.

Contributors

About the author

Ruslan Osipov is a software engineer at Google, an avid traveler, and a part-time blogger. He is a self-taught engineer. He started publishing personal Vim notes in 2012, and became increasingly interested in the intricacies of the editor and its applications in optimizing development workflows.

I'd like to say thank you to Chaitanya, who reached out to me and guided me through the outline; Pooja, who tirelessly edited my drafts; Divya, who meticulously reviewed the code; and everyone else from Packt who worked on this book and I haven't had a chance to meet. A huge thank you to Bram for reviewing this book. A word goes out to the Vim Japan conference organizers—Tatsuhiro Ujihisa (Uji), Taro Muraoka (KaoriYa), Thinca, Aomoririingo, Mopp, Yasuhiro Matsumoto (Mattn), t9md, and Guyon (and anyone else I missed). Thank you for your hospitality! Best regards to my supportive colleagues and cubicle mates at Google, and especially my manager, Patrick, who helped me balance writing this book with my career.

About the reviewer

Bram Moolenaar is the creator and maintainer of Vim. He has been working on it for 27 years, and has no plans to stop improving it, thanks to the many volunteers who provide patches and test new versions.

After studying electronics and inventing parts of digital copying machines, Bram decided that creating open source software was more useful and fun, so he worked on that exclusively for several years. He currently works for Google, one of the few companies that fully embrace open source software. In between, he did voluntary work on a project in Uganda and is still helping poor children there through the I Care Children Foundation(ICCF).

> *I would like to thank all the Vim developers for helping me make Vim into what it is today. Without them, only a fraction of the features would have been implemented and the quality would not have been nearly as high. I would also like to thank all the plugin writers for building on top of Vim and making complex features available to users (so that I don't have to!). And finally, I would like to thank Ruslan for writing a book that not only aids users with Vim's built-in features, but also with getting to know and use plugins.*

Packt is searching for authors like you

If you're interested in becoming an author for Packt, please visit `authors.packtpub.com` and apply today. We have worked with thousands of developers and tech professionals, just like you, to help them share their insight with the global tech community. You can make a general application, apply for a specific hot topic that we are recruiting an author for, or submit your own idea.

Table of Contents

Preface   1

Chapter 1: Getting Started   5
  Technical requirements   6
  Let's start a conversation (about modal interfaces)   6
  Installation   7
    Setting up on Linux   7
    Setting up on MacOS   9
      Using Homebrew   9
      Downloading a .dmg image   13
    Setting up on Windows   15
      Unix-like experience with Cygwin   15
        Installing Cygwin   16
        Using Cygwin   18
      Visual Vim with gVim   21
    Verifying and troubleshooting the installation   24
  Vanilla Vim vs gVim   26
  Configuring Vim with your .vimrc   27
  Common operations (or how to exit Vim)   29
    Opening files   29
    Changing text   31
    Saving and closing files   33
      A word about swap files   34
  Moving around: talk to your editor   36
  Making simple edits in insert mode   40
  Persistent undo and repeat   43
  Read the Vim manual using :help   44
  Summary   48

Chapter 2: Advanced Editing and Navigation   49
  Technical requirements   49
  Installing plugins   50
  Organizing workspace   51
    Buffers   52
    Plugin spotlight – unimpaired   54
    Windows   55
      Creating, deleting, and navigating windows 55
      Moving windows   58
      Resizing windows   64
    Tabs   65
    Folds   66

Folding Python code	67
Types of folds	69
Navigating file trees	**70**
Netrw	70
:e with wildmenu enabled	72
Plugin spotlight – NERDTree	73
Plugin spotlight – Vinegar	75
Plugin spotlight – CtrlP	77
Navigating text	**78**
Jumping into insert mode	82
Searching with / and ?	82
Searching across files	84
ack	86
Utilizing text objects	87
Plugin spotlight – EasyMotion	89
Copying and pasting with registers	**91**
Where do the registers come in?	92
Copying from outside of Vim	94
Summary	**95**
Chapter 3: Follow the Leader - Plugin Management	**97**
Technical requirements	**97**
Managing plugins	**98**
vim-plug	98
Honorable mentions	102
Vundle	102
Do it yourself	104
Pathogen	106
Profiling slow plugins	106
Profiling startup	106
Profiling specific actions	108
Deeper dive into modes	**112**
Normal mode	112
Command-line and ex modes	112
Insert mode	114
Visual and select mode	114
Replace and virtual replace mode	116
Terminal mode	117
Remapping commands	**118**
Mode – aware remapping	120
The leader key	**121**
Configuring plugins	**122**
Summary	**126**
Chapter 4: Understanding the Text	**127**
Technical requirements	**127**

Code autocomplete 127
Built-in autocomplete 128
YouCompleteMe 129
Installation 129
Using YouCompleteMe 131
Navigating the code base with tags 134
Exuberant Ctags 135
Automatically updating the tags 139
Undo tree and Gundo 139
Summary 143

Chapter 5: Build, Test, and Execute 145
Technical requirements 145
Working with version control 146
Quick-and-dirty version control and Git introduction 146
Concepts 147
Setting up a new project 147
Cloning an existing repository 149
Working with Git 149
Adding files, committing, and pushing 149
Creating and merging branches 152
Integrating Git with Vim (vim-fugitive) 154
Resolving conflicts with vimdiff 158
Comparing two files 158
vimdiff and Git 162
git config 163
Creating merge conflict 163
Resolving a merge conflict 164
tmux, screen, and Vim terminal mode 167
tmux 167
Panes are just like splits 168
Windows are just like tabs 171
Sessions are invaluable 172
tmux and Vim splits 172
Screen 174
Terminal mode 174
Building and testing 177
Quickfix list 177
Location list 180
Building code 180
Plugin spotlight: vim-dispatch 181
Testing code 182
Plugin spotlight – vim-test 182
Syntax checking code with linters 183
Using linters with Vim 183
Plugin spotlight – Syntastic 185
Plugin spotlight – ALE 187

Summary	189
Chapter 6: Refactoring Code with Regex and Macros	191
Technical requirements	191
Search or replace with regular expressions	191
Search and replace	192
Operations across files using arglist	196
Regex basics	198
Special regex characters	198
Alternation and grouping	199
Quantifiers or multis	200
More about magic	201
Magic	201
No magic	201
Very magic	202
Applying the knowledge in practice	202
Renaming a variable, a method, or a class	202
Reordering function arguments	204
Recording and playing macros	207
Editing macros	214
Recursive macros	215
Running macros across multiple files	218
Using plugins to do the job	218
Summary	219
Chapter 7: Making Vim Your Own	221
Technical requirements	221
Playing with the Vim UI	221
Color schemes	222
Browsing the color schemes	224
Common issues	224
The status line	225
Powerline	226
Airline	228
gVim-specific configuration	229
Keeping track of configuration files	230
Healthy Vim customization habits	231
Optimizing your workflow	231
Keeping .vimrc organized	232
Summary	235
Chapter 8: Transcending the Mundane with Vimscript	237
Technical requirements	237
Why Vimscript?	238
How to execute Vimscript	238
Learning the syntax	241
Setting variables	241

Surfacing output   243
Conditional statements   244
Lists   246
Dictionaries   249
Loops   250
Functions   253
Classes   255
Lambda expressions   256
Map and filter   257
Interacting with Vim   260
File-related commands   261
Prompts   261
Using :help   266
A word about style guides   266
Let's build a plugin   267
Plugin layout   267
The basics   268
Housekeeping   273
Improving our plugin   276
Distributing the plugin   281
Where to take the plugin from here   282
Further reading   282
Summary   283

Chapter 9: Neovim   285
Technical requirements   285
Why make another Vim?   285
Installing and configuring Neovim   286
Checking health   288
Sane defaults   290
Oni   291
Neovim plugin highlights   294
Summary   295

Chapter 10: Where to Go from Here   297
Seven habits of effective text editing   297
Modal interfaces everywhere   298
A Vim-like web browsing experience   299
Vimium and Vimium-FF   299
Alternatives   302
Vim everywhere else   303
vim-anywhere for Linux and macOS   303
Text Editor Anywhere for Windows   304
Recommended reading and communities   305
Mailing lists   305
IRC   305

Other communities – learning resources | 306

Summary | 306

Other Books You May Enjoy | 309

Index | 313

Preface

Mastering Vim will introduce you to the wonderful world of Vim through examples of working with Python code and tools in a project-based fashion. This book will prompt you to make Vim your primary IDE, since you will learn to use it for any programming language.

Who this book is for

Mastering Vim has been written for beginner, intermediate, and expert developers. The book will teach you to effectively embed Vim in your daily workflow. No prior experience with Python or Vim is required.

What this book covers

Chapter 1, *Getting Started*, introduces the reader to basic concepts and the world of Vim.

Chapter 2, *Advanced Editing and Navigation*, covers movement and more complex editing operations, and introduces a number of plugins.

Chapter 3, *Follow the Leader – Plugin Management*, talks about modes, mappings, and managing your plugins.

Chapter 4, *Understanding the Text*, helps you interact with, and navigate, code bases in a semantically meaningful way.

Chapter 5, *Build, Test, and Execute,* explores options for running code in, or alongside, your editor.

Chapter 6, *Refactoring Code with Regex and Macros*, takes a deeper look at refactoring operations.

Chapter 7, *Making Vim Your Own*, discusses options available for further customizing your Vim experience.

Chapter 8, *Transcending the Mundane with Vimscript*, dives into the powerful scripting language Vim provides.

Chapter 9, *Neovim*, showcases one of Vim's younger siblings.

Chapter 10, *Where to Go from Here*, provides some farewell food for thought and points at a few places on the internet you might be interested in.

Download the example code files

The code bundle for the book is hosted on GitHub at https://github.com/PacktPublishing/Mastering-Vim. In case there's an update to the code, it will be updated on the existing GitHub repository.

We also have other code bundles from our rich catalog of books and videos available at https://github.com/PacktPublishing/. Check them out!

In addition, you can download the example code files for this book from your account at www.packt.com. If you purchased this book elsewhere, you can visit www.packt.com/support and register to have the files emailed directly to you.

You can download the code files by following these steps:

1. Log in or register at www.packt.com.
2. Select the **SUPPORT** tab.
3. Click on **Code Downloads & Errata**.
4. Enter the name of the book in the **Search** box and follow the onscreen instructions.

Once the file is downloaded, please make sure that you unzip or extract the folder using the latest version of:

- WinRAR/7-Zip for Windows
- Zipeg/iZip/UnRarX for Mac
- 7-Zip/PeaZip for Linux

Conventions used

There are a number of text conventions used throughout this book.

`CodeInTxt`: Indicates code words in text, database table names, folder names, filenames, file extensions, pathnames, dummy URLs, user input, and Twitter handles. Here is an example: "Mount the downloaded `WebStorm-10*.dmg` disk image file as another disk in your system."

A block of code is set as follows:

```
" Manage plugins with vim-plug.
call plug#begin()
call plug#end()
```

When we wish to draw your attention to a particular part of a code block, the relevant lines or items are set in bold:

```
" Manage plugins with vim-plug.
call plug#begin()

Plug 'scrooloose/nerdtree'
Plug 'tpope/vim-vinegar'
Plug 'ctrlpvim/ctrlp.vim'
Plug 'mileszs/ack.vim'
Plug 'easymotion/vim-easymotion'

call plug#end()
```

Any command-line input is written as follows:

```
$ cd ~/.vim
$ git init
```

Bold: Indicates a new term, an important word, or words that you see on screen. For example, words in menus or dialog boxes appear in the text like this. Here is an example: "Select **System info** from the **Administration** panel."

 Warnings or important notes appear like this.

Tips and tricks appear like this.

Get in touch

Feedback from our readers is always welcome.

General feedback: If you have questions about any aspect of this book, mention the book title in the subject of your message and email us at customercare@packtpub.com.

Errata: Although we have taken every care to ensure the accuracy of our content, mistakes do happen. If you have found a mistake in this book, we would be grateful if you would report this to us. Please visit www.packt.com/submit-errata, selecting your book, clicking on the Errata Submission Form link, and entering the details.

Piracy: If you come across any illegal copies of our works in any form on the internet, we would be grateful if you would provide us with the location address or website name. Please contact us at copyright@packt.com with a link to the material.

If you are interested in becoming an author: If there is a topic that you have expertise in, and you are interested in either writing or contributing to a book, please visit authors.packtpub.com.

Reviews

Please leave a review. Once you have read and used this book, why not leave a review on the site that you purchased it from? Potential readers can then see and use your unbiased opinion to make purchase decisions, we at Packt can understand what you think about our products, and our authors can see your feedback on their book. Thank you!

For more information about Packt, please visit packt.com.

1
Getting Started

Welcome to Mastering Vim, a book which will teach you to get good with Vim, its plugins, and its ideological successors!

This chapter will establish a foundation for working with Vim. Every tool is built with a particular usage philosophy in mind, and Vim is not an exception. Vim introduces a different way of working with text compared to what most people are used to these days. This chapter focuses on highlighting these differences and establishing a set of healthy editing habits. It will let you approach Vim in a Vim-friendly frame of mind and will ensure you're using the right tools for the job. To make examples concrete, we will be using Vim to create a small Python application throughout this chapter.

The following topics will be covered in this chapter:

- Modal versus modeless interfaces, and why is Vim different from other editors
- Installing and updating Vim
- The gVim - the graphical user interface for Vim
- Configuring Vim for working with Python and editing your `.vimrc` file
- Common file operations: opening, modifying, saving, and closing files
- Moving around: navigating with arrow keys, `hjkl`, by words, paragraphs, and so on

- Making simple edits to files and combining editing commands with movement commands
- Persistent undo history
- Navigating the built-in Vim manual

Technical requirements

Throughout this chapter we will be writing a basic Python application. You don't have to download any code to follow along with this chapter as we'll be creating files from scratch. However, if you ever get lost and need more guidance, you can view the resulting code on GitHub:

```
https://github.com/PacktPublishing/Mastering-Vim/tree/master/Chapter01
```

We will be using Vim to primarily write Python code throughout this book, and it is assumed that the reader is somewhat familiar with the language. Examples assume you're using Python 3 syntax.

> If you must live in the past, you can convert Python 3 examples to Python 2 code by changing the `print()` command syntax. Change all of `print('Woof!')` to `print 'Woof!'` to make the code run in Python 2.

We will also be creating and modifying Vim configuration, which is stored in a `.vimrc` file. The resulting `.vimrc` file is available from the previously mentioned GitHub link.

Let's start a conversation (about modal interfaces)

If you've ever edited text before, you are most likely to be familiar with modeless interfaces. It's the default option chosen by modern mainstream text editors, and that's how many of us learned to work with text.

The term *modeless* refers to the fact that the each interface element has only one function. Each button press results in a letter showing up on screen, or some other action being performed. Each key (or a combination of keys) always does the same thing: the application always operates in a single mode.

But it's not the only way.

Welcome to the modal interface, where each trigger performs a different action based on context. The most common example of a modal interface that we encounter today is a smartphone. Each time we work in different applications or open different menus, a tap on the screen performs a different function.

It's similar when it comes to text editors. Vim is a modal editor, meaning that a single button press might result in different actions, depending on context. Are you in insert mode (a mode for entering text)? Then hitting o would put the letter o on the screen. But as soon as you switch into a different mode, the letter o will change its function to adding a new line below the cursor.

Working with Vim is like having a conversation with your editor. You tell Vim to delete the next three words by pressing d3w (**d**elete **3 w**ords), and you ask Vim to change text inside quotes by pressing ci" (**c**hange **i**nside " [quotes]).

You may hear very frequently that Vim is faster than other editors, but it's not necessarily the point of Vim. Vim lets you stay in the flow when working with text. You don't have to break the pace to reach for your mouse, you don't have to hit a single key exactly 17 times to get to a particular spot on the page. You don't have to drag your mouse millimeter by millimeter to ensure you capture the right set of words to copy and paste.

When working with a modeless editor, workflow is filled with interruptions.

Working with modal editors, and Vim in particular, is like having a conversation with your editor. You ask the editor to perform actions ("delete three words", "change inside quotes") in a consistent language. With Vim, editing becomes a much more deliberate exercise.

Installation

Vim is available on every platform, and comes installed on Linux and Mac OS (however, you may want to upgrade Vim to a more recent version). Find your system in the following paragraphs, and skim through the instructions to set up.

Setting up on Linux

Linux machines come with Vim installed, which is great news! However, it might be rather out of date, and Vim 8 introduces some much-needed optimizations. Pull up your Command Prompt, and run the following code:

```
$ git clone https://github.com/vim/vim.git
$ cd vim/src
$ make
$ sudo make install
```

If you're running into issues as you're installing Vim, you might be missing some dependencies. If you're using a Debian-based distribution, the following command should add common missing dependencies : $ sudo apt-get install make build-essential libncurses5-

```
$ sudo apt-get install make build-essential libncurses5-
dev
   libncursesw5-dev --fix-missing
```

This will make sure you're on the latest major and minor patch of Vim. If you don't care for being on the cutting edge, you can also update Vim using a package manager of your choice. Different Linux distributions use different package managers; the following list includes some common ones:

Distribution	Command to install the latest version of Vim
Debian-based (Debian, Ubuntu, Mint)	`$ sudo apt-get update` `  $ sudo apt-get install vim-gtk`
CentOs (and Fedora prior to Fedora 22)	`$sudo yum check-update` `$sudo yum install vim-enhanced`
Fedora 22+	`$sudo dnf check-update` `$sudo dnf install vim-enhanced`
Arch	`$sudo pacman -Syu` `$sudo pacman -S gvim`
FreeBSD	`$sudo pkg update` `$sudo pkg install vim`

You can see in the preceding table that Vim uses package names for different repositories. Packages like `vim-gtk` on Debian-based distributions or `vim-enhanced` on CentOS come with more features enabled (like GUI support for instance).

Do keep in mind that package manager repositories tend to lag behind from anywhere between a few months to a few years.

That's it, you're now ready to dive into the world of Vim! You can start the editor by typing the following command:

```
$ vim
```

On modern systems, you can also start Vim by invoking `vi`. However, it's not always the case: on older systems the two are different binaries. Vi is **Vim**'s predecessor (Vim stands for **Vi improved**). Today, it's merely an alias pointing to Vim. There are no reasons to use Vi over Vim, unless, for some reason, you're unable to install the latter.

Setting up on MacOS

MacOS comes prepackaged with Vim, but the version can be outdated. There are a few ways to install a fresh version of Vim, and this book will cover two. First, you can install Vim using Homebrew, a package manager for MacOS. You'll have to install Homebrew first, though. Second, you can download a `.dmg` image of MacVim. This experience would be more familiar because Mac users are used to the visual interface.

Since this book covers interactions with the Command line, I recommend taking the Homebrew route. But you're welcome to go forward with installing the image if interacting with the Command line does not interest you.

Using Homebrew

Homebrew is a third-party package manager for MacOS which makes it easy to install and keep packages up to date. Instructions on how to install Homebrew are available on `https://brew.sh`, and, as of the moment of writing this book, consist of a single line executed in the following Command line:

```
$ /usr/bin/ruby -e "$(curl -fsSL
https://raw.githubusercontent.com/Homebrew/install/master/install)"
```

The following screenshot shows the list of operations you will then see Homebrew perform during installation:

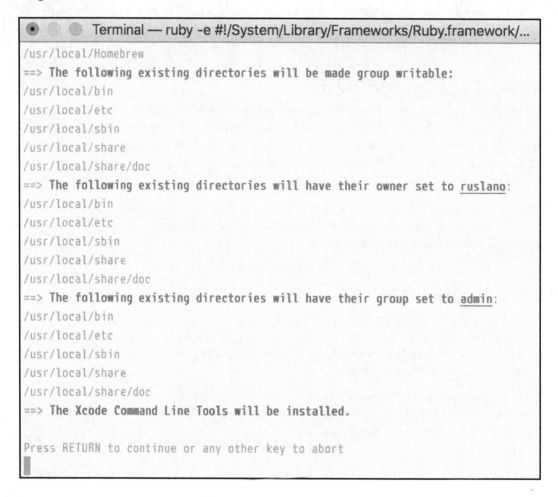

Hit Enter to continue.

If you don't have XCode installed (which is often a prerequisite for any kind of development-related activity on Mac), you'll get an XCode installation pop-up. We won't be using XCode directly, and you can install it with default settings.

This should take a while to run, but you'll have Homebrew installed by the end: a fantastic tool you can use to install a lot more than Vim! You'll see **Installation successful!** in bold font once the installation is complete.

Let's install a new version of Vim now using the following command:

```
$ brew install vim
```

Homebrew will install all the necessary dependencies too, so you won't have to worry about a thing, as can be seen in the following screenshot:

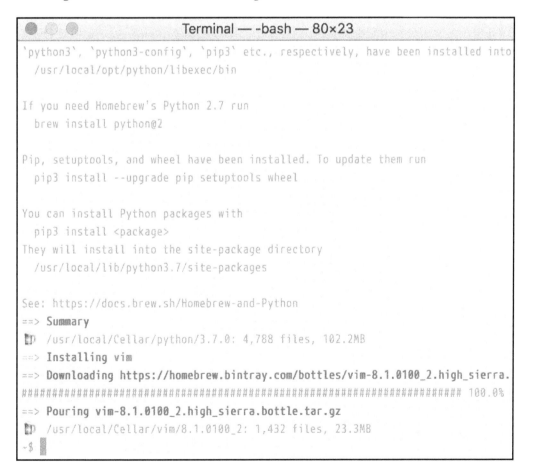

If you already have Homebrew installed, and you have installed Vim in the past, the preceding command will produce an error. You may want to make sure you have the last version of Vim, though, so run the following command:

```
$ brew upgrade vim
```

You should now be ready to enjoy Vim; let's try opening it with the following command:

```
$ vim
```

Welcome to Vim:

```
Terminal — vim -u NONE — 80×24




               VIM - Vi IMproved


               version 8.1.100
             by Bram Moolenaar et al.
       Vim is open source and freely distributable


               Sponsor Vim development!
       type  :help sponsor<Enter>     for information

       type  :q<Enter>                to exit
       type  :help<Enter>  or  <F1>   for on-line help
       type  :help version8<Enter>    for version info


              Running in Vi compatible mode
       type  :set nocp<Enter>          for Vim defaults
       type  :help cp-default<Enter>  for info on this
```

Downloading a .dmg image

Navigate to `https://github.com/macvim-dev/macvim/releases/latest` and download `MacVim.dmg`.

Open `MacVim.dmg`, and then drag the Vim icon into the `Applications` directory, as can be seen in the following screenshot:

Depending on the security settings of your Mac, you might be greeted by an error when navigating to the `Applications` folder and trying to open the `MacVim` app, as demonstrated in the following screenshot:

Open your `Applications` folder, find `MacVim`, right click the icon and select **Open**. The following prompt will pop up:

Now hit **Open**, and `MacVim` can be opened as usual from now on. Give it a shot:

```
● ● ●                        [No Name] - VIM
~
~
~
~
~
~
~                        VIM - Vi IMproved
~
~                           version 8.1.72
~                        by Bram Moolenaar et al.
~                Vim is open source and freely distributable
~
~                        Become a registered Vim user!
~            type  :help register<Enter>    for information
~
~            type  :q<Enter>                 to exit
~            type  :help<Enter>  or  <F1>  for on-line help
~            type  :help macvim<Enter>      for MacVim help
~
~
~
~
~
                                                0,0-1        All
```

Setting up on Windows

Windows provides two primary routes for using Vim: setting up Cygwin and providing a more Unix-like command-line experience, or installing **gVim**—a **graphical version of Vim** (which supports working with `cmd.exe` on Windows). I recommend installing both and picking your favorite: gVim feels slightly more at home on Windows (and it is easier to install), while Cygwin might feel more at home if you're used to the Unix shell.

Unix-like experience with Cygwin

Cygwin is a Unix-like environment and a command-line interface for Windows. It aims to bring powerful Unix shell and supporting tools to a Windows machine.

Installing Cygwin

To begin the installation process, navigate to `https://cygwin.com/install.html` and download either `setup-x86_64.exe` or `setup-x86.exe` depending on the version of Windows you're using (64 bit or 32 bit respectively).

If you're not sure whether your system is 32 bit or 64 bit, you can open **Control Panel | System and Security | System**, and look at **System type**. For example, my Windows machine shows **System type: 64-bit Operating System, x64-based processor**.

Open the executable file, and you will be greeted by the following Cygwin installation window:

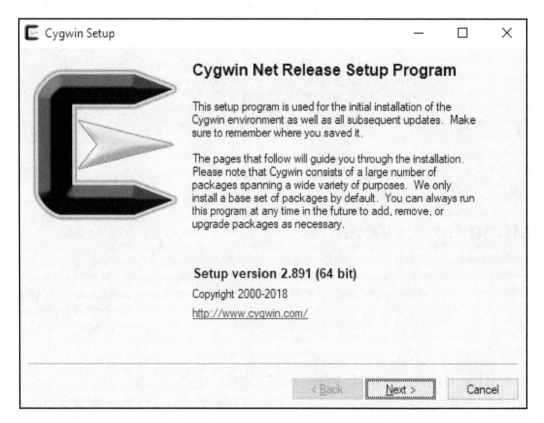

Hit **Next >** a few times, proceeding with the default settings:

- **Download source**: **Install from Internet**
- **Root directory**: C:\cygwin64 (or a recommended default)
- **Install for: all users**
- **Local package directory:** C:\Downloads (or a recommended default)
- **Internet connection: Use System Proxy Settings**
- **Download site:** http://cygwin.mirror.constant.com (or any available option)

After this, you will be greeted with the **Select Packages** screen. Here, we want to select the vim, gvim, and vim-doc packages. The easiest way to do this is to type vim in a search box, expand the **All** |**Editors** category, and click on the arrow-looking icons next to the desired packages, as demonstrated in the following screenshot:

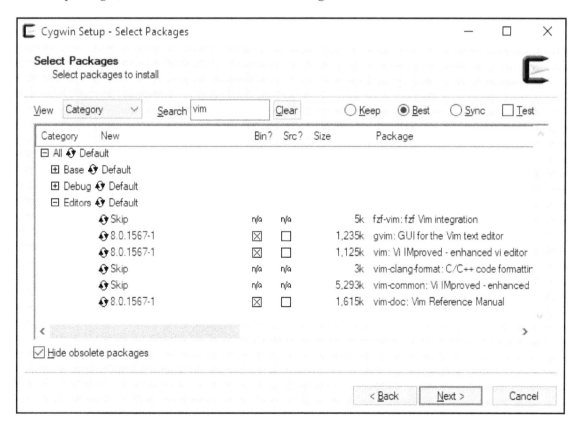

The preceding screenshot shows version **8.0.1567-1**. This is the only version available at the moment of writing this book, November 2018. The primary difference is the absence of the :terminal command (see Chapter 5, *Build, Test, and Execute*) in Vim 8.0 vs 8.1.

> You may want to install curl from under the Net category, and git from under the Devel category, as we'll be using both in chapter 3. It might also be helpful to install dos2unix from under the Utils category, which is a utility used for converting Windows-style line endings to Linux-style line endings (something you might run into once in a while).

Hit **Next >** two more times to proceed, which will begin the installation. Installation will take some time, and now would be a great moment to prematurely congratulate yourself with some coffee!

You might get a few post-install script errors, which you can safely dismiss (unless you see any errors related to Vim—then Google is your friend: search for an error text and try to find a solution).

Hit **Next >** a few more times, proceeding with the defaults:

- **Create icon on Desktop**
- **Add icon to Start Menu**

Congratulations, you now have Cygwin installed with Vim!

> If you ever need to install additional packages in Cygwin, just rerun the installer while selecting the packages you want.

Using Cygwin

Open Cygwin, the program will be called **Cygwin64 Terminal** or **Cygwin Terminal**, depending on the version of your system, as can be seen in the following screenshot:

Open it! You will see the following prompt, familiar to Linux users:

Cygwin supports all of the Unix-style commands we will be using in this book. This book will also say if any commands need to be changed to work with Cygwin. But for now, let's open Vim and proceed onto the next chapter! Type `vim` and hit *Enter* to start Vim, as demonstrated in the following screenshot:

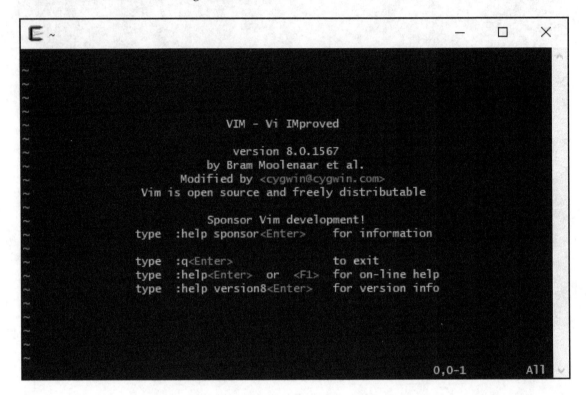

Cygwin is a way to get a Linux-like shell experience on Windows, meaning you'll have to follow Linux specific instructions throughout this book if you decide to use Cygwin.

You'll also want to be careful with Windows-style line endings vs Linux-style line endings, as Windows and Linux treat line endings differently. If you run into an odd issue with Vim complaining about ^M characters its unable to recognize, run the `dos2unix` utility on the offending file to resolve the issue.

Visual Vim with gVim

In this section. you can read more about the graphical version of Vim in *Vanilla Vim vs GVim*.

As it always is with Windows, the process is slightly more visual. Navigate to `www.vim.org/download.php#pc` in your browser and download an executable installer. At the moment of writing this book, November 2018, the binary is called `gvim81.exe`, where `81` stands for version 8.1.

Open the executable and follow the prompts on the screen, as demonstrated by the following screenshot:

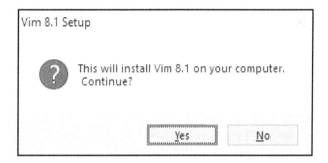

Let's go ahead and hit **Yes,** then **I Agree** until we arrive at the **Installation Options** screen. We're happy with most of the default options gVim has to offer, except that you might want to enable **Create .bat files for command line use**. This option will make the `vim` command work in Windows Command Prompt. Some examples in this book rely on having a Command Prompt, so enabling this option would help you follow along.

Here's a screenshot of the **Installation Options** screen with the proper boxes checked off:

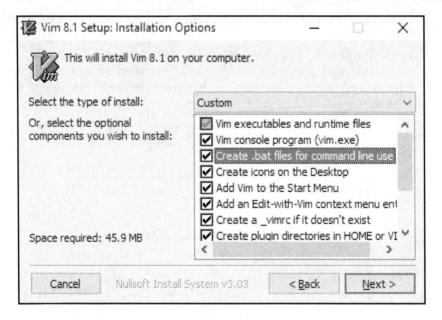

Hit **Next >**. You'll want to continue with the following settings:

- **Select the type of install:** Typical, (after **Create .bat files for command line use** is enabled, type of install value changes to Custom automatically).
- **Do not remap keys for Windows behavior**
- **Right button has a popup menu, left button starts visual mode**
- **Destination Folder:** C:\Program Files (x86)\Vim (or a recommended default)

Once you're done, hit **Install** and then **Close**, as demonstrated in the following screenshot:

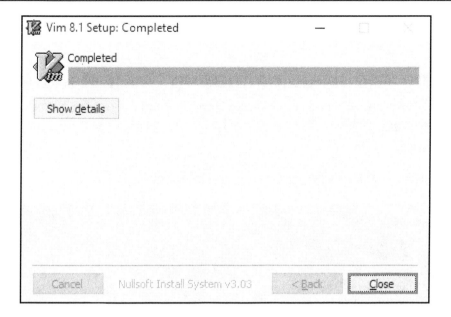

Say **No** to the request to see the README file (who needs a manual, huh?) as seen in the following command:

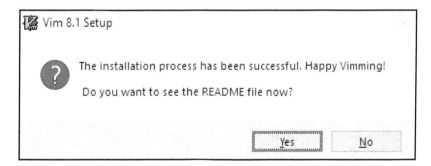

You will now have a few icons pop on your desktop, the most interesting one being gVim 8.1 as shown in the following screenshot:

Start it, and you're ready to proceed! Happy Vimming!

Verifying and troubleshooting the installation

Regardless of the platform you used to install Vim, it's good to make sure that, with Vim, all the right features enabled. On a command line, run the following command:

```
$ vim --version
```

You will see the following output, with a set of features having a + and a – in front of them:

```
ruslan@ann-perkins:~$ vim --version
VIM - Vi IMproved 8.1 (2018 May 18, compiled Aug 13 2018 02:40:26)
Included patches: 1-278
Compiled by ubuntu@ann-perkins
Huge version without GUI.  Features included (+) or not (-):
+acl               +extra_search      +mouse_netterm     +tag_old_static
+arabic            +farsi             +mouse_sgr         -tag_any_white
+autocmd           +file_in_path      -mouse_sysmouse    -tcl
+autochdir         +find_in_path      +mouse_urxvt       +termguicolors
-autoservername    +float             +mouse_xterm       +terminal
-balloon_eval      +folding           +multi_byte        +terminfo
+balloon_eval_term -footer            +multi_lang        +termresponse
-browse            +fork()            -mzscheme          +textobjects
++builtin_terms    -gettext           +netbeans_intg     +timers
+byte_offset       -hangul_input      +num64             +title
+channel           +iconv             +packages          -toolbar
+cindent           +insert_expand     +path_extra        +user_commands
-clientserver      +job               -perl              +vartabs
-clipboard         +jumplist          +persistent_undo   +vertsplit
+cmdline_compl     +keymap            +postscript        +virtualedit
+cmdline_hist      +lambda            +printer           +visual
+cmdline_info      +langmap           +profile           +visualextra
+comments          +libcall           +python            +viminfo
+conceal           +linebreak         -python3           +vreplace
```

In the preceding screenshot, you can see that my Vim was actually compiled with Python 2 support (+python) instead of Python 3 support (-python3). To correct the issue, I'd have to either recompile Vim with +python3 enabled or find a package which distributes a compiled version of Vim with +python3 enabled.

 For a list of all features Vim can have enabled, see `:help feature-list`.

For instance, if we wanted to recompile Vim 8.1 with Python 3 support on Linux, we would do the following:

```
$ git clone https://github.com/vim/vim.git
$ cd vim/src
$ ./configure --with-features=huge --enable-python3interp
$ make
$ sudo make install
```

 We're passing the `--with-features=huge` flag in order to compile Vim with most features enabled. However, `--with-features=huge` does not install language bindings, so we need to explicitly enable Python 3.

In general, if your Vim is not behaving like other Vim installations (including behavior described in this book), you might be missing a feature.

Depending on your system and features you require, the process might be slightly or vastly different. A quick web search along the lines of *Installing Vim <version> with +<feature> on <operating system>* should help.

Vanilla Vim vs gVim

Using instructions given before, you've installed two flavors of Vim: command-line Vim, and gVim. This is how gVim looks on Windows:

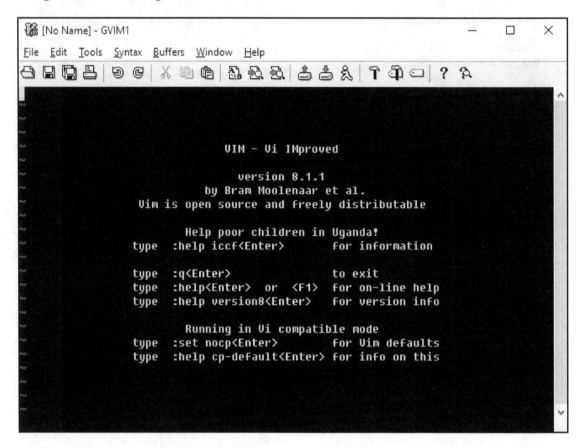

The gVim hooks up a **graphical user interface (GUI)** to Vim, has better mouse support, and adds more context menus. It also supports a wider range of color than many terminal emulators, and provides some quality of life features you'd expect from a modern GUI.

You can launch gVim by running gVim 8.1 executable on Windows, or on Linux and Mac OS by invoking the following command:

```
$ gvim
```

Windows users might favor gVim.

This book focuses on increasing the effectiveness of one's text editing skills, so we will shy away from navigating multiple menus in gVim, as these are rather intuitive, and take the user out of the flow.

Hence, we will focus on a non-graphical version of Vim, but everything that's applicable to Vim also applies to gVim. The two share configuration, and you can swap between the two as you go. Overall, gVim is slightly more newbie friendly, but it doesn't matter which one you choose to use for the purpose of this book.

Try both!

Configuring Vim with your .vimrc

Vim reads configuration from a `.vimrc` file. Vim works out of the box, but there are certain options which make working with code a lot easier.

 In Unix-like systems, files starting with a period `.` are hidden. To see them, run `ls -a` in a Command line.

In Linux and MacOS, `.vimrc` is located in your `user` directory (the full path would be `/home/<username>/.vimrc`). You can also find out your `user` directory by opening a Command Prompt and running the following command:

```
$ echo $HOME
```

Windows does not allow periods in file names, so the file is named `_vimrc`. It's usually located in `C:\Users\<username>\_vimrc`, but you can also locate it by opening the Windows Command Prompt and running the following command:

```
$ echo %USERPROFILE%
```

 If you run into problems, open Vim and type in `:echo $MYVIMRC` followed by *Enter*. It should display where Vim is reading the `.vimrc` from.

Find the proper location for your OS, and place the prepared configuration file there. You can download the `.vimrc` used for this chapter from GitHub at `https://github.com/PacktPublishing/Mastering-Vim/tree/master/Chapter01`. The following code shows the contents of a `.vimrc` file used in this chapter:

```
syntax on                    " Enable syntax highlighting.
filetype plugin indent on    " Enable file type based indentation.

set autoindent               " Respect indentation when starting a new line.
set expandtab                " Expand tabs to spaces. Essential in Python.
set tabstop=4                " Number of spaces tab is counted for.
set shiftwidth=4             " Number of spaces to use for autoindent.

set backspace=2              " Fix backspace behavior on most terminals.

colorscheme murphy           " Change a colorscheme.
```

Lines starting with a double quote " are comments and are ignored by Vim. These settings bring in some sensible defaults, like syntax highlighting and consistent indentation. They also fix one of the common sticking points in a bare-bones Vim installation—inconsistent backspace key behavior across different environments.

When working with Vim configuration, you can try things out before adding them to your `.vimrc` file To do that, type `:` followed by a command, for example, `:set autoindent` (press *Enter* to execute). If you ever want to know the value of a setting, add `?` at the end of the command: for example, `:set tabstop?` will tell you the current `tabstop` value.

I've also changed the `colorscheme` to make screenshots look better in print, but you don't have to.

Vim 8 comes prepackaged with the following color themes: `blue`, `darkblue`, `default`, `delek`, `desert`, `elflord`, `evening`, `industry`, `koehler`, `morning`, `murhpy`, `pablo`, `peachpuff`, `ron`, `shine`, `slate`, `torte`, `zellner`. You can try out a color theme by typing `:colorscheme <name>` and hitting *Enter*, and you can cycle through the available color scheme names by typing `:colorscheme` followed by a space and by hitting *Tab* multiple times. You can read more about configuring Vim and color schemes in `chapter 7`, *Making Vim Your Own*.

Common operations (or how to exit Vim)

Tweet source: `https://twitter.com/iamdevloper/status/435555976687923200`

We will now focus on interacting with Vim without the use of a mouse or navigational menus. Programming is a focus intensive task on its own. Hunting through context menus is nobody's idea of a good time, and keeping our hands on the home row of your keyboard helps trim constant switching between a keyboard and a mouse.

Opening files

First, start your favorite Command Prompt (Terminal in Linux and macOS, Cygwin in Windows). We'll be working on a very basic Python application. For simplicity's sake, let's make a simple square root calculator. Run the following command:

```
$ vim animal_farm.py
```

If you're using gVim—you can open a file by going into a **File** menu and choosing **Open**. Sometimes graphical interface is exactly what you need!

This opens a file named `animal_farm.py`. If the file existed, you'd see its contents here, but since it doesn't, we're greeted by an empty screen, as shown in the following example:

```
"animal_farm.py" [New File]
```

You can tell that the file doesn't exist by the `[New File]` text next to a file name in the status line at the bottom of the screen. Woohoo! You've just opened your first file with Vim!

Vim's status line often contains a lot of useful information. That's the primary way for Vim to communicate with a user, so do keep an eye out for messages in the status line!

If you already have Vim open—you can load a file by typing the following, and hitting *Enter*:

```
:e animal_farm.py
```

You have just executed your first Vim command! Pressing colon character : enters a command-line mode, which lets you enter a line of text which Vim will interpret as a command. Commands are terminated by hitting the *Enter* key, which allows you to perform various complex operations, as well as accessing your system's Command line. Command :e stands for *edit*.

> Vim help often refers to the *Enter* key as a <CR>, which stands for carriage return.

Changing text

By default you're in Vim's normal mode, meaning that every key press corresponds to a particular command. Hit i on your keyboard to enter an insert mode. This will display **-- INSERT --** in a status line (at the bottom), (and, if you're using gVim, it will change the cursor from a block to a vertical line), as can be seen in the following example:

The insert mode behaves just like any other modeless editor. Normally, we wouldn't spend a lot of time in insert mode except for adding new text.

 You've already encountered three of Vim's modes: command-line mode, normal mode, and insert mode. This book will cover more modes, see Chapter 3, *Follow the Leader – Plugin Management* for details and explanation.

Let's create our Python application by typing in the following code. We'll be navigating this little snippet throughout this chapter:

```python
#!/usr/bin/python3

"""Our own little animal farm."""

import sys

def add_animal(farm, animal):
    farm.add(animal)
    return farm

def main(animals):
    farm = set()
    for animal in animals:
        farm = add_animal(farm, animal)
    print("We've got some animals on the farm:", ', '.join(farm) + '.')

if __name__ == '__main__':
    if len(sys.argv) == 1:
        print('Pass at least one animal type!')
        sys.exit(1)
    main(sys.argv[1:])
~
~
-- INSERT --
```

To get back to normal mode in Vim, hit *Esc* on your keyboard. You'll see that **-- INSERT --** has disappeared from the status line. Now, Vim is ready to take commands from you again!

 The preceding code is not showing Python best practices and is provided to illustrate some of Vim's capabilities.

Saving and closing files

Let's save our file! Execute the following command:

`:w`

 Don't forget to hit *Enter* at the end of a command to execute it.

`:w` stands for **write**.

 The write command can also be followed by a filename, making it possible to write to a different file, other than the one that is open. This will save the changes in a new file, and will change the current open file to a new one. Try it, using the following command: `:w animal_farm_2.py`.

Let's exit Vim and check if the file was indeed created. `:q` stands for **quit**. You can also combine write and quit commands to write and exit by executing `:wq`.

`:q`

If you made changes to a file and want to exit Vim without saving the changes, you'll have to use `:q!` to force Vim to quit. Exclamation mark at the end of the command forces its execution.

Many commands in Vim have shorter and longer versions. For instance, :e, :w, and :q are short versions of :edit, :write, and :quit. In the Vim manual, the optional part of the command is often annotated in square brackets ([]). For example, :w[rite] or :e[dit].

Now that we're back in our system's Command line, let's check the contents of a current directory, as seen in the following code:

```
$ ls
$ python3 animal_farm.py
$ python3 animal_farm.py cat dog sheep
```

 In Unix, ls lists contents of a current directory. python3 animal_farm.py executes the script using a Python 3 interpreter, and python3 animal_farm.py cat dog sheep passes three arguments (cat, dog, sheep) to our script.

The following screenshot shows what the three preceding commands should output:

```
ruslan@ann-perkins:~/Mastering-Vim/ch1$ ls
animal_farm.py
ruslan@ann-perkins:~/Mastering-Vim/ch1$ python3 animal_farm.py
Pass at least one animal type!
ruslan@ann-perkins:~/Mastering-Vim/ch1$ python3 animal_farm.py cat dog sheep
We've got some animals on the farm: sheep, dog, cat.
ruslan@ann-perkins:~/Mastering-Vim/ch1$
```

A word about swap files

By default, Vim keeps track of the changes you make to files in swap files. The swap files are created as you edit the files, and are used to recover the contents of your files in case either Vim, your SSH session, or your machine crashes. If you don't exit Vim cleanly, you'll be greeted by the following screen:

```
E325: ATTENTION
Found a swap file by the name ".animal_farm.py.swp"
          owned by: ruslan    dated: Fri Oct 12 23:01:58 2018
         file name: ~ruslan/Mastering-Vim/ch1/animal_farm.py
          modified: YES
         user name: ruslan    host name: ann-perkins
        process ID: 8179
While opening file "animal_farm.py"
             dated: Fri Oct 12 18:05:04 2018

(1) Another program may be editing the same file.  If this is the case,
    be careful not to end up with two different instances of the same
    file when making changes.  Quit, or continue with caution.
(2) An edit session for this file crashed.
    If this is the case, use ":recover" or "vim -r animal_farm.py"
    to recover the changes (see ":help recovery").
    If you did this already, delete the swap file ".animal_farm.py.swp"
    to avoid this message.

Swap file ".animal_farm.py.swp" already exists!
[O]pen Read-Only, (E)dit anyway, (R)ecover, (D)elete it, (Q)uit, (A)bort: ▌
```

You can either hit r to recover the swap file contents, or d to delete the swap file and dismiss the changes. If you decide to recover the swap file, you can prevent the same message from showing up next time you open the file in Vim by reopening a file and running :e, and pressing d to delete the swap file.

By default, Vim creates files like `<filename>.swp` and `.<filename>.swp` in the same directory as the original file. If you don't like your file system being littered by swap files, you can change this behavior by telling Vim to place all the swap files in a single directory. To do so, add the following to your `.vimrc`:

```
set directory=$HOME/.vim/swap//
```

If you're on Windows, you should use `set directory=%USERDATA%\.vim\swap//` (note the direction of the last two slashes).

You can also choose to disable the swap files completely by adding `set noswapfile` to your `.vimrc`.

Moving around: talk to your editor

Vim allows you to navigate content a lot more efficiently than most conventional editors. Let's start with the basics.

You can move your cursor around character by character by using arrow keys or letters *h*, *j*, *k*, and *l*. This is the least efficient and the most precise way to move:

Key	Alternative key	Action
h	Left arrow	Move cursor left
j	Down arrow	Move cursor down
k	Up arrow	Move cursor up
l	Right arrow	Move cursor right

The following diagram is a visual representation which might be a little easier on the eyes:

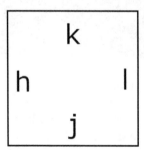

Vi (Vim's predecessor) was created on an old ADM-3A terminal, which didn't have arrow keys. Keys h, j, k, and l were used as arrows.

Image by Chris Jacobs, Wikipedia (CC BY-SA 3.0)

Try it! There's a lot of value to getting used to *hjkl* for movement: your hands stay on the home row of your keyboard. This way you don't have to move your hands and it helps you stay in the flow. Furthermore, many applications treat *hjkl* as arrow keys—you'd be surprised how many tools respond to these.

Now you might be inclined to hit directional keys multiple times to get to a desired position, but there's a better way! You can prefix every command by a number, which would repeat the command that number of times. For example, hitting 5j will move the cursor five lines down, while hitting 14l will move the cursor 14 characters to the left. This works with most commands you encounter in this book.

Calculating the exact number of characters you would like to move is pretty hard (and nobody wants to do it), so there's a way to move by words. Use w to move to the beginning of the next **w**ord, and use e to get to the **e**nd of the closest word. To move **b**ackwards to the beginning of the word, hit b.

You can also capitalize these letters to treat everything but a white space as a word! This allows you to differentiate between the kind of things you'd like to traverse.

 Vim has two kinds of word objects: referred to as lowercase "**word**" and uppercase "**WORD**". In Vim world, word is a sequence of letters, digits, and underscores separated by white space. WORD is a sequence of any non-blank characters separated by white space.

Let's take the following line of code from our example:

```
farm = add_animal(farm, animal)
```

 Notice the cursor position, it's hovering over the first character of add_animal.

Hitting w will move the cursor to beginning of the word add_animal, while hitting W will take you to the beginning of animal. Capitalized W, E, and B will treat any characters bundled together and separated by a space as their own words. This can be seen in the following table:

Key	Action
w	Move forward by word
e	Move forward until the end of the word
W	Move forward by WORD
E	Move forward until the end of the WORD
b	Move backwards to the beginning of the word
B	Move backwards to the beginning of the WORD

The following screenshot shows more examples of how each command behaves:

Key	Initial cursor position	Resulting cursor position
w	farm = add_animal(farm, animal)	farm = add_animal(farm, animal)
e	farm = add_animal(farm, animal)	farm = add_animal(farm, animal)
b	farm = add_animal(farm, animal)	farm = add_animal(farm, animal)
W	farm = add_animal(farm, animal)	farm = add_animal(farm, animal)
E	farm = add_animal(farm, animal)	farm = add_animal(farm, animal)
B	farm = add_animal(farm, animal)	farm = add_animal(farm, animal)

Combine the movements shown with the directional movements you learned earlier to move in fewer keystrokes!

It's also really useful to move in paragraphs. Everything separated by at least two new lines is considered a paragraph, which also means each code block is a paragraph, as can be seen in the following example:

```python
def add_animal(farm, animal):
    farm.add(animal)
    return farm

def main(animals):
    farm = set()
    for animal in animals:
        farm = add_animal(farm, animal)
    print("We've got some animals on the farm:", ', '.join(farm) + '.')
```

The functions `add_animal` and `main` are two separate paragraphs. Use a closing curly brace } to move forward, and an opening curly brace { to move backwards as detailed in the following table:

Command	Action
{	Move back by one paragraph
}	Move forward by one paragraph

Don't forget to combine these two with numbers if you need to move by more than one paragraph.

There are more ways to move around, but these are the most important basics. We'll be covering more complex ways to navigate in `chapter 2`, *Advanced Editing and Navigation.*

Making simple edits in insert mode

When working with Vim, you usually want to spend as little time as possible in the insert mode (unless you're writing and not editing). Since most text operations involve editing, we'll focus on that.

You've already learned to enter the insert mode by pressing i. There are more ways to get to the insert mode. Often times you will want to change some piece of text for another one, and there's a command just for that c. The `change` command allows you to remove a portion of text and immediately enter an insert mode. `Change` is a compound command, meaning that it needs to be followed by a command which tells Vim what needs to be changed. You can combine it with any of the movement commands you've learned before. Here are some examples:

Command	Before	After
cw	`farm = add_animal(farm, animal)`	`farm = add_animal(, animal)`
c3e (comma counts as a word)	`farm = add_animal(farm, animal)`	`farm = add_animal(fa)`
cb	`farm = add_animal(farm, animal)`	`farm = add_animal(farm, mal)`
c4l	`farm = add_animal(farm, animal)`	`farm = add_animal(farm, al)`
cW	`farm = add_animal(farm, animal)`	`farm = add_animal(farm, `

As an odd exception, `cw` behaves like `ce`. This is a leftover from Vi, Vim's predecessor.

As you learn more complex movements commands, you can combine these with a change for quick and seamless editing. We'll also be covering a few plugins which will supercharge a change command to allow for even more powerful editing, like changing text within braces, or replacing the type of quotes on the go.

All of these examples follow the `<command> <number> <movement or a text object>` structure. You can put a number before or after the `<command>`.

For example, if you wish to change `farm = add_animal(farm, animal)` to `farm = add_animal(farm, creature)`, you can execute the following set of commands:

Contents of the line	Action
`farm = add_animal(farm, animal)`	Start with a cursor in the beginning of the line
`farm = add_animal(farm, animal)`	Hit `3W` to move the cursor three WORDs forward to the beginning of `animal`
`farm = add_animal(farm, )`	Press `cw` to delete the word `animal` and enter the insert mode
`farm = add_animal(farm, creature)`	Type `creature`
`farm = add_animal(farm, creature)`	Hit the *Esc* key to return to NORMAL mode

Sometimes we just want to cut things, without putting anything instead, and `d` does just that. It stands for delete. It behaves similarly to `c`, except that the behavior of `w` and `e` is more standard, as can be seen in the following example:

Command	Before	After
dw	`farm = add_animal(farm, animal)`	`farm = add_animal(, animal)`
d3e (comma counts as a word)	`farm = add_animal(farm, animal)`	`farm = add_animal(fa)`
db	`farm = add_animal(farm, animal)`	`farm = add_animal(farm, mal)`
d4l	`farm = add_animal(farm, animal)`	`farm = add_animal(farm, al)`
dW	`farm = add_animal(farm, animal)`	`farm = add_animal(farm, `

There are also two more nifty shortcuts which allow you to change or delete a whole line:

Command	What it does
cc	Clears the whole line and enters insert mode. Preserves current indentation level, which is useful when coding.
dd	Deletes an entire line.

For example, look at the following piece:

```python
def main(animals):
    farm = set()
    for animal in animals:
        farm = add_animal(farm, animal)
    print("We've got some animals on the farm:", ', '.join(farm) + '.')
```

By hitting `dd` you will completely remove a line, as demonstrated in the following example:

```python
def main(animals):
    farm = set()
    for animal in animals:
    print("We've got some animals on the farm:", ', '.join(farm) + '.')
```

Hitting `cc` will clear the line and enter insert mode with the proper indent, as shown in the following example:

```
def main(animals):
    farm = set()
    for animal in animals:
        █
    print("We've got some animals on the farm:", ', '.join(farm) + '.')
```

If you run into difficulties picking the right movement commands, you can also use the visual mode to select text you want to modify. Hit `v` to enter the visual mode and use the usual movement commands to adjust the selection. Run the desired command (like `c` to change or `d` to delete) once you're satisfied with the selection.

Persistent undo and repeat

Like any editor, Vim keeps track of every operation. Press `u` to undo a last operation, and *Ctrl + r* to redo it.

To learn more about Vim's undo tree (Vim's undo history is not linear!) and how to navigate it, see `chapter 4`, *Advanced Workflows*.

Vim also allows you to persist undo history between sessions, which is great if you want to undo (or remember) something you've done a few days ago!

You can enable persistent undo by adding the following line to your `.vimrc`:

```
set undofile
```

However, this will litter your system with an undo file for each file you're editing. You can consolidate the undo files in a single directory, as seen in the following example:

```
" Set up persistent undo across all files.
set undofile
if !isdirectory("$HOME/.vim/undodir")
  call mkdir("$HOME/.vim/undodir", "p")
endif
set undodir="$HOME/.vim/undodir"
```

If you're using Windows, replace the directories with `%USERPROFILE%\_vim\undodir` (and you'll be making changes to `_vimrc` instead of `.vimrc`).

Now, you'll be able to undo and redo your changes across sessions.

Read the Vim manual using :help

The best learning tool Vim can offer is certainly a `:help` command, as can be seen in the following screenshot:

```
help.txt       For Vim version 8.1.  Last change: 2017 Oct 28

                   VIM - main help file
                                                              k
        Move around:  Use the cursor keys, or "h" to go left,        h   l
                      "j" to go down, "k" to go up, "l" to go right.      j
   Close this window:  Use ":q<Enter>".
      Get out of Vim:  Use ":qa!<Enter>" (careful, all changes are lost!).

   Jump to a subject:  Position the cursor on a tag (e.g. bars) and hit CTRL-].
      With the mouse:  ":set mouse=a" to enable the mouse (in xterm or GUI).
                       Double-click the left mouse button on a tag, e.g. bars.
          Jump back:  Type CTRL-T or CTRL-O.  Repeat to go further back.

   Get specific help:  It is possible to go directly to whatever you want help
                       on, by giving an argument to the :help command.
                       Prepend something to specify the context:  help-context

                       WHAT                    PREPEND    EXAMPLE
                      Normal mode command                 :help x
help.txt [Help][RO]

[No Name]
"help.txt" [readonly] 228L, 8583C
```

It's an enormous collection of resources and tutorials which comes installed with Vim. Scroll through using the *Page Up* and *Page Down* keys (bonus point for using *Ctrl + b* and *Ctrl + f* respectively), there is a lot of useful information there.

Whenever you are stuck, or want to learn more about a particular command, try searching it using :help (you can shorten it to :h). Let's try searching for a cc command we've learned :

    :h cc

```
                                                                  cc
["x]cc                    Delete [count] lines [into register x] and start
                          insert linewise.  If 'autoindent' is on, preserve
                          the indent of the first line.


                                                                  C
["x]C                     Delete from the cursor position to the end of the
                          line and [count]-1 more lines [into register x], and
                          start insert.  Synonym for c$ (not linewise).


                                                                  s
["x]s                     Delete [count] characters [into register x] and start
                          insert (s stands for Substitute).  Synonym for "cl"
                          (not linewise).


                                                                  S
["x]S                     Delete [count] lines [into register x] and start
                          insert.  Synonym for "cc" linewise.

{Visual}["x]c    or                                       v_c v_s
change.txt [Help][RO]


[No Name]
"change.txt" [readonly] 1883L, 77104C
```

Help tells us the way the command works, as well as how different options and settings affect the command (for instance autoindent setting preserves the indentation).

:help is a command which navigates a set of help files. As you look through the help files, you'll notice that certain words are highlighted in color. These are tags, and can be searched for using the :help command. Unfortunately, not every tag name is intuitive. For instance, if we wanted to learn how to search for a string in Vim, we could try using the following:

:h search

However, it looks like this command takes us to the entry on expression evaluation, which is not exactly what we were looking for, as demonstrated by the following screenshot:

```
search({pattern} [, {flags} [, {stopline} [, {timeout}]]])      search()
                Search for regexp pattern {pattern}.  The search starts at the
                cursor position (you can use cursor() to set it).

                When a match has been found its line number is returned.
                If there is no match a 0 is returned and the cursor doesn't
                move.  No error message is given.

                {flags} is a String, which can contain these character flags:
                'b'     search Backward instead of forward
                'c'     accept a match at the Cursor position
                'e'     move to the End of the match
                'n'     do Not move the cursor
                'p'     return number of matching sub-Pattern (see below)
                's'     Set the ' mark at the previous location of the cursor
                'w'     Wrap around the end of the file
                'W'     don't Wrap around the end of the file
                'z'     start searching at the cursor column instead of zero
                If neither 'w' or 'W' is given, the 'wrapscan' option applies.
eval.txt [Help][RO]

[No Name]
"eval.txt" [readonly] 11656L, 451265C
```

To find the right entry, type in `:h search` (don't hit *Enter* yet) followed by *Ctrl* + d. This will give you a list of help tags containing the substring `search`. One of the options shown is `search-commands` which is what we'd be looking for. Complete your command in the following way to get to the entry we were looking for:

`:h search-commands`

The following display shows the right help entry for search:

```
1. Search commands                                    search-commands

                                                        /
/{pattern}[/]<CR>          Search forward for the [count]'th occurrence of
                           {pattern} exclusive.

/{pattern}/{offset}<CR> Search forward for the [count]'th occurrence of
                           {pattern} and go {offset} lines up or down.
                           linewise.

                                                        /<CR>
/<CR>                      Search forward for the [count]'th occurrence of the
                           latest used pattern last-pattern with latest used
                           {offset}.

//{offset}<CR>             Search forward for the [count]'th occurrence of the
                           latest used pattern last-pattern with new
                           {offset}.  If {offset} is empty no offset is used.

                                                        ?
pattern.txt [Help][RO]

[No Name]
"pattern.txt" [readonly] 1420L, 59741C
```

Speaking of search functionality, you can search inside help pages (or any file open in Vim) using `/search term` to search forward from the cursor or `?search term` to search backward. See `Chapter 2`, *Advanced Editing and Navigation,* to learn more about how to perform search operations.

Don't forget to use Vim's help system any time you have questions or want to better understand the way Vim behaves.

Summary

The original Vi was developed to work through remote terminals, when bandwidth and speed were limited. These limitations guided Vi towards establishing an efficient and deliberate editing process, which is what's at the core of Vim—Vi Improved today.

In this chapter, you've learned how to install and update Vim and it's graphical counterpart—GVim, on every major platform (in more ways than you will ever need).

You've learned to configure your Vim through tinkering with `.vimrc`, which is something you will often go back to as you customize the editor for your own needs.

You've picked up the basics of working with files, moving around Vim, and making changes. Vim's concept of text objects (letters, words, paragraphs) and composite commands (like `d2w` - **d**elete **2** **w**ords) empower precise text operations.

And if there's one thing you could take away from this chapter, it would be `:help`. Vim's internal help system is incredibly detailed, and it can answer most, if not every, question you might have, as long as you know what you're looking for.

In the next chapter, we'll be looking into getting more out of Vim. You'll learn how to navigate files and get better at editing text.

Advanced Editing and Navigation

2

Throughout this chapter, you will get a lot more comfortable using Vim in your day-to-day tasks. You will be working with a Python code base, which should provide you with a set of real-life scenarios for working with code. If you have a project of your own handy, you can choose to try out the lessons taught in this chapter using your own project files; however, you might find that not every scenario applies to your code base.

The following topics will be covered in this chapter:

- A quick-and-dirty way of installing Vim plugins
- Keeping your workspace organized when working with multiple or long files using buffers, windows, tabs, and folds
- Navigating complex file trees without leaving Vim with Netrw, NERDTree, Vinegar, or CtrlP
- Advanced navigation throughout a file, and covering more types of text objects: using `grep` and `ack` to look for things across files, and EasyMotion, a lightning fast movement plugin
- Copying and pasting with the power of registers

Technical requirements

This chapter will cover working with a Python code base. You can get the code we'll be editing in this chapter from GitHub at `https://github.com/PacktPublishing/Mastering-Vim/blob/master/Chapter02`.

Installing plugins

This chapter will start by introducing Vim plugins. Plugin management is a rather broad subject (and it's covered in Chapter 3, *Follow the Leader - Plugin Management,* as well), but we're starting out with just a few plugins, so we won't have to worry ourselves with that topic yet.

First, let's go through the one-time set up:

1. You'll need to create a directory to store plugins. Execute the following on the command line:

   ```
   $ mkdir -p ~/.vim/pack/plugins/start
   ```

    If you're using GVim under Windows, you'll have to create the `vimfiles` directory under your user folder (usually `C:\Users\<username>`), and then create `pack\plugins\start` folders inside of it.

2. You'll want to tell Vim to load documentation for each plugin, as it doesn't do so automatically. For that, add the following lines to your `~/.vimrc` file:

   ```
   packloadall            " Load all plugins.
   silent! helptags ALL   " Load help files for all plugins.
   ```

Now, every time you want to add a plugin, you'll have to:

1. Find your plugin on GitHub. For example, let's install `https://github.com/scrooloose/nerdtree`. If you have Git installed, find the Git repository URL (in this case, it's `https://github.com/scrooloose/nerdtree.git`) and run the following:

   ```
   $ git clone https://github.com/scrooloose/nerdtree.git
   ~/.vim/pack/plugins/start/nerdtree
   ```

    If you don't have Git installed, or if you're installing a plugin for GVim under Windows, navigate to the plugin's GitHub page, and find a **Clone or download** button. Download the ZIP archive and unpack it into `.vim/pack/plugins/start/nerdtree` in Linux or `vimfiles/pack/plugins/start/nerdtree` in Windows.

2. Restart Vim, and the plugin should be available to use.

Organizing workspace

So far, we've only worked with a single file in Vim. When working with code, you usually have to work with multiple files at once, switching back and forth, making edits across multiple files, and looking up certain bits somewhere else. Luckily, Vim provides an extensive way to deal with many files:

- Buffers are the way Vim internally represents files; they allow you to switch between multiple files quickly
- Windows organize the workspace by displaying multiple files next to each other
- Tabs are a collection of windows
- Folds allow you to hide and expand certain portions of files, making large files easier to navigate

Here's a screenshot illustrating the preceding points:

Let's understand the content in the screenshot:

- Multiple files (labeled `farm.py`, `animals/cat.py`, and `animal_farm.py`) are open as windows
- The bar at the top (listing `3 farm.py` and `a/dog.py`) indicates the tabs
- Lines starting with `+--` indicate folds, hiding away portions of a file

This section will go over windows, tabs, and folds in detail, and you'll be able to comfortably work with as many files as you need.

Buffers

Buffers are internal representations of files. Every file you open will have a corresponding buffer. Let's open a file from the command line: `vim animal_farm.py`. Now, let's see a list of existing buffers:

`:ls`

 Many commands have synonyms, and `:ls` is not an exception: `:buffers` and `:files` will accomplish the same thing. Pick one that's the easiest for you to remember!

Here's what the output of `:ls` looks like (see the bottom three lines):

```
def main(animals):
    animal_farm = farm.Farm()
    for animal_kind in animals:
        animal_farm.add_animal(make_animal(animal_kind))
    animal_farm.print_contents()

if __name__ == '__main__':
    if len(sys.argv) == 1:
        print('Pass at least one animal type!')
:ls
  1 %a   "animal_farm.py"                line 30
Press ENTER or type command to continue
```

The status bar shows some information about the buffers we have open (we only have one right now):

- 1 is the buffer number, and it'll stay constant throughout the Vim session
- % indicates that the buffer is in the current window (see the *Windows* section)
- a signals that the buffer is active: it's loaded and is visible
- "animal_farm.py" is the filename
- line 1 is the current cursor position

Let's open another file:

```
:e animals/cat.py
```

You can see that the file we initially opened is nowhere to be seen and has been replaced with the current file. However, animal_farm.py is still stored in one of the buffers. List all of the buffers again:

```
:ls
```

You can see both filenames listed:

```
class Cat(animal.Animal):

    def __init__(self):
        self.kind = 'cat'
~
~
~
:ls
  1 #    "animal_farm.py"              line 1
  2 %a   "animals/cat.py"             line 1
Press ENTER or type command to continue
```

How do we get to the file, then?

Vim refers to buffers by a number and a name, and both are unique within a single session (until you exit Vim). To switch to a different buffer, use the :b command, followed by the number of the buffer:

```
:b 1
```

You can shorten the previous by omitting the space between :b and the buffer number: :b1.

Voila, you're taken back to the original file! Since buffers are also identified by a filename, you can switch between them using partial filenames. The following will open the buffer containing animals/cat.py:

:b cat

However, if you have more than one match, you'll get an error. Try looking for a buffer with a filename containing py:

:b py

As you can see in the following screenshot, the status line displays an error:

```
E93: More than one match for py
```

That's when you can use tab completion to cycle through the available options. Type in :b py (without hitting *Enter*) and press the *Tab* key to cycle through the available results.

You can also cycle through buffers using :bn (:bnext) and :bp (:bprevious).

Once you're done with the buffer, you can delete it, hence removing it from the list of open buffers without quitting Vim:

:bd

This will return an error if the current buffer is not saved. Hence, you'll get a chance to save the file without accidentally deleting the buffer.

Plugin spotlight – unimpaired

Tim Pope's vim-unimpaired is a plugin that adds a number of handy mappings for existing Vim commands (and a few new ones). I use it daily, as I find mappings more intuitive—]b and [b cycle through open buffers,]f and [f cycle through files in a directory, and so on. It's available from GitHub at https://github.com/tpope/vim-unimpaired (see the *Installing plugins* section earlier in this chapter for installation instructions).

Here are some of the mappings vim-unimpaired provides:

- `]b` and `[b` cycle through buffers

- `]f` and `[f` cycle through files in the same directory as the current buffer

- `]l` and `[l` cycle through the location list (see the *Location List* section in `Chapter 5`, *Build, Test, and Execute*)

- `]q` and `[q` cycle through the quickfix list (see the *Quickfix list* section in `Chapter 5`, *Build, Test, and Execute*)

- `]t` and `[t` cycle through tags (see the *Meet Exuberant Ctags* section in `Chapter 4`, *Understanding the Text*)

The plugin also allows you to toggle certain options with just a few key presses, such as `yos` to toggle spell checking or `yoc` to toggle the cursor line highlighting.

See `:help unimpaired` for a full list of mappings and features that vim-unimpaired provides.

Windows

Vim loads buffers into windows. You can have multiple windows open on the screen at the same time, allowing for split screen functionality.

Creating, deleting, and navigating windows

Let's give working with windows a shot. Open `animal_farm.py` (either from a command line by running `$ vim animal_farm.py` or from Vim with `:e animal_farm.py`).

Open one of our files in a split window:

```
:split animals/cat.py
```

 You can shorten this command to `:sp`.

You can see that `animals/cat.py` was opened above the current file and that your cursor was placed there:

```
"""A cat."""

import animal

class Cat(animal.Animal):

    def __init__(self):
        self.kind = 'cat'
~
~
~
animals/cat.py
#!/usr/bin/python3

"""Our own little animal farm."""

import sys

from animals import cat
from animals import dog
from animals import sheep
import animal
animal_farm.py
"animals/cat.py" 8L, 106C
```

You can split the window vertically as well by running the following code:

```
:vsplit farm.py
```

As you can see, this creates another window in a vertical split (your cursor is now moved to the new window):

```
"""A farm for holding animals."""      """A cat."""

class Farm(object):                     import animal

    def __init__(self):                 class Cat(animal.Animal):
        self.animals = set()
                                            def __init__(self):
    def add_animal(self, animal):               self.kind = 'cat'
        self.animals.add(animal)        ~
                                        ~
    def print_contents(self):           ~
farm.py                                 animals/cat.py
#!/usr/bin/python3

"""Our own little animal farm."""

import sys

from animals import cat
from animals import dog
from animals import sheep
import animal
animal_farm.py
"farm.py" 13L, 332C
```

 :vs is a shorter version of the :vsplit command.

You can combine the :split and :vsplit commands indefinitely to create as many windows as you need.

All of the commands you've learned so far will function as usual within this window, including changing buffers. To move between the windows, use *Ctrl + w*, followed by a directional key: h, j, k, or l. Arrow keys work as well.

If you use windows a lot, you might benefit from binding *Ctrl + h* to go to the split to the left, *Ctrl + j* to go to the split at the bottom, and so on. Add the following to your `.vimrc` file:

```
" Fast split navigation with <Ctrl> + hjkl.
noremap <c-h> <c-w><c-h>
noremap <c-j> <c-w><c-j>
noremap <c-k> <c-w><c-k>
noremap <c-l> <c-w><c-l>
```

Give it a shot: *Ctrl + w* followed by `j` will move you to the window below, and *Ctrl + w*, `k` will move the cursor back up.

You can close the split window in one of the following ways:

- *Ctrl + w*, followed by `q` will close the current window

- `:q` will close the window and unload the buffer; however, this will close Vim if you only have one window open
- `:bd` will delete the current buffer and close the current window
- *Ctrl + w*, followed by `o` (or the `:only` or `:on` command) will close all windows except for the current one

When you have multiple windows open, you can quit them all and exit Vim by executing `:qa`. This can be combined with the `:w` command to save every open file and quit: `:wqa`.

If you want to close a buffer without closing the window it's in, you can add the following command to your `.vimrc` file:

```
command! Bd :bp | :sp | :bn | :bd  " Close buffer without closing window.
```

You'll be able to use `:Bd` to close the buffer while keeping a split window open.

Moving windows

Windows can also be moved, swapped, and resized. Since there's no drag-and-drop functionality in Vim, there are some commands you will have to remember.

You don't have to remember all of these commands, as long as you know what window operations are supported. `:help window-moving` and `:help window-resize` will take you to the corresponding entries in the Vim manual when you inevitably forget the shortcuts.

As with the rest of the window commands, these are prefixed by *Ctrl + w*.

Ctrl + w followed, by an uppercase movement key (`H`, `J`, `K`, or `L`) will move the current window to the corresponding position:

- *Ctrl + w*, `H` moves the current window to the leftmost part of the screen
- *Ctrl + w*, `J` moves the current window to the bottom of the screen
- *Ctrl + w*, `K` moves the current window to the top of the screen
- *Ctrl + w*, `L` moves the current window to the rightmost part of the screen

For example, let's start with the following window layout (which was achieved by opening `animal_farm.py` and running `:sp animals/cat.py`, followed by `:vs farm.py`):

```
"""A farm for holding animals."""          """A cat."""

class Farm(object):                         import animal

    def __init__(self):                     class Cat(animal.Animal):
        self.animals = set()
                                                def __init__(self):
    def add_animal(self, animal):                   self.kind = 'cat'
        self.animals.add(animal)

    def print_contents(self):
farm.py                                     animals/cat.py
#!/usr/bin/python3

"""Our own little animal farm."""

import sys

from animals import cat
from animals import dog
from animals import sheep
import animal
animal_farm.py
"farm.py" 13L, 332C
```

Note the cursor position (in `animals/cat.py`). Here's what happens when we try to move the window containing the `animals/cat.py` buffer in each direction:

- *Ctrl + w*, H migrates `animals/cat.py` all the way to the left:

```
"""A cat."""                          """A farm for holding animals."""

import animal                         class Farm(object):

class Cat(animal.Animal):                 def __init__(self):
                                              self.animals = set()
    def __init__(self):
        self.kind = 'cat'                 def add_animal(self, animal):
~                                             self.animals.add(animal)
~
~                                         def print_contents(self):
~                                     farm.py
~                                     #!/usr/bin/python3
~
~                                     """Our own little animal farm."""
~
~                                     import sys
~
~                                     from animals import cat
~                                     from animals import dog
~                                     from animals import sheep
~                                     import animal
animals/cat.py                        animal_farm.py
```

- *Ctrl + w*, J moves `animals/cat.py` to the bottom of the screen, turning a vertical split into a horizontal split:

```
"""A farm for holding animals."""

class Farm(object):

    def __init__(self):
        self.animals = set()
farm.py
#!/usr/bin/python3

"""Our own little animal farm."""

import sys
animal_farm.py
"""A cat."""

import animal

class Cat(animal.Animal):

    def __init__(self):
animals/cat.py
```

- *Ctrl + w*, K moves `animals/cat.py` to the top of the screen:

```
"""A cat."""

import animal

class Cat(animal.Animal):

    def __init__(self):
animals/cat.py
"""A farm for holding animals."""

class Farm(object):

    def __init__(self):
        self.animals = set()

farm.py
#!/usr/bin/python3

"""Our own little animal farm."""

import sys

animal_farm.py
```

- *Ctrl + w,* L moves `animals/cat.py` to the right of the screen:

```
"""A farm for holding animals."""          """"A cat."""

class Farm(object):                         import animal

    def __init__(self):                     class Cat(animal.Animal):
        self.animals = set()
                                                def __init__(self):
    def add_animal(self, animal):                   self.kind = 'cat'
        self.animals.add(animal)

    def print_contents(self):
farm.py
#!/usr/bin/python3

"""Our own little animal farm."""

import sys

from animals import cat
from animals import dog
from animals import sheep
import animal
animal_farm.py                              animals/cat.py
"farm.py" 13L, 332C
```

You can change the contents of each window by simply navigating to it and selecting the desired buffer using the `:b` command. There are, however, options for swapping window contents:

- *Ctrl + w,* r moves every window within the row or the column (whichever is available—rows are given preference over columns) to the right or downward. *Ctrl + w,* R performs the same operation in reverse.
- *Ctrl + w,* x exchanges the contents of a window with the next one (or a previous one if it's considered a last window).

Internally, Vim refers to windows by number. However, unlike with buffers, the numbers change as your window layout adjusts, and there is no straightforward way to surface window numbers. Some window management commands take the window number as an argument, but this book will not be covering these. For reference, windows are numbered top to bottom, left to right.

Resizing windows

Default 50/50 window proportions might not be exactly what you're looking for, and there are some options for changing sizes.

Ctrl + w followed by = will equalize the height and width of all open windows. This is really useful when you just resized the Vim window and the height of your windows got all messed up.

The `:resize` command increases or decreases the height of a current window, while `:vertical resize` will adjust the width of the window. You can use these as follows:

- `:resize +N` will increase the height of a current window by N rows
- `:resize -N` will decrease the height of a current window by N rows
- `:vertical resize +N` will increase the width of a current window by N columns
- `:vertical resize -N` will decrease the width of a current window by N columns

`:resize` and `:vertical resize` can be shortened to `:res` and `:vert res`. There are also keyboard shortcuts for changing the height and width by one: *Ctrl + w, –* and *Ctrl + w, +* adjust the height, while *Ctrl + w, >* and *Ctrl + w, <* adjust the width.

Both commands can also be used to set the height and the width to a specific number of rows or columns:

- `:resize N` will set the height of the window to N
- `:vertical resize N` will set the width of the window to N

Tabs

In many modern editors, tabs are used to represent different files. While you can certainly do this in Vim, you might want to consider their original purpose.

Vim uses tabs to switch between collections of windows, allowing you to effectively have multiple workspaces. Tabs are often used to work on a slightly different problem or set of files within the same Vim session. Personally, I don't get a lot of use out of tab pages, but if you find yourself often switching context within the project or between projects, then tabs might be exactly what you're looking for.

 Another reason to use tabs would be Vim's diff functionality, which works per tab. You can read more about the vimdiff in `Chapter 5`, *Build, Test, and Execute*.

You can open a new tab with an empty buffer as follows:

`:tabnew`

 You can open an existing file in a new tab by running `:tabnew <filename>`.

As you can see, tabs are displayed on the top of the screen. The tab labeled `3 farm.py` is a tab with three open windows and an active buffer `farm.py`. The `[No Name]` tab is the one we just opened:

You can load a file in it in the usual way: `:e <filename>`. You can also switch to a desired buffer using the `:b` command.

To navigate between tabs, you can use the following:

- gt or :tabnext to move to the next tab
- gT or :tabprevious to move to the previous tab

The tabs can be closed using :tabclose or by closing all of the windows it contains (for example, with :q if it's the only window).

:tabmove N lets you place the tab after the *N*th tab (or as a first tab if N is 0).

Folds

One of the most powerful tools Vim provides for navigating large files is folds. Folds allow you to hide portions of the file, either based on some predefined rules or manual fold markers.

This is how animal_farm.py looks with some sections folded:

```
#!/usr/bin/python3

"""Our own little animal farm."""

import sys

from animals import cat
from animals import dog
from animals import sheep
import animal
import farm

def make_animal(kind):
+--   7 lines: if kind == 'cat':-------------------------------

def main(animals):
+--   4 lines: animal_farm = farm.Farm()-----------------------

if __name__ == '__main__':
+--   4 lines: if len(sys.argv) == 1:--------------------------
~
~
~
```

Method content is hidden, allowing you to view the code from a bird's-eye view.

Folding Python code

Since we're working with Python code throughout this book, let's play with some folds in our code. First, you'll need to change a setting called `foldmethod` to `indent` in your `.vimrc` file:

```
set foldmethod=indent
```

Don't forget to reload your `~/.vimrc` file by either restarting Vim or executing `:source $MYVIMRC`.

This will tell Vim to fold based on indentation (there are multiple ways to work with folds; see the following section, *Types of folds*, for more information).

Open `animal_farm.py` and you will see portions of our file folded away:

```
#!/usr/bin/python3

"""Our own little animal farm."""

import sys

from animals import cat
from animals import dog
from animals import sheep
import animal
import farm

def make_animal(kind):
+--   7 lines: if kind == 'cat':----------------------------

def main(animals):
+--   4 lines: animal_farm = farm.Farm()--------------------

if __name__ == '__main__':
+--   4 lines: if len(sys.argv) == 1:-----------------------
~
~
~
~
```

Navigate your cursor to one of the folded lines. Hitting zo will open the current fold:

```
#!/usr/bin/python3

"""Our own little animal farm."""

import sys

from animals import cat
from animals import dog
from animals import sheep
import animal
import farm

def make_animal(kind):
    if kind == 'cat':
        return cat.Cat()
    if kind == 'dog':
        return dog.Dog()
    if kind == 'sheep':
        return sheep.Sheep()
    return animal.Animal(kind)

def main(animals):
+--  4 lines: animal_farm = farm.Farm()-------------------------------
"animal_farm.py" 32L, 687C
```

Whenever your cursor is over a potential fold (an indented chunk of code in this example), zc will close the fold.

TIP

To visualize where folds are, you can use :set foldcolumn=N, where N is 0..12. This will dedicate the first N columns to the left of the screen to indicate folds with the – (beginning of an open fold), | (contents of an open fold), and + (closed fold) symbols.

You can also use za to toggle folds (open closed folds and close open folds).

You can open and close all folds in the file at the same time using zR and zM, respectively.

Setting an automatic `foldmethod` setting (such as `indent`) will display all files as folded by default. It's a matter of preference, and you may prefer to have the folds open when opening a new file. Adding `autocmd BufRead * normal zR` to your `.vimrc` file will keep the folds open as you open new files. This command tells Vim to execute `zR` (open all folds) when reading a buffer.

Types of folds

Vim is somewhat intelligent when it comes to folding code, and supports multiple ways to fold code. The folding method is guarded by a `foldmethod` option in your `.vimrc` file. Supported fold methods are as follows:

- `manual` allows you to manually define folds. This becomes unrealistic when working with any substantial body of text.
- `indent` supports indentation-based folding, which is perfect for languages and code bases where indentation matters (regardless of the language you're working with, a standardized code base is likely to have some consistent indentation, making `indent` a quick and easy way to fold away bits you don't care for).
- `expr` allows for a regular-expression based folding. This is an extremely powerful tool if you have complex custom rules you'd like to use for defining folds.
- `marker` uses special markup in the text, such as `{{{` and `}}}`. This is useful for managing long `.vimrc` files, but has little use outside of the Vim world since it requires modifying file content.
- `syntax` provides syntax-aware folds. However, not every language is supported out of the box (Python isn't).
- `diff` is automatically used when Vim operates in a diff mode, displaying the difference between two files (see *Vimdiff* in `Chapter 5`, *Build, Test, and Execute*).

Reminder: you can set an option in your `.vimrc` file by adding the following line: `set foldmethod=<method>`.

Navigating file trees

Since software projects contain a lot of files and directories, finding a way to traverse and display these using Vim comes in handy. This section will cover five different ways that you can navigate your files: using the built-in Netrw file manager or using the `:e` command with the `wildemenu` option enabled, as well as using the NERDTree, Vinegar, and CtrlP plugins. All of these provide different ways to interact with files and can be mixed and matched.

Netrw

Netrw is a built-in file manager in Vim (if we want to get technical, it's a plugin that ships with Vim). It allows you to browse directories and functions, similar to any other file manager you've worked with in your favorite OS.

Use `:Ex` (the full command is `:Explore`) to open the file navigation window:

```
"  ==========================================================================
"  Netrw Directory Listing                                    (netrw v156)
"    /home/ruslan/Mastering-Vim/ch2
"    Sorted by        name
"    Sort sequence: [\/]$,\<core\%(\.\d\+\)\=\>,\.h$,\.c$,\.cpp$,\~\=\*$,*,\.o$,\
"    Quick Help: <F1>:help  -:go up dir  D:delete  R:rename  s:sort-by  x:special
"  ==========================================================================
./
./
animals/
.vimrc
README.md
animal.py
animal_farm.py
farm.py
~
~
~
~
~
~
~
```

Netrw is fully integrated with Vim, so executing an edit command on a directory (for example, :e . to open a current directory) actually opens Netrw. This also makes it so that you have one less command to remember.

Here, you can see all of the files within our workspace. Netrw already provides a quick help section in a status bar, but here are the main controls you'll need to know:

- *Enter* opens files and directories
- – goes up a directory
- D deletes a file or directory
- R renames a file or directory

A Netrw window can be open in split windows or new tabs as well:

- :Vex opens Netrw in a vertical split
- :Sex opens Netrw in a horizontal split
- :Lex opens Netrw in a leftmost full-height vertical split

Netrw is a powerful tool, which supports remote editing as well; for instance, to get a directory listing over SFTP, you can run the following:

```
:Ex sftp://<domain>/<directory>/
```

You can substitute :Ex with :e for the same results. You can edit individual files as well. Here's how to open a file over SCP:

```
:e scp://<domain>/<directory>/<file>
```

:e with wildmenu enabled

Another way to explore file trees is to use the `set wildmenu` option in your `.vimrc` file. This option sets an autocomplete menu to operate in enhanced mode, showing possible autocomplete options above the status line. With `wildmenu` enabled, type in `:e` (followed by a space) and hit *Tab*. This will bring up a list of files in the current directory, and you can use the *Tab* key to iterate through these and *Shift + Tab* to move backward (the left and right arrow keys perform the same function):

```
    if kind == 'cat':
        return cat.Cat()
    if kind == 'dog':
        return dog.Dog()
    if kind == 'sheep':
        return sheep.Sheep()
    return animal.Animal(kind)

:e animal
animal.py        animal_farm.py  animals/
animal.py  animal_farm.py  animals/
:e animal_farm.py
```

Pressing *Enter* will open the selected file or directory. The down arrow allows you to drill down into directory under cursor, and the up arrow takes you back up a level.

This also works with partial paths, and entering `:e <beginning_of_filename>` followed by a *Tab* key invokes `wildmenu` as well.

My `.vimrc` file has the following in it:

```
set wildmenu                    " Enable enhanced tab autocomplete.
set wildmode=list:longest,full  " Complete till longest string,
                                " then open the wildmenu.
```

This allows you to autocomplete the path to the longest match possible (and display a list of possible completion options) on a first *Tab* press, and traverse through files with `wildmenu` on a second *Tab* press.

Plugin spotlight – NERDTree

NERDTree is a handy plugin that emulates modern IDE behavior by displaying a file tree in a split buffer to the side of the screen. NERDTree is available from `https://github.com/scrooloose/nerdtree` (see *Installing Plugins* earlier in this chapter for installation instructions).

Once installed, you can invoke NERDTree by typing the following:

```
:NERDTree
```

A list of files in a directory will show up:

```
" Press ? for help                      #!/usr/bin/python3

.. (up a dir)                           """Our own little animal farm."""
</ruslan/Mastering-Vim/ch2/
▯ animals/                              import sys
    cat.py
    dog.py                             from animals import cat
    sheep.py                           from animals import dog
  animal.py                            from animals import sheep
  animal_farm.py                       import animal
  farm.py                              import farm
  README.md
                                       def make_animal(kind):
~                                      +--  7 lines: if kind == 'cat':--------------
~
~                                      def main(animals):
~                                      +--  4 lines: animal_farm = farm.Farm()--------
~
~                                      if __name__ == '__main__':
~                                      +--  4 lines: if len(sys.argv) == 1:----------
~
~
/home/ruslan/Mastering-Vim/ch2  animal_farm.py
```

Use h, j, k, and l or the arrow keys to navigate the file structure, and *Enter* or o to open the file. There are multiple useful shortcuts, and *Shift + ?* brings up a handy cheat sheet.

A notable feature is bookmark support, which allows you to bookmark a directory (when placing the cursor over it in NERDTree) by executing :Bookmark. Press B when in a NERDTree window to display bookmarks at the top of the window.

In the following screenshot, you can see the bookmarks I have for code that supports chapters of this book (the Chapter01/ and Chapter02/ directories):

```
" Press ? for help                    #!/usr/bin/python3

    ----------Bookmarks----------    """Our own little animal farm."""
  ch1 <uslan/Mastering-Vim/ch1/
  ch2 <uslan/Mastering-Vim/ch2/    import sys

.. (up a dir)                        from animals import cat
</ruslan/Mastering-Vim/ch2/          from animals import dog
 animals/                            from animals import sheep
    cat.py                           import animal
    dog.py                           import farm
    sheep.py
  animal.py                          def make_animal(kind):
  animal_farm.py                     +--   7 lines: if kind == 'cat':----------------
  farm.py
  README.md                          def main(animals):
~                                    +--   4 lines: animal_farm = farm.Farm()--------
~
~                                    if __name__ == '__main__':
~                                    +--   4 lines: if len(sys.argv) == 1:----------
~                                    ~
~                                    ~
/home/ruslan/Mastering-Vim/ch2  animal_farm.py
```

You can choose to always display bookmarks in a NERDTree window by setting the `NERDTreeShowBookmarks` option in your `.vimrc` file:

```
let NERDTreeShowBookmarks = 1  " Display bookmarks on startup.
```

You can bring NERDTree up or hide it by executing `:NERDTreeToggle`. If you're interested in having NERDTree up every time you're editing, you might want to add the following to your `.vimrc` file:

```
autocmd VimEnter * NERDTree  " Enable NERDTree on Vim startup.
```

Something I personally found really useful is to close the NERDTree window automatically when it's the last open window. I have the following in my `.vimrc` file:

```
" Autoclose NERDTree if it's the only open window left.
autocmd bufenter * if (winnr("$") == 1 && exists("b:NERDTree") &&
  \ b:NERDTree.isTabTree()) | q | endif
```

These days, I rarely find myself using NERDTree. Before switching to Vim, I often relied on having a project outline in the view when I worked. In my early days of learning Vim, NERDTree was a lifesaver. Vim changed the way I work and having a file outline always on became distracting, so eventually I moved back to using Netrw.

Plugin spotlight – Vinegar

Tim Pope's `vinegar.vim` is a simple plugin that addresses the difficulty of using project drawers with Vim split window functionality. Plugins such as NERDTree become rather disorienting to work with when you have more than one window open in a split.

In the following example, three windows are open (and a fourth NERDTree window on the left):

```
" Press ? for help          """A farm for holding animals."""  """A cat."""

.. (up a dir)               class Farm(object):              import animal
</ruslan/Mastering-Vim/ch2/
▯ animals/                      def __init__(self):          class Cat(animal.Animal):
    cat.py                          self.animals = set()
    dog.py                                                       def __init__(self):
    sheep.py                    def add_animal(self, animal):        self.kind = 'cat'
  animal.py                         self.animals.add(animal)   ~
  animal_farm.py                                               ~
  farm.py                         def print_contents(self):    ~
  README.md                  farm.py                             animals/cat.py
~                            #!/usr/bin/python3
~
~                            """Our own little animal farm."""
~
~                            import sys
~
~                            from animals import cat
~                            from animals import dog
~                            from animals import sheep
~                            import animal
/home/ruslan/Mastering-Vim/ch2  animal_farm.py
```

When pressing *Enter* with the cursor in the NERDTree window, which window will the new file be opened in?

Hint: it's the bottom left one—but you don't have a way of knowing that. NERDTree opens files in the last created window.

Tim Pope solves this problem with a small plugin called **Vinegar**, which makes using Netrw a more seamless experience. It's available over at `https://github.com/tpope/vim-vinegar` (see *Installing plugins* for installation instructions).

If you have NERDTree installed when using Vinegar, you'll get a NERDTree window instead of Netrw. To avoid NERDTree replacing Netrw (and to make commands like - work), set `let NERDTreeHijackNetrw = 0` in your `.vimrc` file.

Vinegar adds a handy new mapping: – (dash) to open Netrw in a current directory. Try it out:

```
.vim/
animals/
.vimrc
README.md
animal.py
animal_farm.py
farm.py




"." is a directory
```

The plugin hides Netrw's help bar, which might be confusing at first. Hit *I* (uppercase i) to bring it back. Another shortcut, *Shift + ~* key, takes you to your home `directory`, which is often where you'll store your projects.

Plugin spotlight – CtrlP

CtrlP is a fuzzy completion plugin that helps you open the files you need quickly, given that you somewhat know what you're looking for. CtrlP is available from `https://github.com/ctrlpvim/ctrlp.vim` (see the *Installing plugins* section earlier in this chapter for installation instructions).

Install it and hit *Ctrl + p*:

This shows the list of files in the project directory. Type in a partial filename or a path, and the list of files will narrow down to string matches. You can use *Ctrl* + j and *Ctrl* + k to navigate up and down the list, and *Enter* to open the file. *Esc* closes the CtrlP window.

CtrlP also allows you to navigate through buffers and most recently used files. With the CtrlP window open, you can use *Ctrl* + *f* and *Ctrl* + *b* to cycle through the available options.

You can invoke these directly by executing `:CtrlPBuffer` for buffers and `:CtrlPMRU` for the most recently used ones. You can also use `:CtrlPMixed` to search through files, buffers, and the most recently used files at the same time.

You can also add custom mappings for these to your `.vimrc` file. For example, to map *Ctrl* + *b* to `:CtrlPBuffer`, you could do the following:

```
nnoremap <C-b> :CtrlPBuffer<cr>   " Map CtrlP buffer mode to Ctrl + B.
```

Navigating text

We've covered some basic movements (by characters, words, and paragraphs), but Vim supports a lot more options for navigation.

Check the following if you want some movement within the current line:

- As you already know, `h` and `l` move the cursor left and right, respectively
- `t` (un**t**il) followed by a character allows you to search the line for that character and place the cursor before the character, while `T` allows you to search backward
- `f` (**f**ind) followed by a character allows you to search the current line for that character and move the cursor to the character, while `F` allows you to search backward
- `_` takes you to the beginning of the line and `$` takes you to the end of the line

A word consists of numbers, letters, and underscores. A WORD consists of any characters except for whitespace (like spaces, tabs, or newlines). This distinction helps with more precise navigation. For instance, `farm.add_animal(animal)` is a single WORD, while `farm`, `add_animal`, and `animal` are individual words.

For free-form movement, you're already familiar with these bits:

- j and l move the cursor down and up, respectively

- w moves you to the beginning of the next word (W for WORD)

- b moves you to the beginning of the previous word (B for WORD)

- e moves you to the end of the next word (E for WORD)

- ge moves you to the end of the previous word (gE for WORD)

- *Shift* + { and *Shift* + } takes you to the beginning and the end of a paragraph

Here are some new free-form movement options:

- *Shift* + (and *Shift* +) takes you to the beginning and the end a sentence

- H takes you to the top of the current window, and L takes you to the bottom of the current window

- *Ctrl* + f (or the *Page Down* key) scrolls the buffer one page down, and *Ctrl* + b (or the *Page Up* key) scrolls one page up

- / followed by a string searches the document for a string and *Shift* + ? to search backward

- gg takes you to the top of the file

- G takes you to the bottom of the file

This handy visualization is based on the Vim movement cheat sheet Ted Nailed published on his blog sometime in 2010:

```
                        gg
                        ?
                      Ctrl-b
                        H
                        {
                        k
  ^ F T ( b ge h    l w e ) t f $
                        j
                        }
                        L
                      Ctrl-f
                        /
                        G
```

You can also move by line numbers. To enable line number display, run :set nu, followed by *Enter* (or add :set number to your .vimrc file). Vim will dedicate a few columns on the left of the screen to display line numbers:

```
 1 #!/usr/bin/python3
 2
 3 """Our own little animal farm."""
 4
 5 import sys
 6
 7 from animals import cat
 8 from animals import dog
 9 from animals import sheep
10 import animal
11 import farm
12
13 def make_animal(kind):
14 +--   7 lines: if kind == 'cat':-----------------------------------
21
22 def main(animals):
23 +--   4 lines: animal_farm = farm.Farm()-----------------------------
27
28 if __name__ == '__main__':
29 +--   4 lines: if len(sys.argv) == 1:-------------------------------
~
~
~
:set nu
```

You can jump to a specific line by typing `:N` followed by *Enter*, where N is the absolute line number. For instance, to jump to line 20, you'll run `:20` followed by *Enter*.

 You can also tell Vim to open a file and immediately place a cursor at a particular line. For that, add +N after the filename when invoking Vim, where N is the line number. For example, to open `animal_farm.py` on line 14, you'd run `$ vim animal_farm.py +14`.

Vim also supports relative line movement. To move down N lines you'll run `:+N` and to move down you'll run `:-N`. You can also ask Vim to display line numbers relative to the current cursor position with `:set relativenumber`. In the following screenshot, our cursor is on line 11, and Vim displays the relative distance to other lines:

```
10 #!/usr/bin/python3
 9
 8 """Our own little animal farm."""
 7
 6 import sys
 5
 4 from animals import cat
 3 from animals import dog
 2 from animals import sheep
 1 import animal
11 import farm
 1
 2 def make_animal(kind):
 3 +--   7 lines: if kind == 'cat'!---------------------------------------
 4
 5 def main(animals):
 6 +--   4 lines: animal_farm = farm.Farm()-------------------------------
 7
 8 if __name__ == '__main__':
 9 +--   4 lines: if len(sys.argv) == 1:----------------------------------
~
~
~
```

For example, you could tell Vim to move to the line containing `def main(animals):` by typing `:+5`, followed by *Enter*.

Jumping into insert mode

You've already learned to enter insert mode using i, which puts you in insert mode at the position of the cursor.

There are a few more convenient shortcuts for entering insert mode:

- a places you in insert mode after the cursor

- A places you in insert mode at the end of the line (equivalent of $a)

- I places you in insert mode at the beginning of the line, but after indentation (equivalent of _i)

- o adds a new line below the cursor before entering insert mode
- O adds a new line above the cursor before entering insert mode
- gi places you in insert mode where you last exited it

You've also learned how to enter insert mode after deleting some code with the change command (c). Here are more ways to chain change commands:

- C deletes text to the right of the cursor (until the end of the line) before entering insert mode
- cc or S deletes the contents of the line before entering insert mode, while preserving indentation
- s deletes a single character (prefix by a number to delete multiple) before placing you in insert mode

Searching with / and ?

Most times one of the fastest ways to navigate somewhere is to search for a particular string. Vim allows you to search for a match by typing in / (which puts you in command-line mode) followed by a search string. Once you hit *Enter*, your cursor will move to the first match.

Cycling through the matches in the same buffer can be done by pressing n to go to the next match and N to the previous match.

A useful option for searching is `set hlsearch` (consider setting it in your `.vimrc` file), since it highlights every match on the screen. For example, this is how running `/kind` in `animal_farm.py` looks with `hlsearch` enabled:

```
from animals import dog
from animals import sheep
import animal
import farm

def make_animal(kind):
    if kind == 'cat':
        return cat.Cat()
    if kind == 'dog':
        return dog.Dog()
    if kind == 'sheep':
        return sheep.Sheep()
    return animal.Animal(kind)

def main(animals):
    animal_farm = farm.Farm()
    for animal_kind in animals:
        animal_farm.add_animal(make_animal(animal_kind))
    animal_farm.print_contents()
```

You can clear the highlights by executing `:noh`.

Another nifty trick is using `set incsearch`. This will make Vim dynamically move you to the first match as soon as you type.

In case you want to search backwards, replace `/` with `?`. This will also affect the way `n` and `N` will behave, showing a next backward match, and a previous backward match respectively.

Searching across files

Vim has two commands to help you search across files, `:grep` and `:vimgrep`:

- `:grep` uses system `grep`, and is a great tool if you're already familiar with how `grep` works
- `:vimgrep` is a part of Vim, and might be easier to use if you are not already familiar with `grep`

We'll focus on `:vimgrep`, since the `grep` tool is outside the scope of this book.

The syntax is as follows: `:vimgrep <pattern> <path>`. `pattern` could either be a string or a Vim-flavored regular expression. `path` will often be a wildcard; use `**` as a path to search recursively (or `**/*.py` to restrict by filetype).

Let's try searching for a `calc` substring in our code base:

```
:vimgrep animal **/* .py
```

This will take us to the first match, displaying the number of matches at the bottom of the screen:

```
"""An animal base class."""


class Animal(object):

+--  2 lines: def __init__(self, kind):----------------------------------------
~
~
~


(1 of 26): """An animal base class."""
```

To navigate through the matches, use `:cn` or `:cp`. However, you might want to open a visual quickfix window by using `:copen`, as follows:

```
"""An animal base class."""


class Animal(object):
+-- 2 lines: def __init__(self, kind):---------------------------------------
~
~
~
~
~
animal.py
animal.py|1 col 7|  """An animal base class."""
animal_farm.py|3 col 19|  """Our own little animal farm."""
animal_farm.py|7 col 6|  from animals import cat
animal_farm.py|8 col 6|  from animals import dog
animal_farm.py|9 col 6|  from animals import sheep
animal_farm.py|10 col 8|  import animal
animal_farm.py|13 col 10|  def make_animal(kind):
animal_farm.py|20 col 12|  return animal.Animal(kind)
animal_farm.py|22 col 10|  def main(animals):
animal_farm.py|23 col 5|  animal_farm = farm.Farm()
[Quickfix List] :vimgrep animal **/*.py                1,1            Top
:copen
```

You can navigate the quickfix list with the `j` and `k` keys and jump to a match by pressing *Enter*. The quickfix window can be closed like any other window by typing `:q` or running *Ctrl + w, q*. You can read more about it in the *Quickfix List* section in `Chapter 5`, *Build, Test, and Execute.*

ack

On Linux, you can use Vim in conjunction with `ack` to search through code bases. `ack` is the spiritual successor of `grep`, and is focused on working with code. Install it using your favorite package manager; here's an example of using `apt-get`:

```
$ sudo apt-get install ack-grep
```

 Visit `https://beyondgrep.com/install` to learn more about `ack` and for installation instructions.

For example, you can now use `ack` from the command line to search for all Python files recursively (starting in the current directory) containing the word `Animal`:

```
$ ack --python Animal
```

The preceding code will produce output similar to `grep`:

```
ruslan@ann-perkins:~/Mastering-Vim/ch2$ ack --python Animal
animal_farm.py
20:    return animal.Animal(kind)

animals/sheep.py
5:class Sheep(animal.Animal):

animals/cat.py
5:class Cat(animal.Animal):

animals/dog.py
5:class Dog(animal.Animal):

animal.py
4:class Animal(object):
ruslan@ann-perkins:~/Mastering-Vim/ch2$
```

Vim has a plugin that integrates the result of `ack` in Vim's quickfix window (see the *Quickfix List* section in Chapter 5, *Build, Test, and Execute*, to learn more about quickfix). The plugin is available from `https://github.com/mileszs/ack.vim`. After installation, you will be able to execute `:Ack` from Vim:

```
:Ack --python Animal
```

This will run `ack` and populate the quickfix window (see the preceding section, as well as *Quickfix List* in `Chapter 5`, *Build, Test, and Execute,* for more information about a quickfix window) with the output:

```
from animals import dog
from animals import sheep
import animal
import farm

def make_animal(kind):
+--   7 lines: if kind == 'cat':------------------------------------------

def main(animals):
+--   4 lines: animal_farm = farm.Farm()---------------------------------

animal_farm.py
animal_farm.py|20 col 19| return animal.Animal(kind)
animals/sheep.py|5 col 20| class Sheep(animal.Animal):
animals/cat.py|5 col 18| class Cat(animal.Animal):
animals/dog.py|5 col 18| class Dog(animal.Animal):
animal.py|4 col 7| class Animal(object):
~
~
~
~
<s -H --nopager --nocolor --nogroup --column --python Animal 1,1          All
```

Utilizing text objects

Text objects are an additional type of object in Vim. Text objects allow you to manipulate text within parentheses or quotes, which becomes really useful when working with code. Text objects are only available when combined with other operators like change or delete or a visual mode (see *Visual and Select Modes* in `Chapter 3`, *Follow the Leader – Plugin Management*).

Let's give it a shot. Navigate your cursor to the text between parentheses:

```
def print_contents(self):
    print("We've got some animals on the farm:",
          ', '.join(animal.kind for animal in self.animals) + '.')
```

Now, type in `di)` (delete inside parentheses). This will delete the text inside parentheses:

```
def print_contents(self):
    print("We've got some animals on the farm:",
          ', '.join() + '.')
```

This works similarly with a change command. Undo the previous change (`u`) and start in the same spot:

```
def print_contents(self):
    print("We've got some animals on the farm:",
          ', '.join(animal.kind for animal in self.animals) + '.')
```

Execute `c2aw` (change the outside of two words) to delete two words (with the surrounding spaces) and enter insert mode:

```
def print_contents(self):
    print("We've got some animals on the farm:",
          ', '.join(animal.kind in self.animals) + '.')
-- INSERT --
```

Text objects come in two flavors—inner objects (prefixed by `i`) and outer objects (prefixed by `a`). Inner objects do not include white space (or other surrounding characters), while outer objects do.

A full list of text objects can be looked up through :help text-objects, but some interesting ones are as follows:

- w and W for words and WORDs
- s for sentences
- p for paragraphs
- t for HTML/XML tags

Pairs of characters that are most often used in programming are all supported as text objects: `, ', ",),], >, and } select the text enclosed by the characters.

One way to think about working with text objects is that it's like constructing sentences. Here are the two examples that we used previously broken down:

Verb	(Number)	Adjective	Noun
d delete		i inside	) parentheses
c change	2	a outside	w word

Plugin spotlight – EasyMotion

EasyMotion has been in an essential part of my kit since I came across it. It simplifies navigation by allowing you to jump to the desired position with speed and precision. It's available from https://github.com/easymotion/vim-easymotion (see *Installing plugins* for installation instructions).

After installing it, you can invoke the plugin by hitting the leader key (\) twice, followed by the desired movement key.

The leader key is often used by plugins to provide additional key mappings. By default, Vim's leader key is \. We'll go into more detail about the leader key in Chapter 3, *Follow the Leader – Plugin Management*.

Try using it with a word-wise motion by invoking \ \ w (backslash, followed by a backslash, followed by w):

```
#!/asr/sin/dython3
g
"""hur kwn little qnimal warm."""
e
rmport tys
y
urom inimals omport pat
zrom xnimals cmport vog
brom nnimals mmport fheep
japort jsimal
jdport jgrm
jh
jkf jlke_animal(jqnd):
    jw jend == ';at':
        ;sturn ;dt.;gt()
    ;h ;knd == ';lg':
        ;qturn ;wg.;eg()
    ;r ;tnd == ';yeep':
        ;uturn ;ieep.;oeep()
    ;pturn ;zimal.;ximal(;cnd)
;v
;bf ;nin(;mimals):
    ;fimal_farm = ;jrm.;;rm()
Target key: ▌
```

You can see that the beginning of every word on the screen have been replaced with a letter (or two letters, once EasyMotion runs out of English letters from the alphabet). Pressing the letter (or two in order) will instantly transport your cursor to that spot on the screen.

EasyMotion supports the following movement commands by default (all prefixed by double tapping the leader key):

- f, to look for a character to the right and F to look for the character on the left
- t, to move until the character on the right and T until the character on the left
- w, to move by word (and W by WORD)

- b, to move backward by word (and B by WORD)
- e, to move forward to the end of the word (and E for the WORD)
- ge, to move backward to the end of the word (and gE for the WORD)
- k and j to go to the beginning of the line up or down
- n and N for jumping through search results on the page (based on the last / or ? search)

EasyMotion leaves many keys unassigned, leaving it up to the user to build their own set of mappings. You should check :help easymotion to see everything EasyMotion can do.

Copying and pasting with registers

You can copy text by using the y (yank) command, followed by a movement or a text object. You can also hit y from a visual mode when you have selected some text.

In addition to all of the standard movement, you can use yy to yank the contents of the current line.

Let's yank the following piece of code by typing ye (yank until the end of the word):

```
        return sheep.Sheep()
    return animal.Animal(kind)

def main(animals):
    animal_farm = farm.Farm()
    for animal_kind in animals:
        animal_farm.add_animal(make_animal())
    animal_farm.print_contents()

if __name__ == '__main__':
    if len(sys.argv) == 1:
```

This will copy `animal_kind` into our default register. Now, place the cursor where you want the text to appear (the text is inserted after the cursor):

```
        return sheep.Sheep()
    return animal.Animal(kind)

def main(animals):
    animal_farm = farm.Farm()
    for animal_kind in animals:
        animal_farm.add_animal(make_animal())
    animal_farm.print_contents()


if __name__ == '__main__':
    if len(sys.argv) == 1:
```

To paste the code, hit p:

```
        return sheep.Sheep()
    return animal.Animal(kind)

def main(animals):
    animal_farm = farm.Farm()
    for animal_kind in animals:
        animal_farm.add_animal(make_animal(animal_kind))
    animal_farm.print_contents()


if __name__ == '__main__':
    if len(sys.argv) == 1:
1 change; before #10   1 seconds ago
```

The delete and change operators also yanks content so that you can paste it later. Oh, and you can prefix the paste command with a number, in case you ever want to duplicate something multiple times.

Where do the registers come in?

Whenever you copy and paste text, it's saved in a register. Vim allows you to operate with many registers, which are identified by letters, numbers, and special symbols.

Registers can be accessed by hitting ", followed by the register identifier, followed for the operation on said register.

Registers a - z are used for holding manually assigned data. For example, to yank a word into the a register, you can run "ayw and paste it using "ap.

 Registers are also used to record macros, which you will learn about in Chapter 6, *Refactoring Code with Regular Expressions and Macros*.

All of the operations you've performed so far have used the unnamed register. If you ever need to access the unnamed register explicitly, it is identified by a double quote character, ". For example, you can use ""p to paste from the unnamed register (which is the same as just invoking p).

Numbered registers are effectively a history of your last 10 delete operations. 0 accesses the last deleted text, 1 the one before it, and so on. For example, if you have stellar memory, you can paste some text you yanked seven yank operations ago by hitting "7p.

 There are some read-only registers you might find handy: % holds the name of the current file, # holds the name of the previously opened file, . is the last inserted text, and : is the last executed command.

You can also interact with buffers from outside of a normal mode. *Ctrl + r* is a convenient shortcut, which allows you to paste a register's contents when you're in insert or command-line modes. For example, while you're in insert mode, *Ctrl + r*, " will paste the contents of the unnamed buffer at the position of the cursor.

You can access the content of a register at any time by running `:reg <register names>`. For instance, if you wanted to check what's inside the a and b registers, you'd run `:reg a b`. Here's the output:

```
from animals import dog
from animals import sheep
import animal
import farm

def make_animal(kind):
    if kind == 'cat':
:reg a b
--- Registers ---
"a   def make_animal(kind):
"b   from animals import cat^]from animals import dog^]from animals import shee
Press ENTER or type command to continue
```

In the preceding example, the a register contains `def make_animal(kind):`, and the b register contains a set of imports (`from animals import ...`) separated by newlines.

In addition, you can list the contents of every register by running `:reg` without any parameters.

Named registers (a-z) can be appended to as well. To append to a register instead of overwriting it, capitalize the register name. For example, to append a, word to register a, run `"Ayw` with a cursor at the beginning of the word.

Copying from outside of Vim

There are two built-in registers that interact with the outside world:

- The * register is the primary system clipboard (the default clipboard in Mac and Windows, and mouse selection inside a Terminal in Linux)
- The + register (only in Linux) is used for Windows-style *Ctrl + c* and *Ctrl + v* operations (referred to as **Clipboard selection**)

You can interact with these registers as you would with any other. For instance, you can use `"*p` to paste from the primary clipboard or use `"+yy` to yank a line into Linux's Clipboard selection.

If you want Vim to work with these registers by default, you can set the `clipboard` variable in your `.vimrc` file. Set it to `unnamed` to copy and paste from the `*` register:

```
set clipboard=unnamed   " Copy into system (*) register.
```

Set it to `unnamedplus` for yank and paste commands to work with the + register by default:

```
set clipboard=unnamedplus   " Copy into system (+) register.
```

You can also tell Vim to use both at once:

```
set clipboard=unnamed,unnamedplus   " Copy into system (*, +) register.
```

Now, `y` and `p` will yank and paste from the specified register by default.

> You can also sometimes choose to paste text from the system clipboard while inside the insert mode. In older Vim versions or in certain Terminal emulators, this will yield some issues, since Vim will try to automatically indent code or extend commented out sections. To avoid this, run `:set paste` before pasting code to disable auto indent and auto comment insertion. Run `:set nopaste` to turn it back on once you're done.
>
> Most of these issues are resolved in bracketed paste mode, which is enabled by default, starting with version 8.0. See `:help xterm-bracketed-paste` for more details.

Summary

You now know how to navigate core concepts Vim operates by: using buffers to represent files, utilizing split windows, and using tabs to organize multiple windows. You've also learned how to use folds to make navigating large files more manageable.

You now should be more confident getting through a large code base by navigating files with plugins such as Netrw, NERDTree, Vinegar, and CtrlP. Oh, and this chapter taught you a quick (even though it's a slightly manual) way to install said plugins.

This chapter covered new movement operations, text objects, ways to quickly dart into insert mode, and how to make even fancier jumps throughout the file using the EasyMotion plugin. We've also dipped into search functionality, searching both within a single file and across the whole code base. You get a bonus point for trying out the `ack` plugin.

Finally, this chapter covered the concept of registers, and how you can use them to supercharge copying and pasting text.

In the next chapter, we'll take a deeper look at plugin management, and we'll go into detail about modes in Vim, as well as creating custom mappings and commands.

Follow the Leader - Plugin Management

Vim plugins are easy to make and the number of available plugins keeps growing every year. Some cater to a very narrow audience and improve on a very particular workflow, while others aim to make Vim more effective to use for the general public. This chapter will take a deep dive into installing plugins and customizing your workflow through remapping keys. This chapter will cover the following topics:

- Ways to manage multiple plugins with vim-plug, Vundle, Pathogen, or a home-made solution
- A way to profile slow plugins
- An in-depth explanation of primary modes in Vim
- Intricacies of remapping commands
- The leader key and how it's useful for all kinds of custom shortcuts
- Configuring and customizing plugins

Technical requirements

In this chapter, you will be working on your `.vimrc` file. If you get lost through this chapter, you can get the resulting file from GitHub: `https://github.com/PacktPublishing/Mastering-Vim/tree/master/Chapter03`

Managing plugins

You have already installed quite a few plugins so far, and the number will only keep going up, especially as you try to solve problems that are specific to whatever it is you're working on. Manually keeping plugins up to date requires quite a bit of work, but luckily there are plugin management solutions out there!

Plugin management becomes even more important if you often change or switch machines and have the need to keep multiple plugins updated.

 For more tips on keeping Vim synced between multiple machines, see Chapter 7, *Making Vim Your Own*.

The plugin management landscape is ever changing, and there's no substitute for good old research when choosing a plugin manager. This chapter covers a few plugin managers that I've used throughout the years, which will hopefully be enough for you to base your own research on.

vim-plug

The newest and the brightest in plugin management is vim-plug, a lightweight plugin that makes it easy to deal with a multitude of plugins. The plugin is available on GitHub at: https://github.com/junegunn/vim-plug (it has a rather friendly README file, but I've captured the gist of it in this section if you're feeling lazy).

There are some neat things about this plugin:

- It's lightweight and fits in a single file, allowing for some straightforward installation options
- It supports parallel plugin load (if Vim is compiled with Python or Ruby enabled, which is true for all modern Vim setups)
- It supports the lazy loading of most plugins, only invoking plugins for a particular command or a file type

In the previous chapter, you manually installed the plugins. This section provides a much better plugin experience, and you'll want to delete the plugins you downloaded manually. In order to do that, remove the manually added plugin directory (`rm -rf $HOME/.vim/pack` in Linux and `rmdir /s %USERPROFILE%\vimfiles\pack` in Windows).

Installing vim-plug is straightforward:

1. Fetch the plugin file from `https://raw.github.com/junegunn/vim-plug/master/plug.vim`.
2. Save the file as `$HOME/.vim/autoload/plug.vim`.

1. To fetch a single file from GitHub, you can use `curl` or `wget` on Linux or macOS, or just open the link in the browser, right-click, and choose **Save as...**. For instance, you could run the following command to fetch the file in Unix:

```
$ curl -fLo ~/.vim/autoload/plug.vim --create-dirs
  https://raw.github.com/junegunn/vim-plug/master/plug.vim
```

2. Update your `.vimrc` file to include vim-plug initializers:

1.
```
" Manage plugins with vim-plug.
call plug#begin()
call plug#end()
```

2. Add some plugins between these two lines, using the last parts of the URL in GitHub (in <username>/<repository> format, for example scrooloose/nerdtree instead of `https://github.com/scrooloose/nerdtree`) to identify the plugins:

   1. ```
      " Manage plugins with vim-plug.
      call plug#begin()

      Plug 'scrooloose/nerdtree'
      Plug 'tpope/vim-vinegar'
      Plug 'ctrlpvim/ctrlp.vim'
      Plug 'mileszs/ack.vim'
      Plug 'easymotion/vim-easymotion'

      call plug#end()
      ```

2. Save your `.vimrc` file and reload it (`:w | source $MYVIMRC`) or restart Vim to apply the changes. Execute `:PlugInstall` to install the plugins.

This will download the aforementioned plugins from GitHub:

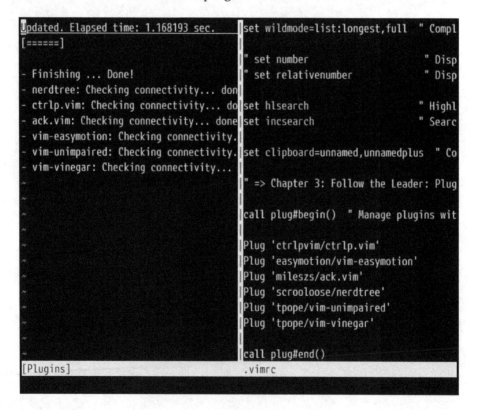
      ```

There are two main commands you will use with vim-plug:

- `:PlugUpdate` will update all of the plugins you have installed.
- `:PlugClean` will delete the plugins you removed from your `.vimrc` file. If you don't run `:PlugClean`, the plugins you deactivated (by either commenting out or removing the relevant `Plug ...` line in your `.vimrc` file) will stay on your system.

> Running `:PlugUpdate` updates every plugin vim-plug manages besides itself. If you want to update vim-plug, you need to run `:PlugUpgrade` and reload your `.vimrc` file by either running `:source $MYVIMRC` or restarting Vim.

Lazy plugin loading is a useful tool to prevent plugins from slowing down Vim. The `Plug` directive supports optional parameters. For instance, if you wanted to load NERDTree when the `:NERDTreeToggle` command is called, you could use the `on` parameter:

```
Plug 'scrooloose/nerdtree', { 'on':  'NERDTreeToggle' }
```

If you wanted to only load a plugin for a particular file type, you could use the `for` parameter:

```
Plug 'junegunn/goyo.vim', { 'for': 'markdown' }
```

> Due to the way vim-plug is installed, its help pages are not available by default. If you'd like to be able to call `:help vim-plug`, add `Plug 'junegunn/vim-plug'` to a list of installed plugins and run `:PlugInstall`.

You can find the list of supported parameters in vim-plug's README file on GitHub at: https://github.com/junegunn/vim-plug.

If you only work on Linux or Mac machines (and Cygwin), you can add a following piece to your `.vimrc` file to install vim-plug whenever you transport your `.vimrc` file to a new machine:

```
" Install vim-plug if it's not already installed.
if empty(glob('~/.vim/autoload/plug.vim'))
   silent !curl -fLo ~/.vim/autoload/plug.vim --create-dirs
      \ https://raw.github.com/junegunn/vim-plug/master/plug.vim
   autocmd VimEnter * PlugInstall --sync | source $MYVIMRC
endif
```

This will install vim-plug (and all the plugins you have listed) next time you open Vim.

You can see a slightly longer solution that works for both Windows and Unix on my blog: `https://www.rosipov.com/blog/cross-platform-vim-plug-setup`.

Honorable mentions

There are many more plugin management alternatives to vim-plug. The following list is not in any way comprehensive, but highlights different styles of plugin management. Pick the one that's more suited to your taste, or maybe search the web for alternatives.

Vundle

Vundle is vim-plug's predecessor (and possibly an inspiration), which works along similar lines. Plugin installation is synchronous, and the plugin packs slightly more weight than vim-plug. One of the differentiating factors is the availability of plugin search; Vundle allows you to search for plugins straight from Vim. In addition, Vundle lets you test out the plugins before permanently installing them. Vundle and its installation instructions are available from GitHub at: `https://github.com/VundleVim/Vundle.vim`.

Vundle works similar to vim-plug, with the `:PluginInstall`, `:PluginUpdate`, and `:PluginClean` commands performing the same functions.

The search feature (possibly the most compelling argument to use Vundle) can be invoked by running `:PluginSearch <string>`. At the moment, Vundle only supports searching by plugin names. For example, let's look for a plugin that helps us manage making comments:

```
:PluginSearch comment
```

We'll get a list of potential matches in return:

```
"Keymap: i - Install plugin; c - Cleanup
; s - Search; R - Reload list
"Search results for: comment
Plugin 'vim-addon-commenting'
Plugin 'CodeCommenter'
Plugin 'toggle_comment'
Plugin 'commentary.vim'
Plugin 'Comment-Squawk'
Plugin 'acomment'
Plugin 'scalacommenter.vim'
Plugin 'simplecommenter'
Plugin 'simple-comment'
Plugin 'commentop.vim'
Plugin 'simple_comments.vim'
Plugin 'CommentAnyWay'
Plugin 'IndentCommentPrefix'
Plugin 'commentToggle'
Plugin 'LineCommenter'
Plugin 'EZComment'
Plugin 'comments.vim'
Plugin 'QuickComment'
Plugin 'F6_Comment'
[Vundle] search [Preview][RO]          [No Name]
41 plugins found
```

Hover your cursor over a small plugin that adds a few useful comment-related key bindings: tComment. Hit i (or execute :PluginInstall) with your cursor over it. The plugin is now immediately available in Vim, without any commitment. You can try using tComment by opening a file (say, your .vimrc file), and executing gcc to comment and uncomment the current line.

This will not install the plugin permanently, and to do so you would have to add the plugin to your .vimrc file.

Do it yourself

You could always decide to take the DIY route and implement your own solution for storing plugins. That's what we effectively did in the previous chapter, albeit with less bells and whistles.

Since most plugins are available on GitHub, a popular way of making sure that the plugins are up to date is installing them as Git submodules. If you're familiar with Git, you can initialize a repository in your .vim folder and install plugins as submodules.

Vim 8 introduced a native way to load plugins, by expecting the files to be in a directory tree under .vim/pack. Vim 8 expects the following structure of the files:

- .vim/pack/<any-directory-name>/opt/ is used for plugins you want to manually load
- .vim/pack/<any-directory-name>/start/ is used for plugins you always load

 If you're the curious type, you could learn more about how each individual plugin folder is structured in Chapter 8, *Transcending the Mundane with VimScript*.

You may want to use some explicit name for a directory under .vim/pack/. For instance, plugins might be a good choice.

You can use the start/ directory for plugins that you always want to load.

On the other hand, `opt/` only loads plugins when you execute `:packadd <plugin-directory-name>`. This lets you add `packadd` commands to your `.vimrc` file. Using the `opt/` and `packadd` commands lets you achieve plugin lazy-loading (just like vim-plug):

```
" Load and run ack.vim plugin on :Ack command.
command! -nargs=* Ack :packadd ack.vim | Ack <f-args>
" Load an run Goyo plugin when opening Markdown files.
autocmd! filetype markdown packadd goyo.vim | Goyo
```

 If you decide to choose this route, do visit `Chapter 7`, *Making Vim Your Own*, which will cover some best practices when it comes to version controlling your Vim configuration.

In addition, you'll want to add the following two lines to your `.vimrc` file to load the documentation for all the plugins:

```
packloadall            " Load all plugins.
silent! helptags ALL   " Load help for all plugins.
```

`packloadall` tells Vim to load every plugin in the `start/` directory (Vim automatically performs this step after `.vimrc` is loaded, but we want to call it earlier). `helptags ALL` loads all available help entries for our plugins, and the `silent!` prefix hides any output and errors you might receive when loading the help entries.

You can manage your plugins yourself (with some overhead) by using Git submodules to download the plugins and keep them up to date.

Initialize a Git repository in the `.vim` directory (a one-time step):

```
$ cd ~/.vim
$ git init
```

Add a plugin as a submodule:

```
$ git submodule add https://github.com/scrooloose/nerdtree.git
pack/plugins/start/nerdtree
$ git commit -am "Add NERDTree plugin"
```

Now, every time you want to update your plugins, you can run the following:

```
$ git submodule update --recursive
$ git commit -am "Update plugins"
```

To delete a plugin, remove the submodule with the following steps:

```
$ git submodule deinit -f -- pack/plugins/start/nerdtree
$ rm -rf .git/modules/pack/plugins/start/nerdtree
$ git rm -f pack/plugins/start/nerdtree
```

DIY is a great route to take if you're a tinkerer, a minimalist, or otherwise enjoy making your life harder than it needs to be.

Pathogen

This section is much more of a history lesson and a noteworthy mention.

By definition, Pathogen is a `runtimepath` manager and not a plugin manager. However, in practice, `runtimepath` manipulation translates into plugin management really well. After Vim 8.0, there's no need to manipulate `runtimepath` to install plugins. However, if you have to use Vim prior to 8.0 (and you don't want to use full-blown package managers), Pathogen might make your life noticeably easier.

Pathogen was one of the earlier takes on plugin management and has heavily influenced the landscape of its successors. Many Vim users still use it today, but the influx of new adopters has stopped.

Pathogen is available from GitHub at: `https://github.com/tpope/vim-pathogen`.

Profiling slow plugins

As you use Vim a lot, you might end up with numerous plugins installed. Sometimes, these plugins can cause Vim to become slow. Often, the culprit is a single unoptimized plugin, either due to the author's oversight or the unique way the plugin interacts with your system. Vim comes with built-in profiling support, which we'll learn to use.

Profiling startup

You can start Vim with a `--startuptime <filename>` flag, which will log every action Vim takes during startup into a file. For instance, here's how you write the startup log into `startuptime.log`:

```
$ vim --startuptime startuptime.log
```

You can launch gvim in a similar manner with `gvim --startuptime startuptime.log`. The commands are the same in the Linux command line and in Windows `cmd.exe`.

Quit Vim, and open `startuptime.log`. You'll be greeted with something like this (I replaced sections of the file with < . . . > to make it easier to read):

```
times in msec
 clock    self+sourced   self:   sourced script
 clock    elapsed:                other lines

000.005  000.005: --- VIM STARTING ---
000.086  000.081: Allocated generic buffers
<...>
009.012  000.936  000.459: sourcing /usr/local/share/vim/vim81/colors/murphy.vim
010.633  001.542  001.542: sourcing /home/ruslan/.vim/autoload/plug.vim
<...>
017.917  017.005  001.936: sourcing $HOME/.vimrc
017.919  000.125: sourcing vimrc file(s)
018.399  000.201  000.201: sourcing /home/ruslan/.vim/plugged/ctrlp.vim/autoload
018.599  000.565  000.364: sourcing /home/ruslan/.vim/plugged/ctrlp.vim/plugin/c
023.826  005.161  005.161: sourcing /home/ruslan/.vim/plugged/vim-easymotion/plu
024.099  000.194  000.194: sourcing /home/ruslan/.vim/plugged/ack.vim/plugin/ack
035.689  011.532  011.532: sourcing /home/ruslan/.vim/plugged/vim-unimpaired/plu
036.010  000.255  000.255: sourcing /home/ruslan/.vim/plugged/vim-vinegar/plugin
036.313  000.073  000.073: sourcing /usr/local/share/vim/vim81/plugin/getscriptP
<...>
041.281  000.319: first screen update
041.283  000.002: --- VIM STARTED ---
```

In the preceding screenshot, you can see a set of timestamps (most in three columns), followed by an action measured by the timestamp. The timestamps are in milliseconds—1/1000 of a second. The first column indicates the number of milliseconds from starting Vim, while the last column indicates how long each action took.

It's the last column which is of interest to us. You'll be looking for any abnormalities in the file.

In our case, we don't have any particularly slow plugins, but for the sake of science, the slowest plugin we have installed is vim-unimpared (at 11 milliseconds—011.532). You'll have to get closer to 500 milliseconds (or half a second) for the plugin to have a noticeable effect on Vim startup times.

Profiling specific actions

If performing a particular action in Vim is slow, you can profile just a particular set of actions.

In this example, I created an obvious performance culprit. I downloaded the Python and Vim repositories from GitHub, and tried running the :CtrlP command that's provided by a CtrlP plugin (which we explored in Chapter 2, *Advanced Editing and Navigation*). :CtrlP will try to index all the files recursively starting at the current directory, which should be slow for such a large number of files.

Start Vim as usual, and execute the following set of commands:

```
:profile start profile.log
:profile func *
:profile file *
```

From now on, Vim will profile every action you'll perform. Run the slow command. In our case, let's run :CtrlP by pressing *Ctrl + p*. After the offending action has been performed, quit Vim (:q).

Open `profile.log`, and you'll be greeted to something like this (you may want to have folds enabled with `set foldmethod=indent`, as the file is large and hard to navigate otherwise):

```
SCRIPT  /home/ruslan/.vim/plugged/ctrlp.vim/autoload/ctrlp.vim
Sourced 1 time
Total time:   0.003392
 Self time:   0.003360

count  total (s)   self (s)
+--2672 lines: " ================================================

SCRIPT  /home/ruslan/.vim/plugged/ctrlp.vim/autoload/ctrlp/utils.vim
Sourced 1 time
Total time:   0.000233
 Self time:   0.000145

count  total (s)   self (s)
+--110 lines: " =================================================

FUNCTION  ctrlp#utils#cachedir()
Called 4 times
Total time:   0.000012
 Self time:   0.000012

count  total (s)   self (s)
    4              0.000010      retu s:cache_dir
```

Scroll to the bottom of the file (`G`) and you'll see a list of functions sorted by how long they took to execute:

```
FUNCTIONS SORTED ON SELF TIME
count  total (s)   self (s)   function
    9   3.898720   0.566486   <SNR>29_GlobPath()
 8220              0.486789   <SNR>29_usrign()
    9   0.802043   0.315247   ctrlp#dirnfile()
  475              0.020151   ctrlp#utils#fnesc()
    2   0.009307   0.009239   ctrlp#utils#writecache()
    1   0.007239   0.007231   ctrlp#rmbasedir()
  474   0.023695   0.003593   <SNR>29_fnesc()
   21   0.006404   0.002002   <SNR>29_mixedsort()
    1              0.001898   <SNR>29_MapNorms()
    1              0.001070   <SNR>29_MapSpecs()
   45              0.000997   <SNR>29_getparent()
    8              0.000959   ctrlp#progress()
   21   0.002034   0.000835   <SNR>29_comparent()
    1   0.001169   0.000720   <SNR>29_Open()
    1   0.001037   0.000707   <SNR>29_opts()
    1   0.917665   0.000663   ctrlp#files()
   21   0.000973   0.000588   <SNR>29_compmatlen()
    1              0.000516   <SNR>29_sublist()
   39              0.000487   <SNR>29_CurTypeName()
    1   0.000514   0.000449   <SNR>29_Close()
```

Many of the slowest functions are prefixed with `ctrlp#`, so it's becoming clear that CtrlP is likely to be the culprit of the slowness (and as we know—it is). If it is not explicitly obvious where the functions come from, we can search the file for the function name. For instance, `<SNR>29_GlobPath()` is responsible for nearly ~3.9 seconds of slowdown (hover over the function name and press * to search for the word under the cursor):

```
FUNCTION  <SNR>29_GlobPath()
Called 9 times
Total time:   3.898720
 Self time:   0.566486

count  total (s)   self (s)
    9              0.072347       let entries = split(globpath(a:dirs, s:glob), "\
n")
    9   0.802176   0.000133       let [dnf, depth] = [ctrlp#dirnfile(entries), a:d
epth + 1]
    9              0.000656       cal extend(g:ctrlp_allfiles, dnf[1])
    9   0.000129   0.000101       if !empty(dnf[0]) && !s:maxf(len(g:ctrlp_allfile
s)) && depth <= s:maxdepth
    8   0.001037   0.000078           sil! cal ctrlp#progress(len(g:ctrlp_allfiles
), 1)
    8   0.025622   0.002863           cal s:GlobPath(join(map(dnf[0], 's:fnesc(v:v
al, "g", ",")'), ','), depth)
    8              0.000007       en

FUNCTION  <SNR>29_InitCustomFuncs()
Called 1 time
Total time:   0.000007
```

As you can see by the number of CtrlP references, this function is likely related to the offending plugin.

If you were to try to profile real issue with Vim, the contents of `profile.log` could tell you which plugins are a likely cause of the slowdowns you are experiencing.

Deeper dive into modes

You've already encountered a few different modes Vim operates in, and this section will cover these and the remaining modes in depth. As you have already learned, Vim uses modes to know how to respond to input: a key press in normal mode will produce different results from a key press in insert or command-line mode.

Vim has seven primary modes, and it's important to understand what each mode does in order to comfortably navigate Vim.

Normal mode

This is where you will (and already have) spend most of your time with Vim. You enter **normal mode** by default when opening Vim, and you can go back to normal mode from other modes by pressing the *Esc* key (sometimes twice).

Command-line and ex modes

Command-line mode is entered by typing a colon (:) or when searching for text with / or ?, and allows you to input a command until you hit *Enter*. Command-line mode provides some useful shortcuts:

- The up and down arrows (or *Ctrl + p* and *Ctrl + n*) let you traverse command history one by one
- *Ctrl + b* and *Ctrl + e* let you go to the **beginning** and the **end** of the line respectively
- The *Shift* or *Ctrl* keys combined with left or right arrows allows you to move by words

A highly useful shortcut is *Ctrl + f*, which opens an editable command-line window with a history of the commands you ran:

```
#!/usr/bin/python3

"""Our own little animal farm."""

import sys

from animals import cat
from animals import dog
from animals import sheep
import animal
import farm

def make_animal(kind):
+--   7 lines: if kind == 'cat':------------------------------------
animal_farm.py
:split farm.py
:wq
:sp animals/cat.py
:bd
:vsp animals/cat.py
:tabnew farm.py
:b1
[Command Line]
```

For editing purposes, it's a regular buffer, so you can find a command you've executed before, edit it (the way you'd edit any text in Vim), and execute it again. You can press *Enter* to execute the line your cursor is on or *Ctrl* + *c* to close the buffer.

You can learn more about working with command-line mode by looking up `:help cmdline-editing`.

Vim has a variation of the command-line mode called **ex mode**, which is entered by pressing *Q*. Ex mode is a compatibility mode with Vim's precursor—*ex*. It allows you to execute multiple commands without exiting the mode after each command, but has very limited uses today.

Insert mode

Insert mode is used to type in text, and that's about it. Hitting *Esc* takes you back to normal mode, which is where you should be performing most of your work. When in insert mode, you can also use *Ctrl + o* to execute a single normal mode command and end up back in insert mode.

Insert mode is indicated by **-- INSERT --** displayed in a status line.

Visual and select mode

Vim's **visual mode** allows for an arbitrary selection of text (usually to perform some sort of operations on). It's useful when you want to work with a section of a file that does not map to an existing text objects (word, sentence, paragraph, and so on). There are three ways to enter visual mode:

- *v* enters a character-wise visual mode (status line text: **-- VISUAL --**)

- *V* enters a line-wise visual mode (status line text: **-- VISUAL LINE --**)

- *Ctrl + v* enters a block-wise visual mode (status line text: **-- VISUAL BLOCK --**)

Once you enter visual mode, you are able to move your cursor using the usual movement commands, which would expand the selection. In the following example, we've entered a character-wise visual mode and moved the cursor by three words and one character to the right (by executing 3e and then 1). You can see animal_farm.add_animal() being selected in visual mode:

```
def main(animals):
    animal_farm = farm.Farm()
    for animal_kind in animals:
        animal_farm.add_animal(make_animal(animal_kind))
    animal_farm.print_contents()

if __name__ == '__main__':
    if len(sys.argv) == 1:
        print('Pass at least one animal type!')
        sys.exit(1)
    main(sys.argv[1:])
-- VISUAL --
```

You can control the selection by doing the following:

- Pressing o to go to the other end of the highlighted text (hence allowing the selection to expand from the other side)
- Pressing o when in block-wise visual mode to the other end of the current line

After you're satisfied with the selection, you can run a command you'd like to execute on a selection. For example, hit d to delete the selected text:

```
def main(animals):
    animal_farm = farm.Farm()
    for animal_kind in animals:
        make_animal(animal_kind))
    animal_farm.print_contents()

if __name__ == '__main__':
    if len(sys.argv) == 1:
        print('Pass at least one animal type!')
        sys.exit(1)
    main(sys.argv[1:])
```

In the preceding screenshot, Vim is back to normal mode (**-- VISUAL --** is not in a status line anymore), and the selection has been deleted. You can always hit *Esc* to come back to normal mode without making a change.

> Text objects become a powerful tool when used in visual mode. See
> *Utilizing Text Objects* in Chapter 2, *Advanced Editing and Navigation*, for
> more information.

Vim also has a **select mode**, which emulates selection mode in other editors: pressing any printable character immediately erases the selected text and enters the insert mode (so the usual movement commands don't work here). Just like the ex mode shown before, select mode has a very specific and limited set of uses. In fact, I have never used it myself, except for when doing research for this book.

You can enter select mode by pressing gh from normal mode or *Ctrl* + *g* from visual mode and exit it by pressing (you guessed it) *Esc*.

Replace and virtual replace mode

Replace mode behaves similarly to those times you accidentally press the *Insert* key on your keyboard and wonder why typing erases text. When working with replace mode, the text you type is placed over existing text (as opposed to moving the existing text in insert mode). This is great when you don't want to change the character count in the original line, for example.

Enter replace mode by hitting *R*:

```
def make_animal(kind):
    if kind == 'cat':
        return cat.Cat()
    if kind == 'dog':
        return dog.Dog()
    if kind == 'sheep':
        return sheep.Sheep()
    return animal.Animal(kind)

def main(animals):
-- REPLACE --
```

You'll see **--REPLACE--** in the status line. Now, you'll be replacing text as you type:

```
def make_animal(kind):
    if kind == 'bat':
        return cat.Cat()
    if kind == 'dog':
        return dog.Dog()
    if kind == 'sheep':
        return sheep.Sheep()
    return animal.Animal(kind)

def main(animals):
-- REPLACE --
```

Hit *Esc* to exit replace mode and go back to normal mode.

You can press r to enter replace mode for a single character press before being switched back to normal mode.

Vim also provides virtual replace mode, which behaves similarly to replace mode, but operates in terms of screen real estate as opposed to characters in a file. The main noticeable differences include *Tab* replacing multiple characters (as opposed to a single character in replace mode) or *Enter* not creating an addition line, but moving onto the next line. You can enter virtual replace mode using gR, and you can read more about it by reading :help vreplace-mode.

Terminal mode

Terminal mode came to Vim in version 8.1, and it allows you to run a Terminal in a split window. You can enter terminal mode by typing the following:

```
:terminal
```

You can shorten the command to :term.

This will open your system's shell (your default shell in Linux, or cmd.exe in Windows) in a horizontal split:

```
ruslan@ann-perkins:~/Mastering-Vim/ch2$ python3 animal_farm.py cat dog
We've got some animals on the farm: dog, cat.
ruslan@ann-perkins:~/Mastering-Vim/ch2$ python3 animal_farm.py
Pass at least one animal type!
ruslan@ann-perkins:~/Mastering-Vim/ch2$
!/bin/bash [ruslan@ann-perkins: ~/Mastering-Vim/ch2]
#!/usr/bin/python3


"""Our own little animal farm."""

animal_farm.py [+]
:term
```

This is a wrapper around your system's Terminal, which lets you work with your shell as you normally would. This window is treated similarly to any other window (you can navigate between split using *Ctrl + w* commands), but the window is effectively locked into insert mode. You may also want to consider using tmux or a screen under Linux or macOS to work with a Terminal alongside Vim.

You can also use :term to execute a single command and place its output in a buffer. For example, we can run animal_farm.py as follows:

```
:term python3 animal_farm.py cat dog
```

The output is immediately available to us in a horizontal split:

```
We've got some animals on the farm: dog, cat.
~
~
~
~
!python3 animal_farm.py cat dog [finished]
#!/usr/bin/python3

"""Our own little animal farm."""

animal_farm.py
:term python3 animal_farm.py cat dog
```

Remapping commands

Now that you are comfortable working with plugins, you may want to consider customizing your Vim further by remapping commands to suit your preferences. Plugins are written by many kinds of different people, and everyone's workflow is different. Vim is infinitely extensible, allowing you to remap nearly every action, change certain default behaviors, and really make Vim your own. Let's talk about remapping commands.

Vim allows you to remap certain keys to be used in place of other keys. `:map` and `:noremap` provide just that:

- `:map` is used for recursive mapping
- `:noremap` is used for non-recursive mapping

This means that commands remapped with `:map` are aware of other custom mappings, while `:noremap` works with system defaults.

 Before you decide to create a new mapping, you may want to see whether the key or sequence you're mapping to is already used somewhere. You can scan through `:help index` for a list of built-in key bindings. The `:map` command lets you view plugin and user-defined mappings. For instance, `:map g` will display every mapping starting with the `g` key.

Let's add a custom mapping to our `.vimrc` file:

```
noremap ; :   " Use ; in addition to : to type commands.
```

In the preceding example, we're remapping `;` to function the same way `:` does. Now, we don't have to press down *Shift* to enter command-line mode. On the downside, we now don't have a command that repeats the last `t`, `f`, `T`, or `F` (find character and find till character) movement.

We're using `noremap` because we still want to enter command-line mode, even if `:` gets remapped to do something else.

 If you ever want to explicitly remove a mapping you or a plugin defined, you'd be looking for `:unmap`. There's also a nuclear option of `:mapclear`, which drops both user-defined and default mappings.

You can use special characters and commands in mappings as well, for example:

```
" noremap <c-u> :w<cr> " Save using <Ctrl-u> (u stands for update).
```

`<c-u>` in the preceding example represents *Ctrl* + *u*. The *Ctrl* prefix in Vim is denoted by `<c-_>` , where _ is some character. Other modifier keys are represented similarly:

- `<a-_>` or `<m-_>` represents *Alt* pressed with some key, for example, `<m-b>` would correspond to *Alt* + b

- `<s-_>` represents a *Shift* press, for example, `<s-f>` would correspond to *Shift* + *f*

Please note that a command is terminated by <cr>, which stands for a carriage return (the *Enter* key). Otherwise, the command will be entered but not executed, and you will be left hanging in command-line mode (unless that's exactly what you want).

By the way, here are all of the special characters you can use:

- <space>: spacebar
- <esc>: *Esc*
- <cr>, <enter>: *Enter*
- <tab>: *Tab*
- <bs>: *Backspace*
- <up>, <down>, <left>, <right>: Arrow keys
- <pageup>, <pagedown>: *Page Up* and *Page Down*
- <f1> to <f12>: Function keys
- <home>, <insert>, <del>, <end>: *Home, Insert, Delete,* and *End*

You can also map a key to <nop> (short for *no operation*) if you want the key to not do anything. This, for instance, could be useful if you're trying to get used to *hjkl*-style movement versus arrow keys. Disabling your arrow keys in .vimrc would look like this:

```
" Map arrow keys nothing so I can get used to hjkl-style movement.
map <up> <nop>
map <down> <nop>
map <left> <nop>
map <right> <nop>
```

Mode – aware remapping

The :map and :noremap commands work for normal, visual, select, and operator pending modes. Vim supports a more fine-grained control over which modes the mappings work in:

- :nmap and :nnoremap: Normal mode
- :vmap and :vnoremap: Visual and select modes
- :xmap and :xnoremap: Visual mode
- :smap and :snoremap: Select mode
- :omap and :onoremap: Operator-pending mode

- `:map!` and `:noremap!`: Insert and command-line modes
- `:imap` and `:inoremap`: Insert mode
- `:cmap` and `:cnoremap`: Command-line mode

 Vim often uses an exclamation mark `!` to force command execution, or to add additional functionality to a command. Try `:help!` for yourself!

For example, if you wanted to add some mappings to alter some insert mode behavior, you could do this:

```
" Immediately add a closing quotes or braces in insert mode.
inoremap ' ''<esc>i
inoremap " ""<esc>i
inoremap ( ()<esc>i
inoremap { {}<esc>i
inoremap [ []<esc>i
```

In the preceding example, we changed the default behavior of a key press in insert mode (for example, the opening square bracket `[`) to insert two characters instead of one (`[]`), leave insert mode, and immediately reenter it (to be placed between both braces, since insert mode is entered before the cursor).

The leader key

You've probably already encountered a key referred to as the **leader key**. The leader key is essentially a namespace for user or plugin defined shortcuts. Within a second of pressing the leader key, any key that's pressed will be in from that namespace.

The default leader key is a backslash `\`, but it's not the most comfortable binding. There are a few alternative keys that are popular in the community, with the comma (`,`) being the most popular. To rebind the leader key, set the following in your `.vimrc` file:

```
" Map the leader key to a comma.
let mapleader = ','
```

You'll want to define your leader key closer to the top of `.vimrc`, as the newly defined leader key will only apply to mappings defined after its definition.

When you rebind a key, it's default functionality is overwritten. For example, comma , this is used to replay the last *t*, *f*, *T*, or *F* movement commands, in the opposite direction.

My personal favorite is to use the spacebar as a leader key. It's a big key, which doesn't have any real use in normal mode (it mimics right arrow key functionality):

```
" Map the leader key to a spacebar.
let mapleader = "\<space>"
```

 The escape character \ is needed before space since `mapleader` doesn't expect special characters (like `space`). Double quotes (") are also necessary for the escape to work, since single quotes (') only allow literal strings.

You can use `leader` in your `.vimrc` mappings like this:

```
" Save a file with leader-w.
noremap <leader>w :w<cr>
```

More often than not, you will use a leader key to map plugin functionality in a way that's easy for you to memorize, as in the following example:

```
noremap <leader>n :NERDTreeToggle<cr>
```

Configuring plugins

Plugins often expose commands for you to map to and variables to change plugin behavior. It's a good idea to review the available options and commands for the plugins you use. Sane plugin defaults make a huge difference in experience. Creating shortcuts that are easy for you to remember will help you remember how to use the plugin you forgot about in a few months.

Vim allows for the creation of global variables, which are primarily used to configure plugins. Global variables are usually prefixed by `g:`. You can find a list of configuration options in the plugin documentation by running `:help <plugin-name>` and looking for options.

For example, opening a help file for the CtrlP plugin (by running :help ctrlp) and searching for options (/options) yields the following:

```
CtrlP ControlP 'ctrlp' 'ctrl-p'
================================================================================
#                                                                              #
#        ::::::::  ::::::::::  ::::::::   :::         ::::::::::                 #
#      :+:    :+:  :+:        :+:    :+:  :+:         :+:      :+:               #
#      +:+          +:+        +:+    +:+ +:+         +:+      +:+               #
#      +#+          +#+        +#++:++#:  +#+         +#++:++#+                  #
#      +#+          +#+        +#+   +#+ +#+          +#+                        #
#      #+#    #+#   #+#        #+#   #+# #+#          #+#                        #
#       ########    ###        ###   ### ##########   ###                       #
#                                                                              #
================================================================================
CONTENTS                                                         ctrlp-contents

    1. Intro.........................................ctrlp-intro
    2. Options.......................................ctrlp-options
    3. Commands......................................ctrlp-commands
    4. Mappings......................................ctrlp-mappings
    5. Input Formats.................................ctrlp-input-formats
    6. Extensions....................................ctrlp-extensions
ctrlp.txt [Help][RO]


[No Name]
/options
```

 You can read more about the CtrlP plugin under Chapter 2, *Advanced Editing and Navigation*.

If we follow the `ctrlp-options` link (by pressing *Ctrl* +]), we will be taken to a list of available options:

```
OPTIONS                                                    ctrlp-options

Overview:

  loaded_ctrlp................Disable the plugin.
  ctrlp_map...................Default mapping.
  ctrlp_cmd...................Default command used for the default mapping.
  ctrlp_by_filename...........Default to filename mode or not.
  ctrlp_regexp................Default to regexp mode or not.
  ctrlp_match_window..........Order, height and position of the match window.
  ctrlp_switch_buffer.........Jump to an open buffer if already opened.
  ctrlp_reuse_window..........Reuse special windows (help, quickfix, etc).
  ctrlp_tabpage_position......Where to put the new tab page.
  ctrlp_working_path_mode.....How to set CtrlP's local working directory.
  ctrlp_root_markers..........Additional, high priority root markers.
  ctrlp_use_caching...........Use per-session caching or not.
  ctrlp_clear_cache_on_exit...Keep cache after exiting Vim or not.
  ctrlp_cache_dir.............Location of the cache directory.
  ctrlp_show_hidden...........Ignore dotfiles and dotdirs or not.
  ctrlp_custom_ignore.........Hide stuff when using globpath().
ctrlp.txt [Help][RO]


[No Name]
/options
```

Let's pick an interesting option to explore, say `ctrlp_working_path_mode`. Move your cursor over to the link, and press *Ctrl +]* to follow it further:

```
                                                    'g:ctrlp_working_path_mode'
When starting up, CtrlP sets its local working directory according to this
variable:
  let g:ctrlp_working_path_mode = 'ra'

  c - the directory of the current file.
  a - the directory of the current file, unless it is a subdirectory of the cwd
  r - the nearest ancestor of the current file that contains one of these
      directories or files:
      .git .hg .svn .bzr _darcs
  w - modifier to "r": start search from the cwd instead of the current file's
      directory
  0 or <empty> - disable this feature.

Note #1: if "a" or "c" is included with "r", use the behavior of "a" or "c" (as
a fallback) when a root can't be found.

Note #2: you can use a b:var to set this option on a per buffer basis.

                                                    'g:ctrlp_root_markers'
ctrlp.txt [Help][RO]


[No Name]
```

It looks like this option guards how CtrlP sets a local working directory. If we wanted to change it to look for a root folder of our Git project (with a fallback to the current working directory), we would change our `.vimrc` file accordingly:

```
" Set CtrlP working directory to a repository root (with a
" fallback to current directory).
  let g:ctrlp_working_path_mode = 'ra'
```

Digging through the available options for plugins takes time; however, it might make you much more productive or even completely change the way you use the plugins.

Remember the leader key? It comes in very handy with plugins, as it provides a full namespace for plugins to use. Some plugins already use the leader key for their default key bindings, others not so much. You can always make your own easy to remember mappings!

For example, all three CtrlP modes can be easily accessed with two key presses:

```
" Remap CtrlP actions to be prefixed by a leader key.
noremap <leader>p :CtrlP<cr>
noremap <leader>b :CtrlPBuffer<cr>
noremap <leader>m :CtrlPMRU<cr>
```

I find it extremely useful to take some time to optimize my key mappings or customize plugin options. Small investment and some mindfulness goes a long way in getting the most out of your setup.

Summary

In this chapter, we've talked about the different ways of managing plugins. The new shiny thing is vim-plug, a lightweight plugin manager that can asynchronously install and update your plugins. Vundle, its predecessor, also allows you to search for and temporarily install new plugins. We've also learned how to manually work with plugins: Vim 8.0 introduced a way to load plugins without the need to manually alter runtimepath for each plugin. If you still use Vim below version 8, then Pathogen provides a way to automate some of the runtimepath manipulation.

We've looked at profiling Vim with a --startuptime flag and the :profile command.

We've revisited modes, covering every major mode: normal mode, command-line and ex modes, insert mode, visual and select modes, and terminal mode.

We've talked about remapping commands to make Vim truly yours. Different key combinations are more convenient and easier to remember for different people. Vim allows you to remap keys based on the mode you're in, meaning you can alter the behavior of every key press. We've covered the leader key, which allows you to access a whole new namespace that's reserved for plugins and user-defined commands.

We've also looked into the ways we can squeeze the most out of our plugins by customizing their configuration options and adding key bindings that make more sense in our own unique workflow.

In the next chapter, we'll cover autocomplete, navigating large code bases with tags, and traversing Vim's undo tree.

4
Understanding the Text

Code bases tend to grow to be large and navigating them often becomes problematic. Luckily, Vim has a few aces up its sleeve when it comes to navigating complex code. This chapter will cover the following topics:

- Autocompleting code using Vim's built-in autocomplete functionality and plugins
- Navigating large code bases using Exuberant Ctags
- Navigating Vim's complex undo tree using Gundo

Technical requirements

We will continue navigating our sample project, and you will continue working on your `.vimrc` file. All of the material is available from GitHub at: `https://github.com/PacktPublishing/Mastering-Vim/tree/master/Chapter04`.

Code autocomplete

One of the most appealing features modern IDEs have is code autocomplete. IDEs allow you to eliminate typos, look up hard to remember variable names, and save time by removing the need to type long variable names over and over again.

Vim has some built-in autocomplete functionality, and there are plugins that expand upon this.

Built-in autocomplete

Vim supports native autocomplete based on words available in open buffers. It's available out of the box starting with Vim 7.0. Start by typing the beginning of a function name and hit *Ctrl + n* to bring up the autocomplete list. You can navigate the list using *Ctrl + n* and *Ctrl + p*. For example, open `animal_farm.py`, enter insert mode, and start typing the first two letters of a function name: `ma` (`make_animal`). Press *Ctrl + n*. This will bring up a list of available options:

```
#!/usr/bin/python3

"""Our own little animal farm."""

import sys

from animals import cat
from animals import dog
from animals import sheep
import animal
import farm

def make_animal(kind):
+--   7 lines: if kind == 'cat':----------------------------------

def main(animals):
    animal_farm = farm.Farm()
    for animal_kind in animals:
        animal_farm.add_animal(make_animal
    animal_farm.print_contents main
                               make_animal
if __name__ == '__main__':
+--   4 lines: if len(sys.argv) == 1:----------------------------
-- Keyword completion (^N^P) match 2 of 2
```

Continue typing to dismiss the list.

In fact, Vim has an insert-completion mode, which supports multiple completion types. Press *Ctrl* + *x* followed by one of the following keys:

- *Ctrl* + l to complete the whole line
- *Ctrl* +] to complete tags
- *Ctrl* + f to complete filenames
- s to complete spelling suggestions (if `:set spell` is enabled)

 These are the commands I found useful in the past, but there are more! Read `:help ins-completion` for a full list of supported commands—everyone's workflow is unique, and you never know which commands you'll find yourself utilizing a lot. You should also check `:help 'complete'`, which is an option that controls where Vim looks for completion (by default, Vim looks in buffers, tag files, and headers).

YouCompleteMe

YouCompleteMe takes a built-in autocomplete engine and pumps steroids into it. YouCompleteMe has a few distinctive features that elevate it beyond built-in autocomplete:

- Semantic (language-aware) autocomplete; YouCompleteMe understands your code a lot better than built-in autocomplete
- Intelligent suggestion ranking and filtering
- An ability to display documentation, rename variables, autoformat code, and fix certain types of errors (language dependent, see `https://github.com/Valloric/YouCompleteMe#quick-feature-summary`)

Installation

First, make sure that you have `cmake` and `llvm` installed, since YouCompleteMe needs to be compiled:

```
$ sudo apt-get install cmake llvm
```

For Windows, you can get cmake from https://cmake.org/download and llvm from https://releases.llvm.org/download.
html. YouCompleteMe requires Vim to be compiled with +python. You can check whether your Vim was compiled with Python support by running vim --version | grep python. If you see -python, you'll have to recompile your Vim with Python support.

If you're using vim-plug, add the following to .vimrc:

```
let g:plug_timeout = 300  " Increase vim-plug timeout for YouCompleteMe.
Plug 'Valloric/YouCompleteMe', { 'do': './install.py' }
```

Save the file and execute it:

```
:source $MYVIMRC | PlugInstall
```

Depending on how fast your machine is, this might take a while. You will be greeted by a successful installation screen:

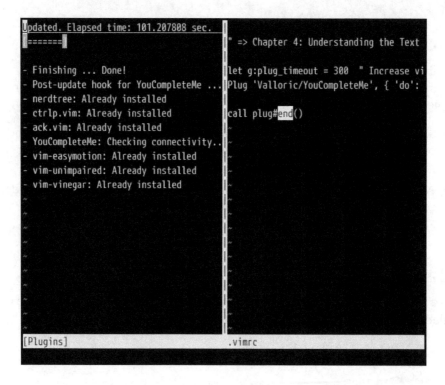

If you're running into an error such as **c++: internal compiler error: Killed (program cc1plus)**, then your machine likely doesn't have enough memory to complete the operation. On Linux, you can perform a swap to increase the available space:

```
$ sudo dd if=/dev/zero of=/var/swap.img bs=1024k
count=1000
$ sudo mkswap /var/swap.img
$ sudo swapon /var/swap.img
```

Using YouCompleteMe

YouCompleteMe doesn't introduce a lot of new key bindings, which makes integrating it into your workflow easier. Enter insert mode and start typing away:

```
#!/usr/bin/python3

"""Our own little animal farm."""

import sys

from animals import cat
from animals import dog
from animals import sheep
import animal
import farm                  make_animal [ID]
                             main        [ID]
                             animal      [ID]
def make_animal(kind):       Animal      [ID]
+--  7 lines: if kind == 'cat' animals   [ID]-----------
                             animal_farm [ID]
def main(animals):           animal_kind [ID]
    animal_farm = farm.Farm() add_animal [ID]
    for animal_kind in animals add_animal [ID]
        animal_farm.add_animal(ma
    animal_farm.print_contents()

if __name__ == '__main__':
+--  4 lines: if len(sys.argv) == 1:--------------
-- INSERT --
```

As you do, autocomplete suggestions will pop up. The *Tab* key will cycle through suggestions. Furthermore, if YouCompleteMe is able to look up function definition, together with a supporting docstring, it will show up in a preview window at the top of the screen:

```
make_animal(kind)

Create an animal class.
[Scratch] [Preview]
import sys

from animals import cat
from animals import dog
from animals import sheep
import animal
import farm

def make_animal(kind):
+--  8 lines: """Create an animal class."""----------------------

def main(animals):
    animal_farm = farm.Farm()
    for animal_kind in animals:
        animal_farm.add_animal(make_animal
        animal_farm.print_contents  make_animal [ID]

if __name__ == '__main__':
animal_farm.py [+]
-- INSERT --
```

The preview window only shows up when YouCompleteMe uses the semantic autocomplete engine. The semantic engine is automatically invoked after typing . (period) in insert mode or manually by pressing *Ctrl* + spacebar.

For Python, YouCompleteMe also allows you to jump to function definition. Add the following mapping to your `.vimrc` file:

```
noremap <leader>] :YcmCompleter GoTo<cr>
```

Now, with the cursor over a function call, press your leader key (backslash (\) by default), followed by]. You will be taken to the function definition:

```
"""A farm for holding animals."""

class Farm(object):

    def __init__(self):
        self.animals = set()

    def add_animal(self, animal):
        self.animals.add(animal)

    def print_contents(self):
        print("We've got some animals on the farm:",
            ', '.join(animal.kind for animal in self.animals) + '.')
~
~
~
~
~
~
~
~
~
~
~
"~/Mastering-Vim/ch4/farm.py" 13L, 332C
```

YouCompleteMe is not the only available autocomplete tool, but merely the author's favorite (and the most popular option at the time of writing this book). There are many alternatives. A quick search along the lines of *Vim autocomplete* will yield plenty of results if you're interested in an alternative.

Navigating the code base with tags

A common task when navigating code bases is trying to figure out where certain methods are defined, and looking for occurrences of a certain method.

Vim has a built-in feature that allows you to navigate to the definition of a variable in the same file. With the cursor over a word, press gd to go to the declaration of the variable. For instance, open `animal_farm.py` and position your cursor at the beginning of `make_animal` on line 26. Press gd, and your cursor will jump to line 13, where the function is defined:

```
 1 #!/usr/bin/python3
 2
 3 """Our own little animal farm."""
 4
 5 import sys
 6
 7 from animals import cat
 8 from animals import dog
 9 from animals import sheep
10 import animal
11 import farm
12
13 def make_animal(kind):
14 +--   8 lines: """Create an animal class."""----------------
22
23 def main(animals):
24     animal_farm = farm.Farm()
25     for animal_kind in animals:
26         animal_farm.add_animal(make_animal(animal_kind))
27     animal_farm.print_contents()
28
29 if __name__ == '__main__':
30 +--   4 lines: if len(sys.argv) == 1:----------------------
```

`gd` will look for a local variable declaration first. There's also `gD`, which will look for a global declaration (starting at the beginning of at the file instead of the beginning of the current scope).

This feature is not syntax aware, as out-of-the-box Vim does not know how your code is structured semantically. However, Vim supports tags—a file of semantically meaningful words and constructs across your files. For example, in Python, likely candidates for tags are classes, functions, and methods.

Exuberant Ctags

Exuberant Ctags is an external utility that generates tag files. Ctags is available at the following link: `http://ctags.sourceforge.net`.

> If you're on a Debian-flavored distribution, you can install Exuberant Ctags by running `sudo apt-get install ctags`.

Ctags introduces a `ctags` binary, which allows you to generate a `tags` file for your code base. Let's navigate to our project and try it out:

```
$ ctags -R .
```

This creates a `tags` file in the directory you're in.

> You may want to set the following option in your `.vimrc` file:
>
> ```
> set tags=tags;  " Look for a tags file recursively in
>                 " parent directories.
> ```
>
> This will make sure that Vim looks for the `tags` file recursively in parent directories to allow you to use a single `tags` file for the whole project. Semicolon (`;`) is what tells Vim to keep looking in parent directories until a `tags` file is found.

Now, open `animal_farm.py` in Vim. Place your cursor over a semantically meaningful keyword, for example, the `add_animal` method on line 26:

```
 1 #!/usr/bin/python3
 2
 3 """Our own little animal farm."""
 4
 5 import sys
 6
 7 from animals import cat
 8 from animals import dog
 9 from animals import sheep
10 import animal
11 import farm
12
13 def make_animal(kind):
14 +--   8 lines: """Create an animal class."""------------------------------
22
23 def main(animals):
24     animal_farm = farm.Farm()
25     for animal_kind in animals:
26         animal_farm.add_animal(make_animal(animal_kind))
27     animal_farm.print_contents()
28
29 if __name__ == '__main__':
30 +--   4 lines: if len(sys.argv) == 1:------------------------------
```

Hit *Ctrl +*] to follow the tag to the definition (which is in a different file—farm.py):

```
"""A farm for holding animals."""

class Farm(object):

    def __init__(self):
        self.animals = set()

    def add_animal(self, animal):
        self.animals.add(animal)

    def print_contents(self):
+--- 2 lines: print("We've got some animals on the farm:",----------------
```

Use *Ctrl + t* to go back in the tag stack (this will place your cursor back to where it was in the previous file).

> Jump list navigation with *Ctrl + o* and *Ctrl + i* also works, however, the two are using different lists.

If you have multiple tags with the same name, you can cycle through the available options by using the :tn (**next tag**) and :tp (**previous tag**) commands.

You can also bring up a list of tags by using the :ts (**tag select**) menu. For example, if you jump to the definition of get_kind (using *Ctrl* +] from animal.get_kind() in farm.py, for instance) and execute :ts, you'll see the following menu:

```
"""An animal base class."""


class Animal(object):

    def __init__(self, kind):
        self.kind = kind

    def get_kind(self):
        return self.kind
  # pri kind tag                  file
> 1 F   m     get_kind            animal.py
                  class:Animal
                  def get_kind(self):
  2 F   m     get_kind            animals/cat.py
                  class:Cat
                  def get_kind(self):
  3 F   m     get_kind            animals/dog.py
                  class:Dog
                  def get_kind(self):
  4 F   m     get_kind            animals/sheep.py
                  class:Sheep
                  def get_kind(self):
Type number and <Enter> (empty cancels): █
```

You can see what file, class, and method the tag refers to, and you can jump to the desired tag by entering a number.

You can also open a tag and select the menu instead of jumping to the tag under the cursor using g].

You can jump to a tag location immediately as you open Vim. From your prompt, execute the following:

```
$ vim -t get_kind
```

This will take you directly to the get_kind tag.

Automatically updating the tags

You probably don't want to have to manually run the ctags -R . command every time you make changes to the code. The simplest way to address this is to add the following to your .vimrc file:

```
" Regenerate tags when saving Python files.
autocmd BufWritePost *.py silent! !ctags -R &
```

The preceding snippet runs ctags -R every time you save a Python file.

> You can replace the preceding *.py extension with different file extensions depending on the language you'd like to work with. For example, the following will generate a tags file for C++ files:
>
> autocmd BufWritePost *.cpp *.h silent! !ctags -R &

Undo tree and Gundo

Most modern editors support an undo stack, with undoing and replaying operations. Vim takes that one step further by introducing an undo tree. If you make a change, X, undo it, and then make a change, Y—Vim still saves the change, X. Vim supports manually browsing undo tree leaves, but there's a better way to do this.

Gundo is a plugin that visualizes the undo tree and is available from GitHub at: https://github.com/sjl/gundo.vim.git.

If you're using `vim-plug` to manage your plugins, add the following to your `.vimrc` file: `Plug 'sjl/gundo.vim'`. Execute `:w | so $MYVIMRC | PlugInstall` and you'll have Gundo installed and ready to go.

Let's say you're working on `animal_farm.py`, with your cursor on line 15:

```
 1 #!/usr/bin/python3
 2
 3 """Our own little animal farm."""
 4
 5 import sys
 6
 7 from animals import cat
 8 from animals import dog
 9 from animals import sheep
10 import animal
11 import farm
12
13 def make_animal(kind):
14     """Create an animal class."""
15     if kind == 'cat':
16         return cat.Cat()
17     if kind == 'dog':
18         return dog.Dog()
19     if kind == 'sheep':
20         return sheep.Sheep()
21     return animal.Animal(kind)
22
23 def main(animals):
```

You're editing the highlighted line: `if kind == 'cat'`. You perform the following operations:

1. Replace the `cat` text with `leopard`
2. Undo the edit using the undo command (`u`)
3. Replace the `cat` text with `lion`

Normally, you'd expect the edit where you changed `cat` to `leopard` to be lost, but since Vim has an undo tree, the change is preserved!

Executing `:GundoToggle` will open two new windows in a split: the visual representation of the tree (top-left) and the difference between that version and a previous snapshot (bottom-left). Here's how it looks:

```
@  [2] 10 seconds ago                         2
|                                             3 """Our own little animal farm.
| o  [1] 13 seconds ago                         """
|/                                            4
o  [0] Original                               5 import sys
__Gundo__                                     6
--- Original                                  7 from animals import cat
+++ 2   2018-10-27 10:24:20 PM                8 from animals import dog
@@ -12,7 +12,7 @@                             9 from animals import sheep
                                             10 import animal
 def make_animal(kind):                      11 import farm
     """Create an animal class."""          12
-    if kind == 'cat':                       13 def make_animal(kind):
+    if kind == 'lion':                      14     """Create an animal class.
         return cat.Cat()                          """
     if kind == 'dog':                       15     if kind == 'lion':
         return dog.Dog()                    16         return cat.Cat()
~                                            17     if kind == 'dog':
~                                            18         return dog.Dog()
~                                            19     if kind == 'sheep':
~                                            20         return sheep.Sheep()
~                                            21     return animal.Animal(kind)
__Gundo_Preview__                            animal_farm.py [+]
```

With your cursor over the Gundo window, you can navigate up and down the the tree with `j` and `k`. Go to the last change at the top of the tree if you're not already on it (you can use `gg` to quickly make your way to the top of the buffer). You can see how we changed the line containing `cat` to contain `lion` in our last change (lines starting with – signify a removal of the line, while lines starting with + show the addition of a line).

Now, hit `j` to go down the tree to a different (now unused) branch:

```
                                              2
 @  [2] 10 seconds ago                        3 """Our own little animal farm.
 |                                              """
 | o  [1] 13 seconds ago                       4
 |/                                            5 import sys
 o  [0] Original                              6
 __Gundo__                                     7 from animals import cat
 --- Original                                  8 from animals import dog
 +++ 1    2018-10-27 10:24:17 PM               9 from animals import sheep
 @@ -12,7 +12,7 @@                            10 import animal
                                             11 import farm
  def make_animal(kind):                     12
      """Create an animal class."""          13 def make_animal(kind):
 -        if kind == 'cat':                   14     """Create an animal class.
 +        if kind == 'leopard':                  """
          return cat.Cat()                   15     if kind == 'lion':
      if kind == 'dog':                       16         return cat.Cat()
          return dog.Dog()                    17     if kind == 'dog':
 ~                                            18         return dog.Dog()
 ~                                            19     if kind == 'sheep':
 ~                                            20         return sheep.Sheep()
 ~                                            21     return animal.Animal(kind)
 __Gundo_Preview__                           animal_farm.py [+]
```

This is the edit we thought we had lost! You can see how we replaced the word `cat` with `leopard`. Hit *Enter*, and Gundo will restore the edit!

Run `:GundoToggle` again to hide the undo tree.

If you're anything like me, you'll use the Gundo tree a lot. I have it mapped to the *F5* key, to make it easier to invoke:

```
noremap <f5> :GundoToggle<cr>   " Map Gundo to <F5>.
```

If you want to learn more about the undo tree, see `:help undo-tree`.

Summary

This chapter covered some of the advanced workflows in Vim. We looked at code autocomplete using Vim's built-in autocomplete functionality. We also looked at YouCompleteMe, a plugin that makes autocomplete syntactically aware. We also looked at Exuberant Ctags as a way to navigate more complex code bases. Lastly, we looked at Vim's undo tree and Gundo, a plugin that makes navigating the undo tree more intuitive.

In the following chapter, we'll dive into combining Vim and version control and dealing with merge conflicts. We'll also dive into ways to build, test, and execute code in a Vim-friendly manner.

Build, Test, and Execute

5

This chapter will focus on version control and the surrounding process, as well as building and testing code. You will learn to do the following:

- Working with version control (and Git in particular) if you haven't already
- Learning to productively use Git and Vim together
- Comparing and merging files with `vimdiff`. Resolve Git conflicts using `vimdiff`
- Using tmux, screen, or Vim terminal mode to multitask and execute shell commands
- Using quickfix and location lists to capture warnings and errors
- Building and testing code using the built-in `:make` command and plugins
- Running syntax checkers manually and by using plugins

Technical requirements

Among other things, this chapter will cover working with version control. Git is the version control system of choice for this chapter; however, the lessons learned are applicable across different systems. A section is dedicated to a quick-and-dirty introduction but, if you want to get the most out of version control systems, you may want to read up on the version control system of your choice.

Throughout this chapter, we'll be making changes to our `.vimrc` file. You can make these changes as you go, or download them from GitHub at `https://github.com/PacktPublishing/Mastering-Vim/tree/master/Chapter05`. Git installation and configuration instructions are also included in the repository.

Working with version control

This section will illustrate working with **version control systems** (often abbreviated to **VCS**) by using Git as an example.

 Git seems to be the most popular version control system as of the time of writing this book. Suggestions in this section can be applied to whichever version control system you choose to work with (or, more likely, whichever VCS you're locked into).

Modern development is nearly impossible without version control and, if you're working with code, it's more than likely you'll have to deal with it. This section gives the reader a refresher on how to use one of the most popular version control systems today—Git. We then cover how to work with Git from within Vim, to make Git commands more robust and interactive.

Quick-and-dirty version control and Git introduction

You can safely skip this section if you're comfortable with Git.

Git lets you track a history of changes to files, and helps ease the pain of multiple people working on the same set of files. Git is a distributed version control system, meaning every developer owns a mirrored copy of the code base on their system.

If you're on a Debian-flavored Linux distribution, you can install Git by running the following:

```
$ sudo apt-get install git
```

If you're on a different system, you can download the binaries or find more instructions from git-scm.com/download. You'll want to configure your username and your email address:

```
$ git config --global user.name 'Your Name'
$ git config --global user.email 'your@email'
```

You're now ready to use Git! If you find yourself stuck, Git has an extensive help system (in addition to a set of tutorials on `git-scm.com`):

```
$ git help
```

Concepts

Git represents history of changes to files using commits—atomic sets of changes to files. In addition to a diff of changes, each commit has a (hopefully) descriptive message attached to it (by the author of the commit), allowing you to determine what changes were made at any given point in time.

Commit history is not just linear and can branch, allowing Git users to work on multiple features without stepping on each other's toes. For example, in the following example (read from bottom to top), `feature A` was built in a master (main) branch, while `feature B` was developed in parallel in its own branch, called `feature-b`:

```
* Merged feature B into a master branch
|\
* | Improved feature A
| * Finished making feature B
| * Started building feature B (feature-b branch)
|/
* Implemented feature A
* Initial commit (master branch)
```

Git is a distributed version control system, meaning that there is no central place to talk to: every developer owns a full copy of the repository.

Setting up a new project

In this example, we'll be working with `Chapter05/animal_farm/` from `https://github.com/PacktPublishing/Mastering-Vim/tree/master/Chapter05/animal_farm`. You can also follow along with any project you'd like. Follow these steps if you're setting up a new Git repository:

1. Initialize the Git repository in the project's root directory:

   ```
   $ cd animal_farm/
   $ git init
   ```

2. Stage all files in a directory to be added to the initial commit:

   ```
   $ git add .
   ```

3. Create an initial commit:

```
$ git commit -m "Initial commit"
```

Here's sample output from the previous commands:

```
$ cd animal_farm/
$ git init
Initialized empty Git repository in /home/ruslan/Mastering-Vim/ch5/animal_farm/.git/
$ git add .
$ git commit -m "Initial commit"
[master (root-commit) e1fec4a] Initial commit
 6 files changed, 89 insertions(+)
 create mode 100644 animal.py
 create mode 100644 animal_farm.py
 create mode 100644 animals/cat.py
 create mode 100644 animals/dog.py
 create mode 100644 animals/sheep.py
 create mode 100644 farm.py
$
```

You should now be ready to work with your newly created repository.

If you want to have your repository backed up somewhere outside of your machine, you may want to use a service such as GitHub. See `github.com/new` to create a new repository, and add the repository URL to your project (where `https://` needs to be replaced with the repository URL— something like `https://github.com/<your-username>/animal-farm.git`):

```
$ git remote add origin <url>
```

Now, you just need to push the changes from your local repository:

```
$ git push -u origin master
```

To keep the repositories in sync, you'll have to push every time you add a new commit; see the *Working with Git* section for details.

Cloning an existing repository

If you already have code in a remote repository (for example, on GitHub), all you need to do is "clone" it—make a local copy. Find the repository URL, either over HTTPS (for example, `https://github.com/vim/vim.git`) or SSH (for example, `git@github.com:vim/vim.git`). Execute the following command (replacing `<url>` with the repository URL):

```
$ git clone <url>
```

This should download the repository to a directory with the project name on your machine.

Your local and remote repositories will now operate independently. If you want to update your local repository with changes from the remote repository (the one you cloned), you'll have to run `git pull --rebase`.

Working with Git

Git is rather extensive, but here are some basic commands to get you started. Let's work in our newly created repository, `animal_farm/`.

Adding files, committing, and pushing

Let's add a file to our repository, `animals/lion.py`:

```python
"""A lion."""

import animal

class Lion(animal.Animal):

    def __init__(self):
        self.kind = 'lion'

    def get_kind(self):
        return self.kind
```

Next let's add a bit to `animal_farm.py` that invokes the file (the added lines are highlighted in bold):

```
...
from animals import dog
from animals import lion
from animals import sheep
...
    if kind == 'dog':
        return dog.Dog()
    if kind == 'lion':
        return lion.Lion()
    if kind == 'sheep':
        return sheep.Sheep()
...
```

You can check the status of your files (to see which changes are going to make it into a commit) by running the following command:

```
$ git status
```

The output of the command will show you that you swap `animal_farm.py` repository and added `animals/lion.py`:

```
$ vim animals/lion.py animal_farm.py
2 files to edit
$ git status
On branch master
Changes not staged for commit:
  (use "git add <file>..." to update what will be committed)
  (use "git checkout -- <file>..." to discard changes in working directory)

        modified:   animal_farm.py

Untracked files:
  (use "git add <file>..." to include in what will be committed)

        animals/lion.py

no changes added to commit (use "git add" and/or "git commit -a")
$
```

Whenever you want to save your files in history, you can stage the files. You can do so individually by executing the following:

```
$ git add <filename>
```

Alternatively, you can stage all of the files at once by running the following:

```
$ git add .
```

If you run `git status`, you'll see that the files are now staged to be committed:

```
$ git add animal_farm.py animals/lion.py
$ git status
On branch master
Changes to be committed:
  (use "git reset HEAD <file>..." to unstage)

        modified:   animal_farm.py
        new file:   animals/lion.py

$
```

To commit a file or a set of files to history, execute the following:

```
$ git commit -m "<informative message describing the changes>"
```

For instance, here's how we would commit our changes to `animals/lion.py` and `animal_farm.py`:

```
$ git commit -m "Added a lion to the animal farm"
[master d2e1693] Added a lion to the animal farm
 2 files changed, 14 insertions(+)
 create mode 100644 animals/lion.py
$
```

To push your changes to a remote repository (if you created one earlier), run the following:

```
$ git push
```

To synchronize your changes with the changes other people made, run the following (in fact, it's usually wise to pull before pushing if you work with multiple people):

```
$ git pull --rebase
```

Now, if you want to view the commit history, run the following:

```
$ git log
```

Here's how the `git log` output looks for our project so far:

```
$ git log
commit d2e1693b795a7dd25b24940830d8e7752652ba13
Author: Ruslan Osipov <ruslan@rosipov.com>
Date:   Mon Oct 29 03:39:36 2018 +0000

    Added a lion to the animal farm

commit e1fec4ab2d14ee331498b6e5b2f2cca5b39daec0
Author: Ruslan Osipov <ruslan@rosipov.com>
Date:   Mon Oct 29 03:13:38 2018 +0000

    Initial commit
$
```

At the top, we can see a commit we just created. Right below it is the initial commit.

If you'd like to pull a particular commit into your working copy (for example, to see how things were at the initial commit), run the following (where `<sha1>` is the alphanumeric commit ID, for example, `e1fec4ab2d14ee331498b6e5b2f2cca5b39daec0` for the `Initial commit` in the previous screenshot):

```
$ git checkout <sha1>
```

Creating and merging branches

Separate branches are often used to create separate chunks of work. Once the feature is ready, the branches are merged back into the master (primary) branch. To create a new branch, run the following:

```
$ git checkout -b <branch-name>
```

For instance, we could create a branch in which we add a new animal type:

```
$ git checkout -b feature-leopard
```

It will appear as the following:

```
$ git checkout -b feature-leopard
Switched to a new branch 'feature-leopard'
$
```

Now, you can perform work on this branch as usual. For instance, we could add a new `animals/leopard.py` and modify `animal_farm.py` just like we did in the previous section:

```
$ vim animals/leopard.py
$ git add animals/leopard.py
$ git commit -m "Add a leopard animal class"
[feature-leopard 0b5d4de] Add a leopard animal class
 1 file changed, 11 insertions(+)
 create mode 100644 animals/leopard.py
$ vim animal_farm.py
$ git add animal_farm.py
$ git commit -m "Add a leopard to the animal farm"
[feature-leopard 7aa382f] Add a leopard to the animal farm
 1 file changed, 3 insertions(+)
$
```

Now that our feature is ready (we've added the leopard), we're ready to merge the `feature-leopard` branch back into the `master` (primary) branch. To see a list of all branches, run the following:

```
$ git branch -a
```

The branch you are currently on is marked with an asterisk (*):

```
$ git branch -a
* feature-leopard
  master
$
```

To move to another branch, run the following:

```
$ git checkout <branch-name>
```

In our case, let's move to the `master` branch:

```
$ git checkout master
```

Now, we just need to merge our feature branch into the branch we're currently on:

```
$ git merge feature-leopard
```

A helpful message will display the result of the merge:

```
$ git checkout master
Switched to branch 'master'
$ git merge feature-leopard
Updating d2e1693..7aa382f
Fast-forward
 animal_farm.py     |  3 +++
 animals/leopard.py | 11 +++++++++++
 2 files changed, 14 insertions(+)
 create mode 100644 animals/leopard.py
$
```

 If your repository is in GitHub, don't forget to run `git push` after you're done, to propagate your changes to the remote repository.

Integrating Git with Vim (vim-fugitive)

This section assumes that you understand the basics of working with Git. If you don't (or it's been a while), see the *Quick and dirty version control and Git introduction* section.

Tim Pope's vim-fugitive is a plugin that makes sure you don't need to leave Vim to interact with Git. Since you're editing the files in Vim, you might as well take care of dealing with version control of said edits in the editor. The plugin is available from `https://github.com/tpope/vim-fugitive`.

 If you're using vim-plug, you can install vim-fugitive by adding `Plug 'tpope/vim-fugitive'` to your `.vimrc` file and running `:w | source $MYVIMRC | PlugInstall`.

A lot of the commands vim-fugitive provides are a mirror of external Git commands. However, the output is often a lot more interactive. Take `git status`, for example, invoked by running the following:

```
:Gstatus
```

You'll see the familiar `git status` output in a split window (you may want to make some changes to the source files without committing them, to have some `git status` output to work with):

```
# On branch master
# Changes not staged for commit:
#   (use "git add <file>..." to update what will be committed)
#   (use "git checkout -- <file>..." to discard changes in working directory)
#
#       modified:   animal_farm.py
#
no changes added to commit (use "git add" and/or "git commit -a")
~
~
~
~
~/Mastering-Vim/ch5/animal_farm/.git/index [Preview][RO]
#!/usr/bin/python3

"""Our own little animal farm."""

import sys

from animals import cat
from animals import dog
from animals import leopard
animal_farm.py
:Gstatus
```

Unlike the `git status` output, this window is interactive. Move your cursor over one of the files (*Ctrl* + *n* and *Ctrl* + *p* allow you to cycle through files as well). Try some of the supported commands:

- – will stage or unstage the file
- `cc` or `:Gcommit` will commit the staged files
- `D` or `:GDiff` will open a diff
- `g?` displays help with more commands

`:Glog` opens a history of commits related to the currently open file. Conveniently, the results are displayed in a quickfix window as follows:

```
#!/usr/bin/python3

"""Our own little animal farm."""

import sys

from animals import cat
from animals import dog
from animals import leopard
from animals import lion
from animals import sheep
<animal_farm/.git//7aa382f6a613bda8e7cb9a87476352dfa7463a4b/animal_farm.py [RO]
fugitive:///home/ruslan/Mastering-Vim/ch5/animal_farm/.git//7aa382f6a613bda8e7cb
9a87476352dfa7463a4b/animal_farm.py|| Add a leopard to the animal farm
fugitive:///home/ruslan/Mastering-Vim/ch5/animal_farm/.git//90116b675f212b72fd5b
2fcdad7b1c237d87bf8f/animal_farm.py|| Revert "Add a leopard to the animal farm"
fugitive:///home/ruslan/Mastering-Vim/ch5/animal_farm/.git//a188d9c698cff0386718
12d1ae66883f4dc42610/animal_farm.py|| Add a leopard to the animal farm
fugitive:///home/ruslan/Mastering-Vim/ch5/animal_farm/.git//d2e1693b795a7dd25b24
940830d8e7752652ba13/animal_farm.py|| Added a lion to the animal farm
fugitive:///home/ruslan/Mastering-Vim/ch5/animal_farm/.git//e1fec4ab2d14ee331498
b6e5b2f2cca5b39daec0/animal_farm.py|| Initial commit
</animal_farm/.git//%H/animal_farm.py::%s' -- animal_farm.py 1,1          All
:copen
```

Use `:copen` to pop open the quickfix window.
The `:cnext` and `:cprevious` commands navigate the quickfix window by displaying different file versions. See the section, *Building and Testing – Quickfix Window,* to learn more about a quickfix window.

`git blame` is a command that lets you quickly figure out who changed every line of the file and when. This way, you can blame other developers (or, most often, yourself in the past) for bugs in your code! `:Gblame` displays interactive `git blame` output in a vertical split window:

```
^e1fec4a (Ruslan Osipov    #!/usr/bin/python3
^e1fec4a (Ruslan Osipov
938471ab (Bram Moolenaar   """Our own little animal farm (somewhat)."""
^e1fec4a (Ruslan Osipov
^e1fec4a (Ruslan Osipov    import sys
^e1fec4a (Ruslan Osipov
^e1fec4a (Ruslan Osipov    from animals import cat
^e1fec4a (Ruslan Osipov    from animals import dog
7aa382f6 (Ruslan Osipov    from animals import leopard
d2e1693b (Ruslan Osipov    from animals import lion
^e1fec4a (Ruslan Osipov    from animals import sheep
^e1fec4a (Ruslan Osipov    import animal
^e1fec4a (Ruslan Osipov    import farm
^e1fec4a (Ruslan Osipov
^e1fec4a (Ruslan Osipov    def make_animal(kind):
938471ab (Bram Moolenaar       """Create an animal class (inefficiently)."""
^e1fec4a (Ruslan Osipov        if kind == 'cat':
^e1fec4a (Ruslan Osipov            return cat.Cat()
^e1fec4a (Ruslan Osipov        if kind == 'dog':
^e1fec4a (Ruslan Osipov            return dog.Dog()
^e1fec4a (Ruslan Osipov        if kind == 'sheep':
^e1fec4a (Ruslan Osipov            return sheep.Sheep()
<vV1Ijko/1.fugitiveblame  animal_farm.py
```

`:Gblame` displays relevant commit ID, name of the commit author, and commit date and time (hidden in the screenshot) next to each line in the file.

Some useful shortcuts for `:Gblame` are as follows:

- C, A, and D resize the blame window up until the commit, author, and date respectively

- *Enter* opens a diff of the chosen commit

- o opens a diff of the chosen commit in a split window

- g? displays help with more commands

`:Gblame` is an extremely useful tool for figuring out when things went wrong.

There are even more really handy wrappers provided in this tool, such as the following:

- `:Gread` checks out the file straight into a buffer for a preview
- `:Ggrep` wraps around `git grep` (Git provides a powerful `grep` command that lets you search through tracked files at any moment in time—see `https://git-scm.com/docs/git-grep` for details)
- `:Gmove` moves the files (while renaming the buffers)
- `:Gdelete` wraps `git remove` commands

Don't forget to use Vim help (for example, `:help fugitive`) to learn more about the plugins!

Resolving conflicts with vimdiff

Often, during the development, you'll find yourself needing to compare some files—be it comparing different output or versions of a file, or dealing with merge conflicts. Vim provides `vimdiff`, a standalone binary that excels at file comparison operations.

Comparing two files

Using `vimdiff` to compare two files is fairly simple. Let's look at two files in `animal_farm/`: `animals/cat.py` and `animals/dog.py`. We'd like to know what's different between the two.

> The files from this example are available from `https://github.com/PacktPublishing/Mastering-Vim/tree/master/Chapter05/animal_farm` move to previous line you can follow this section with any similar but somewhat different files.

Open the files with `vimdiff`:

```
$ vimdiff animals/cat.py animals/dog.py
```

You will be greeted to the following screen (how colorful the screen is will depend on your `colorscheme`):

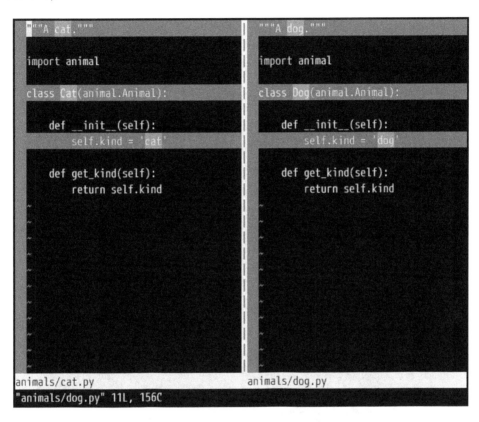

You can see `animals/cat.py` open in a split on the left and `animals/dog.py` in a split on the right. Different lines are highlighted in one color, and different characters are highlighted in another color.

You can navigate from one change to another by using `]c` to move forward and `[c` to move backward.

You can pull and push changes from one file to another:

- `do` or `:diffget` (**do** stands for diff obtain) will move the change to the active window
- `dp` or `:diffput` (stands for diff put) will push the change from the active window

If you want to copy the content of a whole file from one file into another, you can use the `:%diffget` or `:%diffput` commands.

For example, if you want to pull `self.kind = 'cat'` from `animals/cat.py` into `animals/dog.py`, you would navigate to the desired change using `]c` and press `do` to obtain it. The highlighting will disappear and the `animals/dog.py` buffer will now contain the desired change:

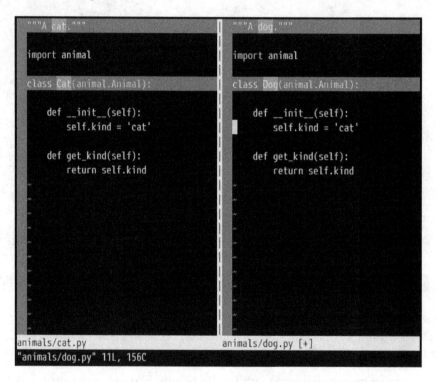

`vimdiff` automatically updates the highlighting if you're using `:diffget` and `:diffput` to move changes between files. If you edit the files manually, you'll have to update the highlighting by running `:diffupdate`, or `:diffu` for short.

You can diff as many files as you'd like at the same time, however, you won't be able to use the `do` and `dp` shortcuts. Let's open three files with `vimdiff`:

```
$ vimdiff animals/cat.py animals/cat.py animals/sheep.py
```

You can see all three side by side:

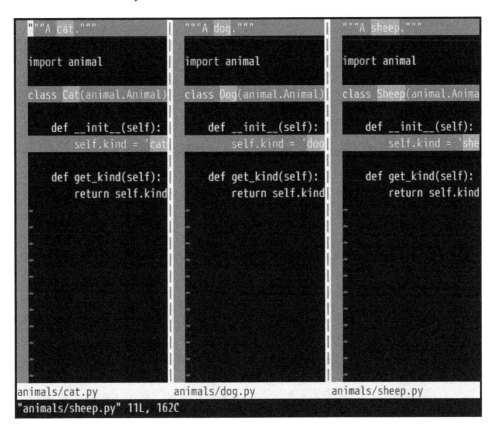

Since there are multiple buffers now, you'll have to specify which buffer you would like to get the changes to or from. Both `:diffget` and `:diffput` (which can be shortened to `:diffg` and `:diffp`) take the buffer specification argument, which can either be a buffer number (look it up from `:ls`!) or a partial buffer name.

For example, while in the `animals/dog.py` window, you can push the change under the cursor into `animals/sheep.py` by running the following:

```
:diffput sheep
```

The desired line will be pushed into the `animals/sheep.py` buffer:

 If you work with `vimdiff` a lot, don't forget to take the time to make useful aliases and key bindings as demonstrated in `Chapter 3`, *Follow the Leader!* The default ones are rather long.

vimdiff and Git

Using `vimdiff` as a Git merge tool can be pretty confusing—Vim bombards you with four windows, a number of keywords, and not a lot of explanation.

git config

First and foremost, configure Git to use `vimdiff` as a merge tool:

```
$ git config --global merge.tool vimdiff
$ git config --global merge.conflictstyle diff3
$ git config --global mergetool.prompt false
```

This will set Git as the default merge tool, will display a common ancestor while merging, and will disable the prompt asking you to open `vimdiff`.

Creating merge conflict

Let's use the `animal_farm/` repository we initialized earlier in this chapter as an example (or you can follow this with your own example if you have a merge conflict you're trying to resolve):

```
$ cd animal_farm/
```

We'll create an additional branch which will conflict with the master branch. In the `animal-create` branch, we'll rename a `make_animal` method to create-animal while, in the master branch, we'll change it to `build_animal`. The order of operations is important in creating the conflict, so you may want to follow closely.

We can start by creating a branch and editing `animal_farm.py`:

```
$ git checkout -b create-animal
$ vim animal_farm.py
```

Let's replace our `make_animal` method with `create_animal`:

```
...
def create_animal(kind):
...
    animal_farm.add_animal(create_animal(animal_kind))
...
```

Now, commit the change:

```
$ git add animal_farm.py
$ git commit -m "Rename make_animal to create_animal"
```

We can now switch back to the master branch to make our next set of changes:

```
$ git checkout master
$ vim animal_farm.py
```

This time, we'll replace `make_animal` with `build_animal`:

```
...
def build_animal(kind):
...
    animal_farm.add_animal(build_animal(animal_kind))
...
```

Commit the file:

```
$ git add animal_converter.py
$ git commit -m "Rename make_animal to build_animal"
```

It's time to merge the `create-animal` branch with `master`:

```
$ git merge create-animal
```

Uh-oh! A merge conflict:

```
$ git merge create-animal
Auto-merging animal_farm.py
CONFLICT (content): Merge conflict in animal_farm.py
Automatic merge failed; fix conflicts and then commit the result.
$
```

Resolving a merge conflict

Start the Git merge tool (which is `vimdiff`, since we configured it earlier):

```
$ git mergetool
```

You will be treated to quite a light show, with four windows and a lot of colors thrown at you:

It's okay to be scared, but it's not as terrifying as it looks.

Local changes (master branch in this case) are in the upper-left window, followed by a closest common ancestor and the `create-animal` branch in the upper-right corner. The result of the merge is in the bottom window.

To get into more detail, from left to right, top to bottom:

- **LOCAL**: This is file from the current branch (or whatever you're merging into)
- **BASE**: The common ancestor—how the file looked before both changes took place
- **REMOTE**: The file you are merging from another branch (`no-dogs` in this case)
- **MERGED**: The merge result—this is what gets saved as output

In the **MERGED** window, you'll see conflict markers. You don't need to interact with them directly, but it's good to have a vague idea of what they mean. Conflict markers are identified by <<<<<<< and >>>>>>>:

```
<<<<<<< [LOCAL commit/branch]
[LOCAL change]
||||||| merged common ancestors
[BASE - closest common ancestor]
=======
[REMOTE change]
>>>>>>> [REMOTE commit/branch]
```

Since we have multiple files, simply running do (:diffget) or dp (:diffput) without arguments would not be enough.

Assuming you want to keep the REMOTE change (from the create-animal branch), move your cursor to the window with MERGED file (the one at the bottom). Now move the cursor to the next change (in addition to regular movement keys, you can use]c and [c to move by changes). Now execute the following:

:diffget REMOTE

This will get the change from the REMOTE file and place it into the MERGED file. You can shorten these commands:

- Get a REMOTE change using :diffg R
- Get a BASE change using :diffg B
- Get a LOCAL change using :diffg L

Repeat for every conflict. Once you're done addressing the conflicts, save the MERGED file and exit vimdiff (running :wqa would be the fastest way) to complete the merge (or move on to the next file if you have more conflicts).

> Merge conflicts tend to leave .orig files in your working directory (for example, animal_farm.py.orig); feel free to discard those once you're done merging.

Don't forget to commit the merge results (git commit -m "Fixed a pesky merge conflict") once you're done.

tmux, screen, and Vim terminal mode

Software development often involves more than just writing code: executing your binaries, running tests, and using command-line tools to accomplish certain tasks. That's where session and window managers come in.

Modern desktop environments allow you to have multiple windows, but we'll focus on how you can manage the tasks you need to accomplish in a single Terminal session.

tmux

tmux is a Terminal multiplexer: it allows you to manage multiple Terminal windows in a single screen.

 If you're on a Debian-based distribution, you can install tmux using `sudo apt-get install tmux`. You can also build tmux from source, which is available from GitHub: `https://github.com/tmux/tmux`.

You can start it by invoking `tmux` in the Terminal:

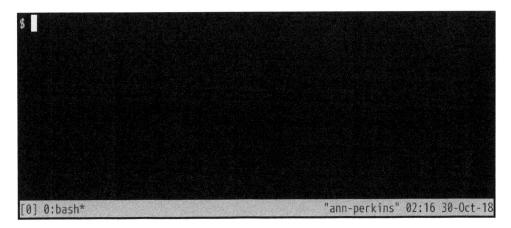

Panes are just like splits

tmux allows you to have multiple panes (the equivalent of windows in Vim) and windows (the equivalent of tabs). To access tmux functionality, you first need to hit a prefix key, followed by a command. The default prefix key is *Ctrl + b*.

You can rebind the default prefix key to something else by creating or editing your `~/.tmux.conf` file. For example, if you wanted to use *Ctrl + * as a prefix instead of *Ctrl + b*, you would add the following:

```
# Use Ctrl-\ as a prefix.
unbind-key C-b
set -g prefix 'C-\'
bind-key 'C-\' send-prefix
```

Restart tmux (or execute *Ctrl + b* followed by `:source-file ~/.tmux.conf`) to apply the configuration.

To split the screen vertically, use *Ctrl + b* followed by `%`:

For some reason, I could never get used to the default bindings. I remember hyphen – is a lot easier for creating vertical splits. My `~/.tmux.conf` file contains the following:

```
# Use - to create vertical splits.
bind - split-window -v
unbind '%'
```

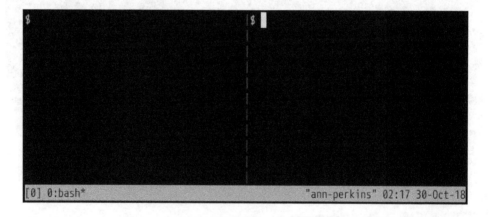

To create a horizontal split, hit *Ctrl + b*, followed by ":

The same as with vertical splits, I find the pipe character | to be a lot easier to remember for creating horizontal split windows. My ~/.tmux.conf file contains the following:

```
# Use | to create horizontal splits.
bind | split-window -h
unbind '"'
```

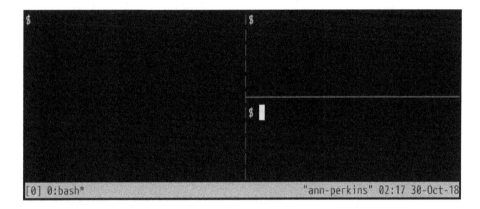

You can navigate the panes by using *Ctrl + b* followed by an arrow key. Every pane operates independently, and you can change directories, execute commands, and (most importantly) use Vim in each one of the panes.

If you're already used to hjkl, arrow key navigation might feel unwieldy. Add the following to your ~/.tmux.conf file to add hjkl movement support:

```
bind h select-pane -L
bind j select-pane -D
bind k select-pane -U
bind l select-pane -R
```

In the following example, I have a file with some code loaded into the left-hand pane; I'm editing .vimrc in the upper-right pane and listing files with ls in the lower-right pane:

```
#!/usr/bin/python3
                                      Plug 'sjl/gundo.vim'
"""Our own little animal farm."""
                                      noremap <f5> :GundoToggle<cr>  " Map Gu
import sys
                                      " => Chapter 5: Build, Test, and Execut
from animals import cat
from animals import dog              Plug 'tpope/vim-fugitive'
from animals import leopard
from animals import lion             call plug#end()
from animals import sheep
import animal
import farm                          $ ls
                                      animal_farm.py        animals
def create_animal(kind):             animal_farm.py.orig   farm.py
+-- 12 lines: """Create an animal class. animal.py         tags
                                      $
def main(animals):
+--  4 lines: animal_farm = farm.Farm()-

if __name__ == '__main__':
+--  4 lines: if len(sys.argv) == 1:----

[0] 0:bash*                                "ann-perkins" 02:18 30-Oct-18
```

Exit the session by executing exit or hitting *Ctrl* + *d* to close the pane.

Windows are just like tabs

You can create a new window by keying in *Ctrl + b* followed by c. You can now see that we have two panes at the bottom of the screen:

```
$ python3 animal_farm.py cat dog sheep
We've got some animals on the farm: cat, dog, sheep.
$
```
```
[0] 0:vim- 1:bash*                        "ann-perkins" 02:27 30-Oct-18
```

Windows are automatically named based on what process is running in an active window within a pane. You can rename the current window by running *Ctrl + b* followed by , :

```
$ python3 animal_farm.py cat dog sheep
We've got some animals on the farm: cat, dog, sheep.
$
```
```
(rename-window) animal-farm
```

You can navigate the windows by pressing *Ctrl + b* followed by n to go forward and *Ctrl + b* followed by p to go backward.

Sessions are invaluable

If you SSH into a machine to work, tmux is an essential tool you can use. tmux allows you to create long-lasting sessions, which outlive a single SSH connection.

If you're in a tmux session, you can detach from it by pressing *Ctrl + b* followed by d. You will be sent back in your shell with the following message:

```
[detached (from session 0)]
```

The session will be alive until your machine is powered off. To list tmux sessions, execute the following:

```
$ tmux list-sessions
0: 2 windows (created Sat Aug 18 19:17:59 2018) [80x23]
```

As you can see, we currently have one session available. Let's open the session, or—in tmux terms—attach to it:

```
$ tmux attach -t 0
```

Running tmux without any arguments always creates a new session.

You can have as many sessions as you want, if you prefer to separate work on different projects using different sessions! It's often helpful to divide projects or different tasks by sessions. You can navigate sessions from within tmux using *Ctrl + b* followed by (or).

You can also name your sessions, either when invoking tmux (tmux new -s name) or from within tmux (*Ctrl + b* and $).

tmux and Vim splits

Developers often use tmux panes and Vim windows to complement each other. You can have Vim open in different tmux panes as a way to isolate Vim instances from each other (and therefore group buffers). Normally, I have a few tmux panes open with Vim in one of them (with its own splits as needed), and shell running in the rest. Everyone treats their panes and windows differently, and you may want to experiment.

tmux and Vim use different key bindings to navigate through windows (or, in tmux terminology, panes). This is rather confusing, and there are solutions in place to fix it! The easiest is to use the vim-tmux-navigator plugin, which is available from `https://github.com/christoomey/vim-tmux-navigator`. vim-tmux-navigator adds support for consistent navigation between Vim windows and tmux panes using the *Ctrl + h*, *Ctrl + j*, *Ctrl + k*, and *Ctrl + l* keys.

In order to use vim-tmux-navigator, your tmux needs to be version 1.8 or higher. You can check your tmux version by running the following:

```
$ tmux -V
```

See the previous *tmux* section for tips on how to install a newer version of tmux.

If you're using vim-plug, you can install vim-tmux-navigator by adding the following line to your `.vimrc` file:

```
Plug 'christoomey/vim-tmux-navigator'
```

Don't forget to run `:w | source $MYVIMRC | PlugInstall` to install the plugin.

Once you have the plugin installed, you'll have to add the following bindings to your `~/.tmux.conf` file (this snippet is available from `https://github.com/christoomey/vim-tmux-navigator`):

```
# Smart pane switching with awareness of Vim splits.
# See: https://github.com/christoomey/vim-tmux-navigator
is_vim="ps -o state= -o comm= -t '#{pane_tty}' \
 | grep -iqE '^[^TXZ ]+ +(\\S+\\/)?g?(view|n?vim?x?)(diff)?$'"
bind-key -n C-h if-shell "$is_vim" "send-keys C-h" "select-pane -L"
bind-key -n C-j if-shell "$is_vim" "send-keys C-j" "select-pane -D"
bind-key -n C-k if-shell "$is_vim" "send-keys C-k" "select-pane -U"
bind-key -n C-l if-shell "$is_vim" "send-keys C-l" "select-pane -R"
bind-key -T copy-mode-vi C-h select-pane -L
bind-key -T copy-mode-vi C-j select-pane -D
bind-key -T copy-mode-vi C-k select-pane -U
bind-key -T copy-mode-vi C-l select-pane -R
```

If you're an advanced tmux user, or don't mind digging around, you may want to use TPM (Tmux Plugin Manager) instead of pasting the snippet into your `.tmux.conf` file. Add the following lines to `.tmux.conf` for TPM to configure the plugin for you:

```
set -g @plugin 'christoomey/vim-tmux-navigator'
run '~/.tmux/plugins/tpm/tpm'
```

You can learn more about TPM (and how to install it) from `https://github.com/tmux-plugins/tpm`.

Screen

Screen is tmux's spiritual predecessor, but it's still used by many today. Screen is not as extensible as tmux, and in fact Vim doesn't play that nicely with Screen out of the box. However, if you're used to Screen and don't want to change your existing workflow, there are a few tweaks you can make to your setup to make the two get along a little nicer.

The *Esc* key doesn't register correctly in Vim when running through Screen. You might want to add the following to your `~/.screenrc` file to fix the *Esc* key behavior:

```
# Wait no more than 5 milliseconds when detecting an input
# sequence, fixes Esc behavior in Vim.
maptimeout 5
```

Screen also sets the `$TERM` variable to `screen`, which Vim does not recognize. Update `.screenrc` to include the following:

```
# Set $TERM to a value Vim recognizes.
term screen-256color
```

There are more minor inconveniences when using Vim and Screen together, such as the *Home* and *End* keys not registering, for example. Vim Wikia has a great in-depth entry on getting Vim and Screen to play along nicely at `http://vim.wikia.com/wiki/GNU_Screen_integration`.

Terminal mode

Historically, you can run shell commands from Vim by using `:!` followed by a shell command. For example, we could execute our Python program as follows:

```
:!python3 animal_farm.py cat dog sheep
```

Vim will pause, and you'll see the output in the Terminal:

```
$ vim animal_farm.py

We've got some animals on the farm: sheep, cat, dog.

Press ENTER or type command to continue
```

Things have got better since then.

In version 8.1, Vim introduced the terminal mode. The terminal mode is effectively a Terminal emulator running within your Vim session. Unlike with tmux, terminal mode plays with Vim out of the box. It's great for running long running commands while you continue to work in Vim.

Terminal mode can be invoked by executing the following:

```
:term
```

This opens a horizontal split with your default shell running:

```
$ python3 animal_farm.py cat dog sheep
We've got some animals on the farm: sheep, cat, dog.
$ 




!/bin/bash [running]
#!/usr/bin/python3

"""Our own little animal farm."""

import sys

from animals import cat
from animals import dog
from animals import leopard
from animals import lion
animal_farm.py
:term
```

The Terminal window is treated like any other window, and can be resized and moved as usual (see the *Windows* section in Chapter 10, *Neovim*). The window is running in a terminal-job mode, something akin to an insert mode. But there are a few specific key bindings:

- *Ctrl + w, N* enters a terminal-normal mode, which behaves just like a normal mode. Operations that take you back to insert mode (such as i or a) will take you back to a terminal-job mode.
- *Ctrl + w,* " followed by a register will paste the contents of a register into a terminal. For example, to paste something you yanked with yw, you can execute *Ctrl + w,* " to paste from the default register.
- *Ctrl + w, Ctrl + c* sends *Ctrl + c* to the running command in a Terminal.

The best feature of a terminal mode is that you can invoke terminal mode with a specific command, and get full access to the output. Try running the following from within Vim:

```
:term python3 animal_farm.py cat dog sheep
```

This will execute a command and, once it is done running, open a buffer with the resultant output:

If you so desire, you can open a Terminal in a vertical split by running `:vert term`.

> If you use the *Ctrl + hjkl* shortcuts from `Chapter 2`, *Advanced Editing and Navigation*,to navigate your Vim windows, you may want to add an additional set of bindings to your `.vimrc` file to work with the terminal mode:
>
> ```
> tnoremap <c-j> <c-w><c-j>
> tnoremap <c-k> <c-w><c-k>
> tnoremap <c-l> <c-w><c-l>
> tnoremap <c-h> <c-w><c-h>
> ```

For best results, you can combine Vim terminal mode with tmux: tmux can manage your sessions for you (for when you need to switch focus between tasks), while terminal mode can manage windows. For instance, you could use Vim terminal windows to organize work on your project and tmux windows (or tabs in Vim terminology) to switch focus and work on different tasks.

Building and testing

As you work on your code, you will have to compile (in compiled languages, which does not apply to Python) it and run accompanying tests.

Vim supports populating build and test failures through quickfix and location lists, which we will cover in this section.

Quickfix list

You've already had a brush with a quickfix window in `Chapter 2`, *Advanced Editing and Navigation*, but let's dig a bit deeper into it.

Vim has an additional mode that makes jumping to certain parts of files easier. Some Vim commands use it to navigate between positions in files, such as jumping to compile errors for `:make` or search terms for `:grep` or `:vimgrep`. Plugins such as linters (syntax checking) or test runners use the quickfix list as well.

Let's try using a quickfix list by running a `:grep` command to search for the `animal` keyword recursively (`-r`) in every Python file (`--include="*.py"`), starting in the current directory (`.`):

```
:grep -r --include="*.py" animal .
```

This will open the first match in a current window. To open a quickfix window and see all of the matches, execute the following:

```
:copen
```

You can see the results a horizontal split now:

```
"""Our own little animal farm."""

import sys

from animals import cat
from animals import dog
from animals import leopard
from animals import lion
from animals import sheep
import animal
./animal_farm.py
./animal_farm.py|3| """Our own little animal farm."""
./animal_farm.py|7| from animals import cat
./animal_farm.py|8| from animals import dog
./animal_farm.py|9| from animals import leopard
./animal_farm.py|10| from animals import lion
./animal_farm.py|11| from animals import sheep
./animal_farm.py|12| import animal
./animal_farm.py|15| def create_animal(kind):
./animal_farm.py|16| """Create an animal class."""
./animal_farm.py|27| return animal.Animal(kind)
<ckfix List] :grep -n -r --include "*.py" animal . /dev/null 1,1          Top
:copen
```

You can navigate the quickfix window as usual with k and j keys to move up and down, *Ctrl* + *f* and *Ctrl* + *b* to scroll by pages, and / and ? to search forward and backward. *Enter* will open a file with a match in the buffer you were searching from. It will also place your cursor in the desired position.

For example, if you wanted to open a match in a file, `animals/sheep.py`, you can navigate to the desired line by running `/sheep`, followed by n (next) until the cursor is at the right line, and pressing *Enter*. The file will be opened in the original window with the cursor located where the match is:

```
"""A sheep."""

import animal

class Sheep(animal.Animal):

    def __init__(self):
        self.kind = 'sheep'

    def get_kind(self):
        return self.kind
./animals/sheep.py
./animal_farm.py|31| for animalKind in animals:
./animal_farm.py|32| animal_farm.add_animal(create_animal(animalKind))
./animal_farm.py|33| animal_farm.print_contents()
./animal_farm.py|37| print('Pass at least one animal type!')
./animals/sheep.py|3| import animal
./animals/sheep.py|5| class Sheep(animal.Animal):
./animals/lion.py|3| import animal
./animals/lion.py|5| class Lion(animal.Animal):
./animals/leopard.py|3| import animal
./animals/leopard.py|5| class Leopard(animal.Animal):
<ckfix List] :grep -n -r --include "*.py" animal . /dev/null 17,1-11    52%
"./animals/sheep.py" 11L, 162C
```

You can close the quickfix list with `:cclose` (or `:bd` to delete the quickfix buffer if it's in an active window).

You can also navigate the quickfix list without opening the quickfix window:

- `:cnext` (or `:cn`) navigates to the next entry in the quickfix list
- `:cprevious` (or `:cp`, `:cN`) navigates to the previous entry in the list

Lastly, you can choose to only open the quickfix window if errors (such as compile errors) are found: `:cwindow` (or `:cw`) will toggle the quickfix window only if errors are present.

Location list

In addition to a quickfix list, Vim also has a location list. It behaves just like a quickfix list, except that it stays local to the current window. While you can have only one quickfix list in a single Vim session, you can have as many location lists as you want.

To populate a location list, you can prefix most quickfix-operating commands with the letter *l* (such as :lgrep or :lmake).

Shortcuts also replace the :c prefix with the :l prefix:

- :lopen opens the location window
- :lclose closes the window
- :lnext navigates to the next item in a location list
- :lprevious navigates to the previous item in a location list
- :lwindow toggles the quickfix window only if the errors were present

In general, you will use a quickfix list when the results need to be accessed in multiple windows, while a location list is great for capturing output relevant to a single window.

Building code

Building doesn't necessarily apply to Python (since there isn't much compiling going on), but it's definitely worth going over to understand how Vim deals with executing code.

Vim provides a :make command, which wraps around the Unix make utility. In case you're not familiar, Make is a build management solution as old as time (and if it ain't broke...) that allows you to recompile parts of a bigger program (or all of it) as needed.

Some relevant options you'd want to be aware of are as follows:

- :compiler lets you specify a different compiler plugin, which also modifies the expected format output for the compiler
- In particular, :set errorformat defines a set of recognized error formats
- :set makeprg sets what program to execute when running :make

Want to learn more about one of these options? Don't forget that you can run :help <anything> to look up an entry in the Vim manual.

The two can be used in conjunction to work with any compiler. For example, if you wanted to compile a C file you're working on, you could invoke `gcc` (standard issue C compiler) by running the following:

```
:compiler gcc
:make
```

What makes `:make` important is that it allows Vim users to implement syntax checkers, test runners, or just about anything else that spits out references to lines as a compiler plugin, giving us access to quickfix or location windows!

Terminal mode, introduced in Vim 8.1, is also a solid candidate for long-running builds, as `:term make` will call make asynchronously while you continue working on your code. See the *Terminal mode* section for more about terminal mode.

Plugin spotlight: vim-dispatch

Tim Pope supercharges the `:make` command, makes it asynchronous, and adds a whole bunch of syntactic sugar and additional commands to support its use. A big chunk of vim-dispatch became obsolete with Vim 8.1 rolling out terminal mode support, however, depending on your preferred workflow, integration with different terminal emulators can be very useful. You can get vim-dispatch from GitHub at `https://github.com/tpope/vim-dispatch`.

> If you're using vim-plug, you can install vim-dispatch by adding `Plug 'tpope/vim-dispatch'` to a list of your plugins and running `:w | source $MYVIMRC | PlugInstall`.

Here are some highlights:

- `:Make` allows you to run a task in a different window (only if you're using `tmux`, `iTerm`, or `cmd.exe`)
- `:Make!` kicks off a task in the background (only in `tmux`, Screen, `iTerm`, or `cmd.exe`)
- `:Dispatch` allows you to combine `:compiler <compiler-name>` and `:make` into a single command, for example, `:Dispatch testrb test/models/user_test.rb`
- `:Dispatch` can also just run arbitrary commands, for example, `:Dispatch bundle install`

If you find yourself using built-in `:make` a lot, you may want to give vim-dispatch a shot.

Technically, you can also run tests from vim-dispatch, but since tests normally don't provide standardized output, vim-dispatch cannot automatically populate the quickfix or the location lists.

Testing code

Test output happens to be a lot less uniform than compile errors, so your bet here is using test-runner-specific plugins you can find online. There are as many plugins as there are test runners, if not more.

In addition, terminal mode, added in Vim 8.1, provides a good way to run tests while continuing to work on your code.

Plugin spotlight – vim-test

This is the most popular test runner, as it provides a set of compilers (as well as handy mappings) for plugging into a lot of test runners. For Python, vim-test supports djangotest, django-nose, nose, nose2, pytest, and PyUnit. It's available from `https://github.com/janko-m/vim-test`. You'll have to make sure you have the desired test runner already installed before using vim-test.

 If you're using vim-plug, you can install vim-test by adding `Plug 'janko-m/vim-test'` to your `.vimrc` file and running `:w | source $MYVIMRC | PlugInstall`.

vim-test supports the following commands:

- `:TestNearest` runs the test nearest to the cursor
- `:TestFile` runs the tests in the current file
- `:TestSuite` runs the entire test suite
- `:TestLast` runs the last test

vim-test also allows you to specify test strategy, as in, what method to use for running tests. Strategies such as make, neomake, MakeGreen, and dispatch (or `dispatch_background`) populate a quickfix window, which is exactly what you'd be looking for in a plugin like this.

For example, if you wanted to run your tests through vim-dispatch (to run a test in a different Terminal window, for instance), you would add the following to your `.vimrc` file:

```
let test#strategy = "dispatch"
```

You can visit `https://github.com/janko-m/vim-test` for more information about vim-test.

Syntax checking code with linters

Syntax checking (also known as linting) has essentially become a staple in any multi-person software project. There are many linter programs available online, which support different languages and styles.

Python code has it easier than many languages out there, as it tends to adhere to a single standard—PEP8 (`https://www.python.org/dev/peps/pep-0008`). The most common linters that make sure the code adheres to PEP8 are Pylint, Flake8, and autopep8.

Before proceeding, make sure one of these (the following examples work with Pylint) is installed on your machine, as Vim merely calls external linters.

 If you're on a Debian-flavored distribution, you can run `sudo apt-get install pylint3` to install Pylint for Python3.

Using linters with Vim

A lot of common linters have associated plugins, which you can use to avoid dealing with the intricacies of each linter. However, if you have to support a custom linter, Vim lets you populate a quickfix list however you want.

You can leverage Vim's `:make` command, which populates a quickfix list. By default, it runs the Unix `make` command (no surprise here), but you can override that by setting the `makeprg` variable.

Quickfix expects `:make` output to be in a particular format, and you can try to get a linter to output in a desired format. This is error-prone, and has possible compatibility issues (if the underlying linter changes).

Add the following to your `.vimrc` file to override the `:make` behavior only when working on Python files:

```
autocmd filetype python setlocal makeprg=pylint3\ --reports=n\ --msg-

template=\"{path}:{line}:\ {msg_id}\ {symbol},\ {obj}\ {msg}\"\ %:p
autocmd filetype python setlocal errorformat=%f:%l:\ %m
```

Now, if you run `:make | copen` while in a Python file, you'll see a populated quickfix list:

```
        return sheep.Sheep()
    return animal.Animal(kind)


def main(ANIMALS):
    animal_farm = farm.Farm()
    for animalKind in ANIMALS:
        animal_farm.add_animal(create_animal(animalKind))
    animal_farm.print_contents()


if __name__ == '__main__':
    if len(sys.argv) == 1:
animal_farm.py
|| No config file found, using default configuration
|| ************* Module animal_farm
animal_farm.py|29| C0103 invalid-name, main Invalid argument name "ANIMALS"
animal_farm.py|29| C0111 missing-docstring, main Missing function docstring
animal_farm.py|31| C0103 invalid-name, main Invalid variable name "animalKind"
~
~
~
~
~
< /home/ruslan/Mastering-Vim/ch5/animal_farm/animal_farm.py  3,1         All
```

If you're not accustomed to using linters, you might be wondering how to silence warnings you don't care for. For Pylint, it's done by adding a statement such as `disable-invalid-name,missing-docstring` to `~/.pylintrc` or by commenting `# pylint: disable=invalid-name` on the offending line. Each linter has its own syntax for silencing warnings.

Plugin spotlight – Syntastic

Syntastic is the go-to plugin when it comes to syntax checking. It supports over 100 languages (and can be extended with smaller syntax checker plugins). Syntastic is available from `https://github.com/vim-syntastic/syntastic`.

If you're using vim-plug, you can install Syntastic by adding `Plug 'vim-syntastic/syntastic'` to your `.vimrc` file and running `:w | source $MYVIMRC | PlugInstall`.

Syntastic does not provide newbie-friendly defaults, so you may want to have the following in your `.vimrc` file:

```
set statusline+=%#warningmsg#
set statusline+=%{SyntasticStatuslineFlag()}
set statusline+=%*

let g:syntastic_always_populate_loc_list = 1
let g:syntastic_auto_loc_list = 1
let g:syntastic_check_on_open = 1
let g:syntastic_check_on_wq = 0

let g:syntastic_python_pylint_exe = 'pylint3'
```

Now, as long as you have a Python syntax checker (such as Pylint) installed on your system, you will see the following when you open a Python file:

```
def create_animal(kind):
+-- 12 lines: """Create an animal class."""-----------------------


>>def main(ANIMALS):
    animal_farm = farm.Farm()
>>  for animalKind in ANIMALS:
        animal_farm.add_animal(create_animal(animalKind))
    animal_farm.print_contents()


if __name__ == '__main__':
+-- 4 lines: if len(sys.argv) == 1:---------------------------
[Syntax: line:29 (3)]
animal_farm.py|29 col 1 warning| [invalid-name] Invalid argument name "ANIMALS"
animal_farm.py|29 col 1 warning| [missing-docstring] Missing function docstring
animal_farm.py|31 col 9 warning| [invalid-name] Invalid variable name "animalKin
d"
~
~
~
~
~
~
[Location List] :SyntasticCheck pylint (python)          1,1            All
[invalid-name] Invalid argument name "ANIMALS"
```

There are a few things going on here, from top to bottom:

- Lines with syntactic errors are highlighted with >>
- Offending characters or strings are highlighted as well
- A location list is open, listing everything wrong with the current file
- A status line is displaying the error on a currently open line

Since this is a regular location list, you can use the usual location list shortcuts to navigate (for example, :lnext or :lprevious).

If you were to fix the error, the syntax error list updates as soon as you save the file:

```
def create_animal(kind):
+-- 12 lines: """Create an animal class."""----------------

>>def main(animals):
    animal_farm = farm.Farm()
>>  for animalKind in animals:
        animal_farm.add_animal(create_animal(animalKind))
    animal_farm.print_contents()


if __name__ == '__main__':
+-- 4 lines: if len(sys.argv) == 1:--------------------------
[Syntax: line:29 (2)]
animal_farm.py|29 col 1 warning| [missing-docstring] Missing function docstring
animal_farm.py|31 col 9 warning| [invalid-name] Invalid variable name "animalKin
d"







[Location List] :SyntasticCheck pylint (python)              1,1        All
"animal_farm.py" 39L, 885C written
```

Plugin spotlight – ALE

Asynchronous Lint Engine (**ALE**) is a more recent player on the field, but it's been getting nearly as much traction as Syntastic has. Its primary selling point is that ALE displays lint errors as you type, and it runs the linters asynchronously. ALE is available from GitHub at `https://github.com/w0rp/ale`.

> If you're using vim-plug, you can install ALE by adding
> `Plug 'w0rp/ale'` to your `.vimrc` file and running `:w | source`
> `$MYVIMRC | PlugInstall`. ALE requires Vim 8+ or Neovim for
> asynchronous calls to work.

It's ready to be used out of the box, and the output looks very similar to Syntastic. Here's a screenshot of a file with ALE enabled (I've opened the location window using `:lopen`):

```
def create_animal(kind):
+-- 12 lines: """Create an animal class."""-------------------

--def main(animals):
    animal_farm = farm.Farm()
--  for animalKind in animals:
        animal_farm.add_animal(create_animal(animalKind))
    animal_farm.print_contents()

if __name__ == '__main__':
+-- 3 lines: if len(sys.argv) == 1:-----------------------------
animal_farm.py
animal_farm.py|29 col 1 warning| missing-docstring: Missing function docstring
animal_farm.py|31 col 9 warning| invalid-name: Invalid variable name "animalKind
"




<] /home/ruslan/Mastering-Vim/ch5/animal_farm/animal_farm.py 2,1          All
invalid-name: Invalid variable name "animalKind"
```

You can see the line with an error highlighted with >>, and the status line displays the relevant `linmessage` at the bottom.

You can toggle ALE on and off by running `:ALEToggle` if you don't like to be nagged by it.

ALE is a lot more than just a linter though, and is a full-blown language server protocol client: it supports autocompletion, traveling to definitions, and so on. It's not as established and popular as, say, YouCompleteMe (see the *Autocomplete* section in Chapter 4, *Understanding the Text*)—but it has a loyal fan base and it's growing quickly.

For reference, you can jump to definitions by running `:ALEGoToDefinition` and look for references using `:ALEFindReferences`. In order to enable autocomplete, you'll need the following line in your `.vimrc` file:

```
let g:ale_completion_enabled = 1
```

You can learn more about ALE and decide whether it's a tool worth investing your time in at `https://github.com/w0rp/ale`.

Summary

In this chapter, you learned (or got a refresher on) how to use Git, including a quick brush-up on core concepts and setting up and cloning existing projects, and a rundown of the most frequent commands. You learned about vim-fugitive, a Vim plugin that makes Git a lot more interactive from inside Vim.

We covered vimdiff, a separate tool packaged with Vim made for comparing files and moving changes between files. We learned how to compare and move changes between multiple files. Furthermore, we got some practice at resolving nasty Git merge conflicts, which will hopefully make them less intimidating.

This chapter covered multiple ways of running shell commands when working with Vim, be it through tmux, screen, or Vim terminal mode

We also learned about (global) quickfix and (local) location lists, which can be used to store pointers to certain lines in files. We combined those with the output of `:grep` and `:make` commands to get some easy-to-navigate results! We learned how `:make` works to call an external compiler, and covered the vim-dispatch plugin to expand the `:make` functionality, and the vim-test plugin to make running tests smoother.

Lastly, we covered a set of solutions for running syntax checkers in Vim, including building our own solution for Pylint. We've looked at ALE, an asynchronous linter, and Syntastic, a similarly popular syntax checker.

In the next chapter, we will cover refactoring operations using Vim regular expressions and macros.

6
Refactoring Code with Regex and Macros

This chapter will focus on features provided by Vim to support refactoring operations.

We will cover the following topics:

- Using search or replace functionality with `:substitute`
- Using regular expressions to make searches and substitutions smarter
- Using arglist to perform operations on multiple files
- Examples of refactoring operations, such as renaming methods and reordering arguments
- Macros, which let you record and replay keystrokes

Technical requirements

This chapter works with multiple code samples, which can be found on GitHub under `https://github.com/PacktPublishing/Mastering-Vim/tree/master/Chapter06`.

You can work with that repository, or, if you're feeling more comfortable, use your own project throughout this chapter.

Search or replace with regular expressions

Regular expressions (or regexes) are wonderful, and you should know how to use them. Vim, as is custom among regex implementations, has its own flavor of regex. However, once you learn one, you're comfortable with all of them.

First, let's talk about the regular (that is, the normal) search and replace command.

Search and replace

Vim supports search and replace through the `:substitute` command, most often abbreviated to `:s`. By default, `:s` will replace one substring with another in a current line. It has the following format:

```
:s/<find-this>/<replace-with-this>/<flags>
```

The flags are optional, and you shouldn't worry about them for now. To try it, open `animal_farm.py`, navigate to the line containing `cat` (for example, with `/cat`), and execute the following:

```
:s/cat/dog
```

As you can see in the screenshot, this replaces the first occurrence of `cat` in the current line:

```
from animals import dog
from animals import dog
from animals import sheep
import animal
import farm

def make_animal(kind):
    """Create an animal class."""
    if kind == 'cat':
        return cat.Cat()
    if kind == 'dog':
:s/cat/dog
```

Now, let's look at the flags you can pass to the substitute command:

- `g`—global replace: replace every occurrence of the pattern, not just the first one
- `c` —confirm each substitution: prompt the user before replacing the text
- `e` —do not show errors if no matches are found
- `i` —ignore case: make the search case-insensitive
- `I` —make the search case-sensitive

You can mix and match these (except for `i` and `I`) as you see fit. For example, running `:s/cat/dog/gi` will turn the string `cat.Cat()` into `dog.dog()`.

`:substitute` can be prefixed by a range, which tells it what to operate on. The most common range used with `:substitute` is `%`, which makes `:s` operate on the current file.

For instance, if we wanted to replace each instance of `animal` in a file with `creature`, we would run the folxlowing:

```
:%s/animal/creature/g
```

If you try it on `animal_farm.py`, you'll see, as in the screenshot, that every instance of `animal` was replaced with `creature`:

```
import creature
import farm

def make_creature(kind):
    """Create an creature class."""
    if kind == 'cat':
        return cat.Cat()
    if kind == 'dog':
        return dog.Dog()
    if kind == 'sheep':
        return sheep.Sheep()
    return creature.Animal(kind)

def main(creatures):
    creature_farm = farm.Farm()
    for creature_kind in creatures:
        creature_farm.add_creature(make_creature(creature_kind))
    creature_farm.print_contents()
    creature_farm.act('a farmer')

if __name__ == '__main__':
    if len(sys.argv) == 1:
        print('Pass at least one creature type!')
19 substitutions on 15 lines
```

The `:substitute` command conveniently tells us how many matches were replaced in the status line at the bottom of the screen.

It seems as if we just completed a very simple case of refactoring!

`:substitute` supports more ranges. Here are some common ones:

- numbers—a line number
- $—the last line in the file

- %—a whole file (this is one of the most used ones)
- /search-pattern/—lets you find a line to operate on
- ?backwards-search-pattern?—does the same thing as the previous flag, but searches backwards

Furthermore, you can combine the ranges with a ; operator. For example, 20;$ will let you search from line 20 until the end of the file.

To demonstrate, the following command will search for and replace every instance of animal with creature from line 12, up to and including the line where it encounters dog:

```
:12;/dog/s/animal/creature/g
```

As you can see in the following screenshot, two instances of animal were replaced on lines 13 and 14, but not on lines 10 or 21 (I've enabled line number display by running :set nu):

```
 1 #!/usr/bin/python3
 2
 3 """Our own little animal farm."""
 4
 5 import sys
 6
 7 from animals import cat
 8 from animals import dog
 9 from animals import sheep
10 import animal
11 import farm
12
13 def make_creature(kind):
14     """Create an creature class."""
15     if kind == 'cat':
16         return cat.Cat()
17     if kind == 'dog':
18         return dog.Dog()
19     if kind == 'sheep':
20         return sheep.Sheep()
21     return animal.Animal(kind)
22
23 def main(animals):
:12;/dog/s/animal/creature/g
```

You can also select a range in a visual mode, and run :s without any explicit ranges to operate on a selected text. See :help cmdline-ranges for more information on ranges.

If you find yourself working with Linux file paths (or anything with / in them), you can escape them by prefixing with a backslash (\), or change the separator. For example, `:s+path/to/dir+path/to/other/dir+gc` is (with a separator changed to +) equivalent to `:s/path\/to\/dir/path\/to\/other\/dir/gc`.

Most often, you will find yourself replacing all occurrences in the whole file by running the following:

```
:%s/find-this/replace-with-this/g
```

When replacing text, you may want to only search for the whole word. You can use `\<` and `\>` for this purpose. For example, given the following file, we can search for `/animal` (`:set hlsearch` is enabled to highlight all results), but we also get results we're not exactly interested in, such as `animals`:

```python
#!/usr/bin/python3

"""Our own little animal farm."""

import sys

from animals import cat
from animals import dog
from animals import sheep
import animal
import farm

def make_creature(kind):
    """Create an creature class."""
    if kind == 'cat':
        return cat.Cat()
    if kind == 'dog':
        return dog.Dog()
    if kind == 'sheep':
        return sheep.Sheep()
    return animal.Animal(kind)

def main(animals):
/animal
```

However, if we search for /\<animal\>, we'll be able to match whole words only, without falsely detecting `animals`, as follows:

```
#!/usr/bin/python3

"""Our own little animal farm."""

import sys

from animals import cat
from animals import dog
from animals import sheep
import animal
import farm

def make_creature(kind):
    """Create an creature class."""
    if kind == 'cat':
        return cat.Cat()
    if kind == 'dog':
        return dog.Dog()
    if kind == 'sheep':
        return sheep.Sheep()
    return animal.Animal(kind)

def main(animals):
/\<animal\>
```

Operations across files using arglist

Arglist allows you to perform the same operation on multiple files, without having to have them preloaded in buffers first.

Arglist provides a few commands, as follows:

- :arg defines the arglist.
- :argdo allows you to execute a command on all the files in the arglist.
- :args displays the list of files in the arglist.

For example, if we wanted to replace all instances of `animal` in every Python file (recursively), we would do the following:

```
:arg **/*.py
:argdo %s/\<animal\>/creature/ge | update
```

This command work as follows:

- `:arg <pattern>` adds a set of files matching a pattern to the arglist (each argument in arglist also has a corresponding buffer).
- `**/*.py` is a wildcard for every `.py` file, recursively starting with the current directory.
- `:argdo` executes a command on every item in the argument list.
- `%s/\<animal\>/creature/ge` replaces every occurrence of `animal` with `creature`, in every file, without raising errors if the matches are not found.

 As mentioned above, `\<` and `\>` around `animal` tell Vim to only replace a whole word, so we won't be replacing occurrences like `animal_farm` or `animals`.

`:update` is equivalent to `:write`, but it only saves the file if the buffer has been modified.

You need to use `:update` in arglist commands, because Vim doesn't like when you switch buffers without saving their contents. An alternative would be to use `:set hidden` to silence these warnings, and save all files at the end by running `:wa`.

Give it a shot, and you'll see that every occurrence of a word has been replaced (you can check by running `git status` or `git diff` if you have a repository checked into Git). You can also view the contents of the arglist by running the following without any arguments:

```
:args
```

Arglist is actually left over from the Vi days—it was used in a similar way to how we use buffers today. Buffers expand upon an argument list: every arglist entry is in the buffer list, but not every buffer is in the arglist.

Technically, you can also use `:bufdo` to perform an operation on every open buffer (since arglist entries are reflected in the buffer list). However, I would advise against it, since there is a risk of running a command on buffers you unintentionally had open before populating the argument list.

Regex basics

Regular expressions work in substitution commands, as well as in search. Regex introduces special patterns that can be used to match a set of characters; for example, see the following:

- `\(c\|p\)arrot` matches both `carrot` and `parrot`—the `\(c\|p\)` denotes either c or p.
- `\warrot\?` matches `carrot`, `parrot`, and even `farro`—the `\w` signifies any word character, and the `t\?` means that the `t` is optional.
- `pa.\+ot` matches `parrot`, `patriot`, or even `pa123ot`—the `.\+` denotes one or more of any character.

If you're familiar with other variations of regex, then you'll notice that unlike in many other regex flavors, most special characters need to be escaped with \ to work (the default mode for most characters is non-regex, with a few exceptions such as `.` or `*`). This behavior can be reversed by using magic mode, as we will cover below.

Special regex characters

Let's dig deeper into regex:

Symbol	Meaning
.	Any character, except for end of the line
^	The beginning of the line
$	The end of the line
_	Any character, including end of the line
\<	The beginning of a word
\>	The end of a word

You can see the full list of these using `:help ordinary-atom`.

There are also what Vim calls character classes:

Symbol	Meaning
\s	Whitespace (*Tab* and Space)
\d	A digit
\w	A word character (digits, numbers or underscores)
\l	A lowercase character
\u	An uppercase character
\a	An alphabetic character

These classes have the opposite effect when capitalized; for example, \D matches all non-digit characters, whereas \L matches everything but lowercase letters (note that this is different to just matching uppercase letters).

You can see the full list by checking out :help character-classes.

You can also specify a set of characters explicitly, using square brackets ([]). For instance, [A-Z0-9] will match all uppercase characters and all digits, while [,4abc] will only match commas, the number 4, and letters a, b, and c.

For sequences (such as numbers or letters of the alphabet), you can use a hyphen (-) to represent a range. For instance, [0-7] will include numbers from 0 to 7, and [a-z] will include all lowercase letters from a to z.

Here's one more example, including letters, numbers, and underscores: [0-9A-Za-z_].

Finally, you can negate an entire range by prefixing it with a caret (^). For instance, if you wanted to match all non-alphanumeric characters, you would put [^0-9A-Za-z].

Alternation and grouping

Vim has a few more special operators:

Symbol	Meaning
|	alternation
\(\)	grouping

The alternation operator is used to signify *or*. For example, `carrot\|parrot` matches both `carrot` and `parrot`.

Grouping is used to put multiple characters in a group, which can serve two purposes. Firstly, you can combine operators with each other. For example, `\(c\|p\)arrot` is a nicer way to match both `carrot` and `parrot`.

Grouping can also be used to later refer to each section in parentheses. For example, if you wanted to turn the string `cat hunting mice` into `mice hunting cat`, you could use the following `:substitute` command:

```
:s/\(cat\) hunting \(mice\)/\2 hunting \1
```

This becomes relevant during refactoring; for example, when reordering arguments—but more on that later.

Quantifiers or multis

Each character (be it a literal or a special character) or a range of characters is followed by a quantifier, or a *multi* in Vim terms.

For example, `\w\+` will match one or more word characters, and `a\{2,4}` will match two to four `a` characters in succession (such as `aaa`, for example).

Here is the list of most common quantifiers:

Symbol	Meaning
`*`	0 or more, greedy
`\+`	1 or more, greedy
`\{-}`	0 or more, non-greedy
`\? or \=`	0 or 1, greedy
`\{n,m}`	n to m, greedy
`\{-n,m}`	n to m, non-greedy

The full list of quantifiers is available through `:help multi`.

You may have encountered two new terms in the table given: greedy and non-greedy. **Greedy** search refers to trying to match as many characters as possible, while **non-greedy** search tries to match as few characters as possible.

For example, given a string `foo2bar2`, greedy regex `\w\+2` will match `foo2bar2` (as many characters as it can until encountering a final 2), while non-greedy `\w\{-1,}2` will only match `foo2`.

More about magic

Escaping special characters with backslashes \ is no trouble if you're only occasionally spicing up your searches and substitutions with regular expressions. If you want to write longer expressions without having to escape every special character, you could switch to the magic mode for that expression.

Magic mode determines how Vim parses regex-enabled strings (like those in search or substitute commands).

Vim has three magic modes: magic, no magic, and very magic.

Magic

The default mode. Most special characters need to be escaped, but some (such as . or *) don't have to be.

You can prefix your regex strings with \m (for example, `/\mfoo` or `:s/\mfoo/bar`) to explicitly set magic.

No magic

This mode is similar to magic mode, but every special character needs to be escaped with a backslash, \.

For example, in default magic mode, you'd search for a line containing any text with `/^.*$` (here, ^ is for beginning of line, .* searches for every character repeatedly, and $ is for end of line). However, in no magic mode, you'd have to escape each one of those: `/\^\.\*\$`.

You can explicitly set no magic mode by prefixing your regex strings with \M (for example, /\Mfoo or :s/\Mfoo/bar). No magic can be also set in your .vimrc by adding set nomagic, but it's highly discouraged: by changing the way Vim treats regular expressions, you're more than likely to break several plugins you're using (as their creators will not have built them to work in no magic mode).

Very magic

Very magic mode treats every character apart from letters, numbers, and underscores as a special character.

You can set very magic mode for a command by prefixing your regex strings with \v (for example, /\vfoo or :s/\vfoo/bar).

Very magic mode is often used when many special characters are to be used. For instance, we used the following example to replace cat hunting mice with mice hunting cat:

```
:s/\(cat\) hunting \(mice\)/\2 hunting \1
```

In very magic mode, this can be rewritten as follows:

```
:s/\v(cat) hunting (mice)/\2 hunting \1
```

Applying the knowledge in practice

Many tasks when refactoring code involve renaming or reordering things, and regular expressions are perfect tools for this.

Renaming a variable, a method, or a class

Oftentimes, we rename things when refactoring, and these changes need to be reflected throughout the code base. However, simple search and replace often won't cut it, since you'll risk accidentally renaming unrelated things.

For example, let's try renaming our Dog class as Pitbull. Since we need to carry this out in multiple files, we'll use arglist:

```
:arg **/*.py
```

Now, move your cursor over the class name you'd like to rename (`Dog`), and enter the following(here, `\<[Ctrl + r, Ctrl + w]\>` signifies pressing *Ctrl + r* followed by *Ctrl + w* and not typing in square brackets):

```
:argdo %s/\<[Ctrl + r, Ctrl + w]\>/Pitbull/gec | update
```

Once you run it, you'll be prompted for every match:

```
import sys

from animals import cat
from animals import dog
from animals import sheep
import animal
import farm

def make_animal(kind):
    """Create an animal class."""
    if kind == 'cat':
        return cat.Cat()
    if kind == 'dog':
        return dog.Dog()
    if kind == 'sheep':
        return sheep.Sheep()
    return animal.Animal(kind)

def main(animals):
    animal_farm = farm.Farm()
    for animal_kind in animals:
        animal_farm.add_animal(make_animal(animal_kind))
    animal_farm.print_contents()
replace with Pitbull (y/n/a/q/l/^E/^Y)?
```

Press y to approve each change, or n to reject it.

Here's what's going on here:

- `:argdo` runs the operation on every arglist entry (which we loaded with `:arg`)
- `%s/.../.../gec` substitutes every occurrence (`g`) throughout the whole file (`%`), without raising errors if no entries were found (`e`), and asking the user before making changes (`c`)

- \<...\> ensures we're looking for a whole word, and not just partial matches (otherwise we'll also rename another class called `Dogfish`, which we don't want to do)
- *Ctrl + r, Ctrl + w* is a shortcut to insert the word under the cursor in the current command (which would insert `Dog`)

This approach has the disadvantage of locking you into dialog windows, without you being able to look around the file first. If you'd like more control, another alternative would be to use `:vimgrep` to find the matches first:

```
:vimgrep /\<Dog\>/ **/*.py
```

You'll be able to look at matches, and step through them with `:cn` or `:cp` (or open the quickfix window with `:copen` and navigate from there):

```
import animal
import farm

def make_animal(kind):
    """Create an animal class."""
    if kind == 'cat':
        return cat.Cat()
    if kind == 'dog':
        return dog.Dog()
    if kind == 'sheep':
        return sheep.Sheep()
(1 of 2): return dog.Dog()
```

In this particular example, you could replace the word using the usual change word command (`cw` followed by `Pitbull` followed by *Esc*), and then replay the changes by pressing dot (`.`), or run a non-global `:substitute` command (`:s/\<Dog\>/Pitbull`).

Reordering function arguments

Another common refactoring operation is to change the function arguments. Let's look at reordering arguments, since findings from this example can also be applied to other situations.

Here is a sample method in `animal.py`:

```
def act(self, target, verb):
    return 'Suddenly {kind} {verb} at {target}!'.format(
            kind=self.kind,
            verb=verb,
            target=target)
```

The order of arguments in this method doesn't seem very intuitive. We might be better off changing it to look like this:

```
def act(self, verb, target):
    return 'Suddenly {kind} {verb} at {target}!'.format(
            kind=self.kind,
            verb=verb,
            target=target)
```

However, there are quite a few callers for this method already, since we also use the method in `farm.py` (the code is intentionally repetitive for illustration purposes):

```
def act(self, target):
    for animal in self.animals:
        if animal.get_kind() == 'cat':
            print(animal.act(target, 'meows'))
        elif animal.get_kind() == 'dog':
            print(animal.act(target, 'barks'))
        elif animal.get_kind() == 'sheep':
            print(animal.act(target, 'baas'))
        else:
            print(animal.act(target, 'looks'))
```

This looks like a job for regular expressions! Let's write one up:

```
:arg **/*.py
:argdo %s/\v<act>\((\w{-1,}), ([^,]{-1,})\)/act(\2, \1)/gec | update
```

Give it a shot, and you will be greeted by a confirmation screen for every one of your matches (as we specified the c flag for the :substitute command):

```
"""A farm for holding animals."""

class Farm(object):

    def __init__(self):
        self.animals = set()

    def add_animal(self, animal):
        self.animals.add(animal)

    def act(self, target):
        for animal in self.animals:
            if animal.get_kind() == 'cat':
                print(animal.act('meows', target))
            elif animal.get_kind() == 'dog':
                print(animal.act(target, 'barks'))
            elif animal.get_kind() == 'sheep':
                print(animal.act(target, 'baas'))
            else:
                print(animal.act(target, 'looks'))

    def print_contents(self):
        print("We've got some animals on the farm:",
replace with act(\2, \1) (y/n/a/q/l/^E/^Y)?
```

To break it down, we have the following:

- \v sets the magic mode for this string to very magic, to avoid having to escape every special character.
- <act>\(matches the literal string act (, ensuring that act is a whole word (so partial matches such as react (would not be picked up).
- (\w{-1,}), ([^,]{-1,})\) defines two groups separated by a comma and a space, and followed by a closing parenthesis. The first group is a word of at least one character, while the second is any character string of at least one character, excluding commas (this way we'll match act(target, 'barks'), but not act(self, target, verb)).
- Finally, act(\2, \1) places the two matching groups in reverse order.

Recording and playing macros

Macros are an extremely powerful tool that allow you to record and replay a set of actions.

Let's perform the same operation as before, using macros. We have the following code in `farm.py`:

```
...
def act(self, target):
    for animal in self.animals:
        if animal.get_kind() == 'cat':
            print(animal.act(target, 'meows'))
        elif animal.get_kind() == 'dog':
            print(animal.act(target, 'barks'))
        elif animal.get_kind() == 'sheep':
            print(animal.act(target, 'baas'))
        else:
            print(animal.act(target, 'looks'))
...
```

We'd like to reorder arguments in `animal.act` calls. Open `farm.py`, and move your cursor to the top of the file with `gg`:

```
"""A farm for holding animals."""

class Farm(object):

    def __init__(self):
        self.animals = set()

    def add_animal(self, animal):
        self.animals.add(animal)

    def act(self, target):
        for animal in self.animals:
            if animal.get_kind() == 'cat':
                print(animal.act(target, 'meows'))
            elif animal.get_kind() == 'dog':
                print(animal.act(target, 'barks'))
            elif animal.get_kind() == 'sheep':
                print(animal.act(target, 'baas'))
            else:
                print(animal.act(target, 'looks'))

    def print_contents(self):
        print("We've got some animals on the farm:",
"farm.py" 24L, 758C
```

Enter macro recording mode using q followed by any register (let's pick a), as follows: qa. You'll see `recording @a` in a status line, which indicates that the macro is recording:

```
"""A farm for holding animals."""

class Farm(object):

    def __init__(self):
        self.animals = set()

    def add_animal(self, animal):
        self.animals.add(animal)

    def act(self, target):
        for animal in self.animals:
            if animal.get_kind() == 'cat':
                print(animal.act(target, 'meows'))
            elif animal.get_kind() == 'dog':
                print(animal.act(target, 'barks'))
            elif animal.get_kind() == 'sheep':
                print(animal.act(target, 'baas'))
            else:
                print(animal.act(target, 'looks'))

    def print_contents(self):
        print("We've got some animals on the farm:",
recording @a
```

Every movement or edit you make when in macro mode will be repeated when you replay the macro later on. That's why it's important to be deliberate when recording macros, and try to consider replayability when moving or performing actions.

Let's navigate to the first instance by searching for `/animal.act`:

```
    def act(self, target):
        for animal in self.animals:
            if animal.get_kind() == 'cat':
                print(animal.act(target, 'meows'))
            elif animal.get_kind() == 'dog':
                print(animal.act(target, 'barks'))
            elif animal.get_kind() == 'sheep':
                print(animal.act(target, 'baas'))
            else:
                print(animal.act(target, 'looks'))
recording @a
```

We're searching (and not navigating by line numbers, for instance) to make it possible to apply the macro to the rest of the text.

Now, move your cursor to the word `target`. You can move by word (`4w`), or navigate to the opening parenthesis (`f(`) followed by moving one character to the right (`l`):

```
    def act(self, target):
        for animal in self.animals:
            if animal.get_kind() == 'cat':
                print(animal.act(target, 'meows'))
            elif animal.get_kind() == 'dog':
                print(animal.act(target, 'barks'))
            elif animal.get_kind() == 'sheep':
                print(animal.act(target, 'baas'))
            else:
                print(animal.act(target, 'looks'))
recording @a
```

Since we want to paste `target` later, let's copy it into a register. `"bdw` will delete the word target into the `b` register, as follows:

```
def act(self, target):
    for animal in self.animals:
        if animal.get_kind() == 'cat':
            print(animal.act(, 'meows'))
        elif animal.get_kind() == 'dog':
            print(animal.act(target, 'barks'))
        elif animal.get_kind() == 'sheep':
            print(animal.act(target, 'baas'))
        else:
            print(animal.act(target, 'looks'))
recording @a
```

Now, let's delete the remaining comma (for this we don't need a special register, and we don't need to worry about overwriting `target` as it's been moved to its own register):

```
def act(self, target):
    for animal in self.animals:
        if animal.get_kind() == 'cat':
            print(animal.act('meows'))
        elif animal.get_kind() == 'dog':
            print(animal.act(target, 'barks'))
        elif animal.get_kind() == 'sheep':
            print(animal.act(target, 'baas'))
        else:
            print(animal.act(target, 'looks'))
recording @a
```

Now navigate to the end of `meows` with `f'`:

```
def act(self, target):
    for animal in self.animals:
        if animal.get_kind() == 'cat':
            print(animal.act('meows'))
        elif animal.get_kind() == 'dog':
            print(animal.act(target, 'barks'))
        elif animal.get_kind() == 'sheep':
            print(animal.act(target, 'baas'))
        else:
            print(animal.act(target, 'looks'))
recording @a
```

Add the missing comma followed by a space: a (to enter insert after the cursor), , ,
followed by *Esc*:

```
def act(self, target):
    for animal in self.animals:
        if animal.get_kind() == 'cat':
            print(animal.act('meows', ))
        elif animal.get_kind() == 'dog':
            print(animal.act(target, 'barks'))
        elif animal.get_kind() == 'sheep':
            print(animal.act(target, 'baas'))
        else:
            print(animal.act(target, 'looks'))
-- INSERT --recording @a
```

Now paste from the register b: "bp:

```
def act(self, target):
    for animal in self.animals:
        if animal.get_kind() == 'cat':
            print(animal.act('meows', target))
        elif animal.get_kind() == 'dog':
            print(animal.act(target, 'barks'))
        elif animal.get_kind() == 'sheep':
            print(animal.act(target, 'baas'))
        else:
            print(animal.act(target, 'looks'))
recording @a
```

Done! Hit q to finish recording the macro, you'll see that the `recording @a` line has
disappeared.

Fantastic! Now you can replay the macro using @a:

```
def act(self, target):
    for animal in self.animals:
        if animal.get_kind() == 'cat':
            print(animal.act('meows', target))
        elif animal.get_kind() == 'dog':
            print(animal.act('barks', target))
        elif animal.get_kind() == 'sheep':
            print(animal.act(target, 'baas'))
        else:
            print(animal.act(target, 'looks'))
```

 A handy shortcut is @@. @@ replays the last macro you ran.

You can repeat the macro multiple times by prefixing it with a number: 2@a. However, if, for instance, you are searching as part of your macro, the search may wrap back to the beginning of the file and replay a macro on a portion of file you've already modified:

```
def act(self, target):
    for animal in self.animals:
        if animal.get_kind() == 'cat':
            print(animal.act('meows', 
        elif animal.get_kind() == 'dog':
            print(animal.act('barks', target))
        elif animal.get_kind() == 'sheep':
            print(animal.act('baas', target))
        else:
            print(animal.act('looks', target))
```

That's where working with macros can get messy. All macros do is record your actions and replay them back.

So, how can we make this macro not do this?

A macro stops executing if it encounters an error. If there are no patterns we're searching for below the cursor, Vim just looks for one above the cursor—without producing an error. So we just need to manually produce an error, to make sure the macro doesn't continue running when it doesn't have to.

In this particular case, we can tell search to stop wrapping back around, and, instead, produce an error when reaching the end of the file:

```
:set nowrapscan
```

If you replay the macro, you'll now get an error:

```
def act(self, target):
    for animal in self.animals:
        if animal.get_kind() == 'cat':
            print(animal.act('meows', target))
        elif animal.get_kind() == 'dog':
            print(animal.act('barks', target))
        elif animal.get_kind() == 'sheep':
            print(animal.act('baas', target))
        else:
            print(animal.act('looks', target))
E385: search hit BOTTOM without match for: animal.act
```

Now you can safely execute this macro any number of times.

Due to errors like these, or if you're not confident about the matches, sometimes it's useful to carry out a separate search. It might make sense to search for an occurrence outside the macro (such as /animal.act), and then play the macro if you decide that the change is warranted.

Then, you can run n to search for the next search occurrence of animal.act, decide whether you'd like to make changes, and run the macro again with @a or @@.

Editing macros

Macros are stored in registers (the same ones used by yank and paste operations). You can view the contents of all your registers by executing `:reg`:

```
                elif animal.get_kind() == 'dog':
                    print(animal.act('barks', target))
                elif animal.get_kind() == 'sheep':
                    print(animal.act('baas', target))
                else:
                    print(animal.act('looks', target))

        def print_contents(self):
            print("We've got some animals on the farm:",
:reg
--- Registers ---
""      ,
"1    target
"2    target
"3    target
"4    target
"a    /animal.act^M4w"bdwdwf'a, ^["bp
"b    target
"-      ,
".      ,
":    reg
"%    farm.py
"/    animal.act
Press ENTER or type command to continue
```

Close to the middle of the list you can see `"a`, the register containing our macro. You can also view the contents of, say, register a by executing `:echo @a`.

In the preceding screenshot, many special characters are represented differently. For instance, `^[` signifies the *Esc* key, and `^M` is an *Enter* key.

In fact, macros are nothing but registers: the q command lets you add keystrokes to the register, while @ lets you replay the keystrokes from that register.

Since the macro is just a register, you can paste it using p. Open a new buffer with `:new`, and paste the contents of the register using `"ap`:

```
/animal.act^M4w"bdwdwf'a, ^["bp
~
~
~
~
~
~
~
~
~
```

Now you can edit your macro without having to retype the whole thing.

When you're finished editing, copy it back into the register: `_"ay$`. `_` will place you to the beginning of the line, `"a` will tell `yank` to use register a, and `y$` will copy the text until the end of the line.

That's it. Paste the register with `"ap`, and place it back when you've finished editing using `_"ay$`.

 As with many Vim commands, you shouldn't try to remember the exact letters, but focus on what the command does. This one, for instance, goes to the beginning of the line and yanks the rest of the line into register a. That's much easier to remember than `_"ay$`.

Recursive macros

Earlier we ran macros multiple times by prefixing `@` with a number. That's not very computer science-like, and we can do better.

Vim supports recursive macros, but there are a few quirks to be aware of.

First, you'll need to make sure the register you will be recording to is empty. You can do this by entering macro recording mode, and immediately exiting it. For instance, if you wanted to empty register b, you'll run `qbq` to clear it.

Then, record your macro as usual, and insert that same register into itself (for example, by using `@b`).

Let's say we wanted to swap keys with values in a Python dictionary:

```
animal_noises = {
    'bark': 'dog',
    'meow': 'cat',
    'silence': 'dogfish',
}
```

We could record a macro as follows, starting with the cursor in the beginning of the line `'bark': 'dog'`:

Let's record the macro into register b. First, we'll need to flush it and enter macro recording mode: qbqqb (qbq empties register b, and qb enters macro recording mode).

Now, as we want to swap `bark` and `dog`, we could yank one of these words into some temporary register (say c), and then move `dog` over using the default register.

Let's go ahead: `"cdi'` (delete inside single quotes into buffer c):

Move over `'dog'` (W) and run `di'` to yank `dog` into the default register:

Move one character to the left (either with `h` or `b`) and insert the word `bark` from register `c` (`"cp`):

```
animal_noises = {
        '': 'bark',
        'meow': 'cat',
        'silence': 'dogfish',
}
```

Now, move back to the beginning of the line (`_`) and paste `dog` from the default register (`p`):

```
animal_noises = {
        'dog': 'bark',
        'meow': 'cat',
        'silence': 'dogfish',
}
```

Almost there! Go down one line (`j`), and move your cursor to the beginning of the line (`_`):

```
animal_noises = {
        'dog': 'bark',
        'meow': 'cat',
        'silence': 'dogfish',
}
```

Now, replay macro `b`: `@b`. Nothing will happen, since register `b` is still empty. Finish recording the macro (`q`).

Now replay the macro using `@b` once, and it will iterate through every line in your file:

```
animal_noises = {
        'dog': 'bark',
        'cat': 'meow',
        'dogfish': 'silence',
}
```

That's it! You can make any macro recursive by appending to the register. To append to a register, you use the uppercase version of the register identifier. For example, if you wanted to make a macro in a register b recursive, run qB@bq to append @b to the end of the macro.

Running macros across multiple files

If you wanted to replay a macro across multiple files, you can use (you guessed it) arglist. Arglist allows you to execute normal mode commands with :normal command. For instance, you could run a macro from register a, as follows:

```
:arg **/* .py
:argdo execute ":normal @a" | update
```

Here, :normal @a will execute macro a in normal mode, and update will save the buffer contents. You'll probably want to use arglist with recursive macros.

Using plugins to do the job

"Wait," you ask. "There were plugins to do this all along?" Indeed, there are plugins that support refactoring operations—be it modifying parameters, renaming, or method extraction.

However, when working with existing refactoring solutions, I always find they do almost, but not quite, what I need. That's why I continue to write fancy substitute commands for refactoring. I find the cost of incorporating a refactoring plugin into my workflow, only to switch to :substitute commands for some of my refactoring needs, too high.

At the time of writing this book, there's no go-to refactoring plugin. Some are language-specific, and some focus on only certain aspects of refactoring. For instance, plugins like YouCompleteMe provide semantically-aware renaming commands (such as :YcmComplete RefactorRename).

Your best bet is to figure out for yourself which operations you want to perform, and try out a few plugins based on that. A web search along the lines of "Vim refactoring plugins" should do the trick.

Summary

In this chapter, we covered the `:substitute` command and macros—two powerful tools we can use for refactoring.

We covered the `:substitute` command and its flags. We looked into arglist, which is a way to execute a command across multiple files.

The `:substitute` command also supports regular expressions, which make your life a lot easier by allowing you to go beyond literal matches. We covered the basics of regular expressions and Vim magic modes (which are ways of interpreting special characters when parsing regex-enabled strings).

Finally, we looked at macros: a feature that lets you record and later replay a set of keystrokes. Macros can be edited the same way that registers can, and can also be made recursive to play as many times as needed.

In the next chapter, we'll cover customizing Vim for a personalized editing experience.

7
Making Vim Your Own

This chapter will cover Vim customization, and how to make Vim work for you. Everyone's needs are different, and this chapter tries to help you develop your own style.

This chapter will cover the following topics:

- Color schemes and making your Vim look pretty
- Enhancing the status line with additional information
- GUI configuration specific to gVim
- Healthy habits when customizing your workflow
- Methodologies for organizing your .vimrc

Technical requirements

In this chapter, we will be covering ways to keep your .vimrc file organized. There's no supporting code – you're welcome to bring along your .vimrc file and try out the techniques suggested in this chapter.

In addition, we'll be installing some packages with pip, so you may want to make sure you have pip installed. You can install pip by running:

```
$ curl https://bootstrap.pypa.io/get-pip.py -o get-pip.py && python3
get-pip.py.
```

Playing with the Vim UI

Vim has extensible UI, and it doesn't always have to look like it's stuck in the 90s. You can change its themes, tweak the way certain UI elements are displayed, and enhance the information displayed in a status line. If you're a gVim user, there are even more customization options available to you!

Color schemes

Vim has a plethora of beautiful color schemes available, both packaged with Vim and made by community members.

You can change the color scheme by changing the `colorscheme` setting in your `.vimrc`, as follows:

```
:colorscheme elflord
```

To get a list of currently installed color schemes, execute `:colorscheme` *Ctrl + d*. This will list every installed color scheme:

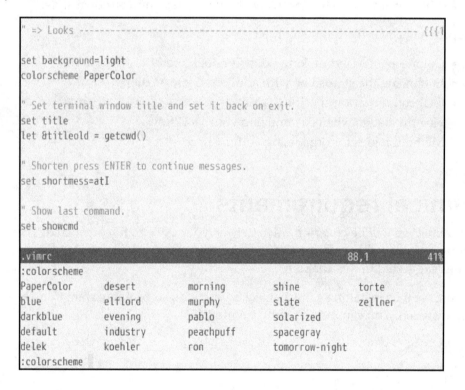

In the preceding example, I'm using `:colorscheme PaperColor` from `https://github.com/NLKNguyen/papercolor-theme`.

You can further customize the color scheme by setting the `background` option to either light or dark (the option must precede the `colorscheme` call).

For example, this is how the same color scheme as in the preceding screenshot (`PaperColor`) looks with `set background=dark`:

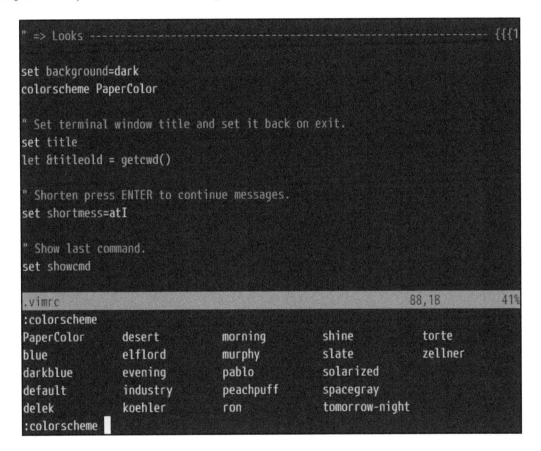

Browsing the color schemes

There are many color schemes available online, since tastes differ so significantly. There's no single indisputably authoritative resource for color schemes. Your best bet is looking around and trying to find what catches your eye.

If you manage to get your hands on lots of color schemes while you're trying to find the one you like, you can use a helpful plugin called `ScrollColors`. Now, `ScrollColors` adds a `:SCROLL` command that lets you interactively cycle through your color schemes.

 If you're using vim-plug, you can install `ScrollColors` by adding `Plug 'vim-scripts/ScrollColors'` to your `.vimrc` and running `:w | source $MYVIMRC | PlugInstall`.

There's also a collection of color schemes available at `https://github.com/flazz/vim-colorschemes`, with what looks like a few hundred of the most popular color schemes. I found all of my personal favorites in that list, so it might be a good resource for someone who's trying to decide on a few favorite color schemes.

This plugin and `ScrollColors` can be used together to browse through a gallery of the most popular color schemes.

 `vim-colorschemes` can be installed with vim-plug by adding `Plug 'flazz/vim-colorschemes'` to your `.vimrc` and running `:w | source $MYVIMRC | PlugInstall`.

Common issues

Sometimes you'll find that the color schemes you're trying out don't look as nice or don't display as many colors as you see in screenshots online.

This is most likely due to the fact that your Terminal emulator mistakenly tells Vim that it only supports 8 colors, and not the 256 most likely available in modern Terminal emulators. For that, you'll have to properly set the `$TERM` environment variable.

It's most common when using tmux and GMU Screen, as they might wrongly report the number of colors available.

If you find 256 colors to be not enough, certain Terminals support 24-bit colors, often referred to as "truecolor". If your Terminal supports 24-bit truecolor (a quick web search would help), add `set termguicolors` to your `~/.vimrc`.

To view the current content of the `$TERM` environment variable, run the following in your shell:

```
$ echo $TERM
```

If you're using tmux, add the following to your `.tmux.conf`:

```
set -g default-terminal "xterm-256color"
```

If you're a GNU Screen user, add the following to your `.screenrc`:

```
term "xterm-256color"
```

If the preceding didn't apply to you, add the following to your `.bashrc`:

```
TERM=xterm-256color
```

However, overriding `$TERM` in your `.bashrc` is rarely a good idea, and you may want to do some deeper research into what sets your `$TERM` environment variable to the wrong format.

The status line

The status line is that lovely bar at the bottom of the screen that is used to display information. You can make it even more useful with some minor configuration tweaks:

```
" Always display a status line (it gets hidden sometimes otherwise).
set laststatus=2

" Show last command in the status line.
set showcmd
```

If you want to go even further, there are plugins to enhance your status line. Powerline is an everything-in-one powerhouse, while Airline is its lighter alternative.

Powerline

Powerline provides an enhanced status line for Vim, as well as providing other functions, such as extending your shell prompt or tmux status line. It is available (along with detailed installation instructions) from https://github.com/powerline/powerline. When enabled in Vim, it looks something like this:

As you can see, it displays a plethora of information, including current mode, Git branch, filename, status of a current file, file type, encoding, and how far along you are in a current file. It's fully customizable, and lets you display as much or as little information as you want.

It's a bit of trouble to install, since it's not just a Vim plugin. First, you'll need to install the powerline-status package through pip:

```
$ python3 -m pip install powerline-status
```

If you don't have pip installed, see the technical requirements at the beginning of this chapter for setup instructions.

You'll also need to make sure $HOME/.local/bin (the default scripts location for pip) is on your path by adding the following to your .bashrc:

```
PATH=$HOME/.local/bin:$PATH
```

Finally, set laststatus to 2 (to make sure the status line is always displayed), and load Powerline in your .vimrc:

```
" Always display status line (or what's the purpose of having powerline?)
set laststatus=2

" Load powerline.
python3 from powerline.vim import setup as powerline_setup
python3 powerline_setup()
python3 del powerline_setup
```

Now, reload your Vim configuration (`:w | source $MYVIMRC`), and you'll see the fancy new status line at the bottom of your screen:

```
" Enable syntax highlighting.
syntax on

" Language dependent indentation.
filetype plugin indent on

" Reasonable indentation defaults.
set autoindent
set expandtab
set shiftwidth=4
set tabstop=4
set softtabstop=4

" Set a colorscheme.
colorscheme murphy

" Install vim-plug if it's not already installed.
if empty(glob('~/.vim/autoload/plug.vim'))
  silent !curl -fLo ~/.vim/autoload/plug.vim --create-dirs
    \ https://raw.github.com/junegunn/vim-plug/master/plug.vim
  autocmd VimEnter * PlugInstall --sync | source $MYVIMRC
endif
```

```
NORMAL    ~/.vimrc                           unix   utf-8   vim      2%        1:1
```

Airline

Airline is a great alternative if you don't want anything extra, and don't like the idea of a Python daemon continuously running in the background. It provides an informative, nice-looking prompt, as in the following screenshot:

```
import util


class Animal:

    def __init__(self, kind, name):
        self.kind = kind
        self.name = name

    def introduce(self):
        print('This is', self.name, 'and it\'s a', self.kind)

    def act(self, verb, target):
        print(self.name, verb, 'at', target)


class Dog(Animal):

    def __init__(self, name):
        super().__init__(self, 'dog', name)
```

```
 NORMAL  ⎇ mas  animals.py                          pyt   3% ☰   1:  1  ☰ [18]tra
"animals.py" 32L, 574C
```

Airline is available from `https://github.com/vim-airline/vim-airline`, and has no additional dependencies.

 You can install Airline with vim-plug by adding `Plug 'vim-airline/vim-airline'` to your `.vimrc` and running `:w | source $MYVIMRC | PlugInstall`.

gVim-specific configuration

gVim is a standalone application, and lets you configure more than out-of-the box Vim does. In fact, gVim supports having its own configuration file (in addition to reading `.vimrc`): `.gvimrc`.

The primary option for managing how the GUI looks is `guioptions`. This configuration string takes a set of letters, which enable options. Some relevant settings might include the following:

- `a` and `P`—automatically yank the visual selection into the system clipboard (for `*` and `+` registers respectively, see *Registers* in `Chapter 2`, *Advanced Editing and Navigation*)
- `c`—use console dialogs instead of pop-ups
- `e`—display tabs using GUI components
- `m`—display a menu bar
- `T`—include a toolbar
- `r`, `l`, and `b`—make right, left, and bottom scroll bars always visible

For example, if you wanted to display a menu bar, a toolbar, and always display a bottom scroll bar, you could do so by adding the following to your `.vimrc`:

```
" GUI: Enable menu bar, toolbar, always display bottom scrollbar.
set guioptions=mTb
```

The changes will look like this (this screenshot depicts gVim in Windows):

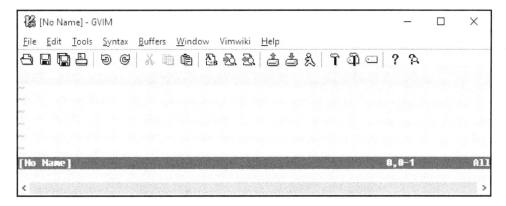

You can learn more about gVim-specific options by reading `:help gui`.

Keeping track of configuration files

Chances are, you won't spend the next ten years using the same computer. It's also possible you have multiple machines you work across—so you should probably find a way to synchronize your configuration files across multiple environments.

As usual, there's no single right way to do this, but a common practice is to store files in a Git repository (often called `dotfiles`, since configuration files in Linux tend to start with a dot), and pointing symlinks from the files in the home directory to the files in the `dotfiles` directory. All you'll have to do is commit, push, and pull the configuration with Git on each machine to stay up to date.

The easiest way would probably be to create a repository using a service such as GitHub, and utilize it to synchronize your configuration. Just don't store any sensitive information like passwords in version control!

Most frequently, the process of changing my configuration files is as follows (I store mine in `$HOME/.dotfiles` on Linux and Mac, and `%USERPROFILE%\_dotfiles` on Windows):

```
$ cd ~/.dotfiles
$ git pull --rebase
# Make the desired changes, like editing .vimrc
$ git commit -am "Updated something important"
$ git push
```

 The `.dotfiles` should be a git repository, see *Quick and dirty* in Chapter 5, *Build, Test, and Execute* to learn how to create one and if you'd like a refresher on Git.

For example, you might have a repository in `~/dotfiles`, which contains `.vimrc` and `.gvimrc` files, as well as a `.vim` directory. You could create links manually (`ln -s ~/dotfiles/.vimrc .vimrc`), or by writing a small Python script like this:

```python
import os

dotfiles_dir = os.path.join(os.environ['HOME'], 'dotfiles')
for filename in os.listdir(dotfiles_dir):
    os.symlink(
        os.path.join(dotfiles_dir, filename),
        os.path.join(os.environ['HOME'], filename))
```

You can get infinitely creative with solutions to this problem. Here are just a few examples of where you can take this:

- Make the preceding Python script work cross-platform (for instance, `.vim` directory becomes `vimfiles` in Windows)
- Periodically synchronize the Git repository using a cron job
- Use some form of file sync instead of Git (trading informative commit messages for near-instant update across machines)

Healthy Vim customization habits

As you continue to work with Vim, you will find yourself making a lot of configuration changes. It's important to take time to go back, reflect, and make sure your `.vimrc` doesn't become a pile of unneeded aliases, functions, and plugins.

Once in a while, take the time to go back into your `.vimrc` and clean up unnecessary functions and plugins, or remove key bindings you don't use any more. If you don't know what something does, you're probably better off deleting it, since you won't get much use out of configurations you don't understand.

It's also helpful to take some time to read about the options you have set and plugins you have installed with the built-in `:help` command—you'll never know what useful feature you'll discover!

Optimizing your workflow

Everyone's workflow is unique, and no two people use Vim in exactly the same way. It's useful to find ways to compliment your style by enhancing and optimizing the way you do things in Vim.

Find yourself using a particular command a lot? Create a custom key binding!

For example, I use the CtrlP plugin quite a lot (both for navigating the file tree and the buffer list), and I have the following custom mappings:

```
nnoremap <leader>p :CtrlP <cr>
nnoremap <leader>t :CtrlPTag <cr>
```

I also often find myself running the :Ack command (provided by the ack-vim plugin) on a word under cursor, so I have the following in my .vimrc:

```
nnoremap <leader>a :Ack! <c-r><c-w><cr>
```

The <c-r> and <c-w> inserts the word under cursor into the command line. Use :grep for a similar purpose? Not a problem:

```
nnoremap <leader>g :grep <c-r><c-w> */**<cr>
```

Accidentally find yourself hitting ; instead of : to enter command-line mode? Remap it:

```
nnoremap ; :
vnoremap ; :
```

Whenever you catch yourself doing something a lot, take a moment to add a relevant key binding to make your life easier.

Keeping .vimrc organized

If you use and customize Vim a lot, your .vimrc file tends to grow rather quickly, and it's important to make it easy to navigate. If you ever take a break from working with your .vimrc and come back later, you'll thank yourself.

Comments are crucial for making sure you remember what's going on. If you take just one thing from this chapter, make sure it is comments. Just like when working with code, comments save you wasting time trying to understand what's going on.

I try to make a point of documenting every configuration bit with a corresponding comment:

```
" Show last command in the status line.
set showcmd

" Highlight cursor line.
set cursorline

" Ruler (line, column and % at the right bottom).
set ruler

" Display line numbers if terminal is wide enough.
if &co > 80
  set number
endif
```

```
" Soft word wrap.
set linebreak

" Prettier display of long lines of text.
set display+=lastline

" Always show statusline.
set laststatus=2
```

Some people might prefer to place the comments on the same line as the configuration bits:

```
set showcmd            " Show last command in the status line.

set cursorline         " Highlight cursor line.

set ruler              " Ruler (line, column and % at the right bottom).

if &co > 80            " Display line numbers if terminal is wide enough.
  set number
endif

set linebreak          " Soft word wrap.

set display+=lastline  " Prettier display of long lines of text.

set laststatus=2       " Always show statusline.
```

For plugins in particular, I find it extremely useful to add a quick comment explaining what each one of them does. This makes it easy to revise the list of plugins once I don't need certain ones anymore:

```
Plug 'EinfachToll/DidYouMean'           " filename suggestions
Plug 'Lokaltog/vim-easymotion'          " better move commands
Plug 'NLKNguyen/papercolor-theme'       " colorscheme
Plug 'ajh17/Spacegray.vim'              " colorscheme
Plug 'altercation/vim-colors-solarized' " colorscheme
Plug 'christoomey/vim-tmux-navigator'   " better tmux integration
Plug 'ervandew/supertab'                " more powerful Tab
Plug 'junegunn/goyo.vim'                " distraction-free writing
Plug 'kien/ctrlp.vim'                   " Ctrl+p to fuzzy search
Plug 'mileszs/ack.vim'                  " ack integration
Plug 'scrooloose/nerdtree'              " prettier netrw output
Plug 'squarefrog/tomorrow-night.vim'    " colorscheme
Plug 'tomtom/tcomment_vim'              " commenting helpers
Plug 'tpope/vim-abolish'                " change case on the fly
Plug 'tpope/vim-repeat'                 " repeat everything
Plug 'tpope/vim-surround'               " superchange surround commands
Plug 'tpope/vim-unimpaired'             " pairs of helpful shortcuts
```

```
Plug 'tpope/vim-vinegar'            " - to open netrw
Plug 'vim-scripts/Gundo'            " visualize the undo tree
Plug 'vim-scripts/vimwiki'          " personal wiki
```

There are many ways to make configuration easier to navigate. My organizational method of choice is marker folds. I break down my configuration into categories, such as *looks*, *editing*, or *movement and search*. Then I use manual fold markers ({{{1) to indicate folds.

I also tend to add some ASCII art in the form of arrows => and lines --- to make each section look more like a header:

```
...

" => Editing ----------------------------------------------------- {{{1
syntax on

...

" => Looks ------------------------------------------------------- {{{1

set background=light
colorscheme PaperColor

...
```

This way, if I want an overview of my `.vimrc` file, I can close all folds using zM, and I'll get a nice overview as follows:

Summary

In this chapter, we've covered ways to enhance Vim's user interface and personalize Vim.

We've looked at color schemes, ways to configure them, finding them, and browsing them. We've also looked at ways to enhance Vim's status line with a heavyweight Powerline or a lightweight Airline plugin.

We've looked at GUI configuration specific to gVim, and how to customize the way gVim looks.

Finally, as you use Vim more, you'll develop your own style and personal workflow. This workflow is best enhanced by bindings and shortcuts. As your `.vimrc` grows, there are a number of ways to get it organized, well documented, and easy to navigate.

In the next chapter we'll learn Vimscript, an extensive scripting language which comes packaged with Vim.

Transcending the Mundane with Vimscript

8

This chapter will cover Vimscript in all its glory. We will go into quite a bit of detail, but since we only have so many pages the coverage will be somewhat spotty. Hopefully, this chapter will get you interested in Vimscript enough to start your own research, and maybe you can use it as a reference as you build your early plugins and scripts. In this chapter, we will look at the following:

- The basic syntax, from declaring variables to using lambda expressions
- Style guides, and how to keep sane when developing in Vimscript
- A sample plugin from start to finish—from the first line to publishing it online

Technical requirements

This chapter walks you through learning Vimscript by using numerous examples. All the examples are available on GitHub: `https://github.com/PacktPublishing/Mastering-Vim/tree/master/Chapter08`. You can create the scripts on your own as we're working through this chapter, or download the files from the repository to play around with.

Why Vimscript?

You've already encountered Vimscript when you worked on your `.vimrc`. What you may not have known is that Vimscript is actually a Turing-complete scripting language—there's no limit to what you can do. So far, you've used it to set variables and perform a few comparison operations, but it can do so much more!

You will learn how Vimscript not only helps you understand Vim configuration better, but lets you solve text editing problems you encounter by writing functions and plugins.

It's pretty awesome.

How to execute Vimscript

Vimscript is made up of commands you run in command-line mode, and really is just a sequence of Vim commands in a file. You can always execute Vimscript by running each command in command mode (the one you prefix with `:`), or by executing the file with commands using a `:source` command. Historically, Vim scripts have a `.vim` extension.

As you're following along with this section, you may want to create `*.vim` files to experiment in. You can execute the files by running this:

```
:source <filename>
```

A much shorter version of that is this:

```
:so %
```

Here, `:so` is a short version of `:source`, and `%` refers to the currently open file.

For example, I just created a `variables.vim` file to play around with Vim's variables. I could execute its contents with `:so %`:

```
let g:animal = 'cat'

echo 'I am about to print an animal name'
echo g:animal
echo 'I just printed the animal name'
~
~
~
~
~
~
~
~
~
~
~
~
~
I am about to print an animal name
cat
I just printed the animal name
Press ENTER or type command to continue
```

Alternatively, I could run each command in command mode. For example, if I wanted to print the contents of a variable, `g:animal`, I would run the following:

```
:echo g:animal
```

I will do just that, as in, print `cat` into our status line:

```
let g:animal = 'cat'

echo 'I am about to print an animal name'
echo g:animal
echo 'I just printed the animal name'
~
~
~
~
~
~
~
~
~
~
~
~
~
~
cat
```

Normally, I run longer scripts with `:so %`, and perform debugging operations through command-line mode (`:`).

Additionally, if you're entering commands in command-line mode, you'll stay in command-line mode if you enter a function or a flow control operator (such as `if`, `while`, or `for`):

```
~
~
~
:if has('win32')
:   echo 'this is windows'
:   else
:   echo 'this is probably unix'
this is probably unix
:   endif
```

In this example, I did not have to type : on every line. Additionally, each line gets executed as you hit *Enter* (as you can see by `this is probably unix` being printed on the screen).

Learning the syntax

Let's take a lightning-fast deep dive into Vimscript's syntax.

 This section assumes you're comfortable with at least one programming language, conditional statements and loops in particular. If that's not the case, you will most certainly be better off finding a more extensive tutorial. Vimscript deserves its own book, and Steve Losh wrote just that: *Learn Vimscript the Hard Way* is easily the best Vimscript tutorial available (and it's free on the web!).

Setting variables

You've already discovered some basics of Vimscript syntax. To set internal Vim options, you use the `set` keyword:

```
set background=dark
```

To assign a value to a non-internal variable, use the `let` keyword:

```
let animal_name = 'Miss Cattington'
```

Vimscript doesn't have explicit booleans, so `1` is treated as true and `0` as false:

```
let is_cat = 1
```

Since we're assigning variables, let's talk about scopes. Vim handles variable and function scopes with prefixes, like so:

```
let g:animal_name = 'Miss Cattington'
let w:is_cat=1
```

Each letter has a unique meaning, in particular the following:

- `g`: global scope (default if scope is not specified)
- `v`: global defined by Vim
- `l`: local scope (default within a function if scope is not specified)
- `b`: current buffer
- `w`: current window
- `t`: current tab
- `s`: local to a `:source`'d Vim script
- `a`: function argument

In this example, `g:animal_name` is a global variable (it could also be written as `let animal_name='Miss Cattington'`, but explicit scope declarations are always better), and `w:is_cat` is a window scope variable.

As you might remember, you can also set registers with `let`. For example, if you wanted to set register `a` to hold `cats are weird`, you could do this:

```
let @a = 'cats are weird'
```

You can also access Vim options (the ones you can change with `set`) by prefixing the variable with `&`, for example:

```
let &ignorecase = 0
```

You can use the usual mathematical operations on integers (+, −, *, /). String concatenation is performed using the `.` operator:

```
let g:cat_statement = g:animal_name . ' is a cat'
```

If you wanted to use a single quote within a single-quoted string, you can do so by typing it twice (`''`).

Oh, and like in many languages, single quotes identify literal strings, while double quotes identify non-literal strings. This becomes slightly confusing because comments also start with a double quote. Due to this behavior, certain commands in Vimscript can't be followed by a comment.

Surfacing output

You can print the content of a variable (or the results of any operation) into a status line using echo:

```
echo g:animal_name
```

One thing about echo, though, is that the output does not get logged anywhere and there's no way to view the message once it's dismissed.

For that, there's :echomsg (or :echom for short):

```
echom g:animal_name . ' is an animal'
echom 'here is an another message'
```

To see the log of messages from this sessions, execute the following command:

```
:messages
```

Now, you can see every message we printed:

```
Messages maintainer: Bram Moolenaar <Bram@vim.org>
cat is an animal
here is an another message
Press ENTER or type command to continue
```

In fact, many operations log messages via `echom`. For instance, file write using `:w` does so:

```
~
~
~
Messages maintainer: Bram Moolenaar <Bram@vim.org>
cat is an animal
here is an another message
"messages.vim" [New] 1L, 1C written

Press ENTER or type command to continue
```

Messages can be a powerful tool for debugging and trying to figure out what went wrong with your script. Learn more about messages via `:help message-history`.

Conditional statements

Conditional statements are performed using `if` statements:

```
if g:animal_kind == 'cat'
  echo g:animal_name . ' is a cat'
elseif g:animal_kind == 'dog'
  echo g:animal_name . ' is a dog'
else
  echo g:animal_name . ' is something else'
endif
```

You can also make this operation inline:

```
echo g:animal_name . (g:is_cat ? 'in'is a cat' : 'in'is something else')
```

Vim supports all of the logical operators you're used to from other languages:

- `&&` - and
- `||` - or
- `!` - not

For example, you can do this:

```
if !(g:is_cat || g:is_dog)
  echo g:animal_name . ' is something else'
endif
```

In the previous example, you'll get to `g:animal_name . ' is something else'` only if neither `g:is_cat` or `g:is_dog` are true.

This can also be written with the `&&` operator:

```
if !g:is_cat && !g:is_dog
  echo g:animal_name . ' is something else'
endif
```

Since text editing implies operating on strings, Vim has additional text-specific comparison operators:

- `==` compares two string; case sensitivity depends on user's settings (see later)
- `==?` explicitly case insensitive comparison
- `==#` explicitly case sensitive comparison
- `=~` checks a match against an expression on the right (`=~?` or `=~#` to make those explicitly case insensitive or sensitive)
- `!~` checks that a string does not match an expression on the right (`=~#`or `!~#` to make those explicitly case insensitive or sensitive)

The default behavior of `==`, as well as `=~` and `!~` (case sensitive or case insensitive) depends on the `ignorecase` setting.

Here are some examples:

```
'cat' ==? 'CAT'                    " true
'cat' ==# 'CAT'                    " false
set ignorecase | 'cat' == 'CAT'    " true
'cat' =~ 'c.\+'                    " true
'cat' =~# 'C.\+'                   " false
'cat' !~ '.at'                     " false
'cat' !~? 'C.\+'                   " false
```

Lists

Vim also supports more complex data structures, such as lists and dictionaries. Here's an example of a list:

```
let animals = ['cat', 'dog', 'parrot']
```

Operations to modify lists are similar to the ones in Python. Let's take a look at some common operations.

You can get elements by index using the `[n]` syntax. Here are some examples:

```
let cat = animals[0]      " get first element
let dog = animals[1]      " get second element
let parrot = animals[-1]  " get last element
```

Slices work in a similar way to Python, for instance:

```
let slice = animals[1:]
```

The value of `slice` would be `['dog, 'parrot']`. The main difference from Python is that the end of the range is inclusive:

```
let slice = animals[0:1]
```

The value of `slice` would be `['cat', 'dog']`.

To append to the list, use `add`:

```
call add(animals, 'octopus')
```

 Something to pay attention to is this: in Vimscript, we explicitly call functions with `call` unless they're a part of an expression. Don't worry too much about it yet, we'll get into more detail in a bit.

This will turn our list into `['cat', 'dog', 'parrot', 'octopus']`. While it's an in-place operation, it also returns the modified list, so you can assign to it as well:

```
let animals = add(animals, 'octopus')
```

You can also prepend to the list using `insert`:

```
call insert(animals, 'bobcat')
```

This will modify the list to be `['bobcat', 'cat', 'dog', 'parrot', 'octopus']`.

You can also provide an optional index argument. For instance, if you wanted to insert `'raven'` at index 2 (where the `'dog'` currently is) in the previous list, you would do the following:

```
call insert(animals, 'raven', 2)
```

The list will become `['bobcat', 'cat', 'raven', 'dog', 'parrot', 'octopus']`.

There are a few ways to remove the elements. For example, you can use unlet to remove an element at index 2 (`'raven'`):

```
unlet animals[2]
```

The list will be back to `['bobcat', 'cat', 'dog', 'parrot', 'octopus']`.

You can also use `remove`:

```
call remove(animals, -1)
```

This will leave us with `['bobcat', 'cat', 'dog', 'parrot']`.

Additionally, `remove` also returns the item itself:

```
let bobcat = remove(animals, 0)
```

You can also use ranges with both `unlet` and `remove`. Here's an example of deleting everything up to and including the second element:

```
unlet animals[:1]
```

If you were to do this with `remove`, you'll have to specify boundaries explicitly:

```
call remove(animals, 0, 1)
```

You can concatenate the lists using + or `extend`. For example, given the lists `mammals` and `birds`:

```
let mammals = ['dog', 'cat']
let birds = ['raven', 'parrot']
```

We could create a new list:

```
let animals = mammals + birds
```

Here, `animals` will contain `['dog', 'cat', 'raven', 'parrot']`. We could also extend the existing list:

```
call extend(mammals, birds)
```

This will extend `mammals` to contain `['dog', 'cat', 'raven', 'parrot']`.

You can sort the list in place using `sort`. If we to use sort on a previous example, we would write:

```
call sort(animals)
```

The result would be `['cat', 'dog', 'parrot', 'raven']` (sorted alphabetically).

You can get an index of an element using index. For instance, if you wanted to get an index of `parrot` from the previous list, you would run this:

```
let i = index(animals, 'parrot')
```

In this case, `i` would be equal to 2.

You can check whether a list is empty using (an aptly named) `empty`:

```
if empty(animals)
  echo 'There aren''t any animals!'
endif
```

The length of a list is retrieved using `len`:

```
echo 'There are ' . len(animals) . ' animals.'
```

Finally, Vim lets you count the number of elements in a list:

```
echo 'There are ' . count(animals, 'cat') . ' cats here.'
```

 You can get a full list of operations by checking out the help page: `:help list`.

Dictionaries

Dictionaries are also supported in Vim:

```
let animal_names = {
    \ 'cat': 'Miss Cattington',
    \ 'dog': 'Mr Dogson',
    \ 'parrot': 'Polly'
    \ }
```

As you may have noticed, you need to explicitly outline the line breaks with a backslash \ if you're defining a dictionary on multiple lines.

Dictionary modification operations are similar to the ones familiar to you from Python. Elements can be accessed in two ways:

```
let cat_name = animal_names['cat']    " get an element
let cat_name = animal_names.cat       " another way to access an element
```

Accessing an element via . only works if the key contains numbers, letters, and underscores.

You can set or override a dictionary entry as follows:

```
let animal_names['raven'] = 'Raven R. Raventon'
```

Entries are removed using `unlet` or `remove`:

```
unlet animal_names['raven']
let raven = remove(animal_names, 'raven')
```

Dictionaries can be merged using extend (in place):

```
call extend(animal_names, {'bobcat': 'Sir Meowtington'})
```

This will make `animal_names` look as follows:

```
let animal_names = {
    \ 'cat': 'Miss Cattington',
    \ 'dog': 'Mr Dogson',
    \ 'parrot': 'Polly',
    \ 'bobcat': 'Sir Meowtington'
    \ }
```

In case the second argument to `extend` contains duplicate keys, the original entries will be overwritten.

Similarly to lists, you can measure dictionary length and check whether the dictionaries are empty:

```
if !empty(animal_names)
  echo 'We have names for ' . len(animal_names) . ' animals'
endif
```

Lastly, you can check whether a key is present in a dictionary using `has_key`:

```
if has_key(animal_names, 'cat')
  echo 'Cat''s name is ' . animal_names['cat']
endif
```

> You can get a full list of operations by checking out the help page: `:help dict`.

Loops

You can loop through lists and dictionaries using the `for` keyword. For example, do this to go through a list:

```
for animal in animals
  echo animal
endfor
```

And here's you iterating through a dictionary:

```
for animal in keys(animal_names)
  echo 'This ' . animal . '''s name is ' . animal_names[animal]
endfor
```

You can also access both the key and the value of the dictionary simultaneously using `items`:

```
for [animal, name] in items(animal_names)
  echo 'This ' . animal . '''s name is ' . name
endfor
```

You can control the iteration flow with `continue` and `break`. Here's an example of using `break`:

```
let animals = ['dog', 'cat', 'parrot']
for animal in animals
  if animal == 'cat'
    echo 'It''s a cat! Breaking!'
    break
  endif
  echo 'Looking at a ' . animal . ', it''s not a cat yet...'
endfor
```

The output from this would be the following:

```
~
~
~
loops.vim                                    1,1            All
Looking at a dog, it's not a cat yet...
It's a cat! Breaking!
Press ENTER or type command to continue
```

And this is how you would use continue:

```
let animals = ['dog', 'cat', 'parrot']
for animal in animals
  if animal == 'cat'
    echo 'Ignoring the cat...'
    continue
  endif
  echo 'Looking at a ' . animal
endfor
```

And the output from this would be the following:

```
~
~
~
~
loops.vim                                                    8,1        All
Looking at a dog
Ignoring the cat...
Looking at a parrot
Press ENTER or type command to continue
```

while loops are also supported:

```
let animals = ['dog', 'cat', 'parrot']
while !empty(animals)
  echo remove(animals, 0)
endwhile
```

This will print the following:

```
~
~
~
~
loops.vim                                                    4,8        All
dog
cat
parrot
Press ENTER or type command to continue
```

You can use `break` and `continue` the same way with `while` loops:

```
let animals = ['cat', 'dog', 'parrot']
while len(animals) > 0
  let animal = remove(animals, 0)
  if animal == 'dog'
    echo 'Encountered a dog, breaking!'
    break
  endif
  echo 'Looking at a ' . animal
endwhile
```

This will output the following:

```
~
~
~
loops.vim                                          3,29          All
Looking at a cat
Encountered a dog, breaking!
Press ENTER or type command to continue
```

Functions

Just like most other programming languages, Vim supports functions:

```
function AnimalGreeting(animal)
  echo a:animal . ' says hello!'
endfunction
```

 In Vim, user-defined function names must start with a capital letter (unless they're within a script scope or behind a namespace). You'll get an error if you try to define a function starting with a lowercase letter.

You can try calling the function and you'll get the following output:

```
:call AnimalGreeting('cat')
cat says hello!
```

You can see that function arguments are accessed via the a: scope.

Functions, of course, can return values:

```
function! AnimalGreeting(animal)
  return a:animal . ' says hello!'
endfunction
```

 Something to keep in mind is that in Vim a single script can get loaded multiple times (for example, when the user runs :source on a file). Redefining a function would throw an error, and a way to get around this is to use function! to define your functions, as shown before.

Now, `echo` the return value of the function so we can see it:

```
:echo AnimalGreeting('dog')
dog says hello!
```

Vim also supports a variable number of arguments via the . . . notation (an equivalent to Python's `*args`):

```
function! AnimalGreeting(...)
   echo a:1 . ' says hi to ' . a:2
endfunction
```

Invoking this with the arguments `'cat'` and `'dog'` will produce the following result:

```
:call AnimalGreeting('cat', 'dog')
cat says hi to dog
```

You can access a list of all of the arguments with `a:000`:

```
function ListArgs(...)
   echo a:000
endfunction
```

Try invoking it with a few arguments:

```
:call ListArgs('cat', 'dog', 'parrot')
['cat', 'dog', 'parrot']
```

You can also combine variable arguments with explicitly specified arguments, just like you would in Python:

```
function! AnimalGreeting(animal, ...)
   echo a:animal . ' says hi to ' . a:1
endfunction
```

And here's the output:

```
:call AnimalGreeting('cat', 'dog')
cat says hi to dog
```

You can (and should) use local scope for your functions to keep them inaccessible from outside the file they are defined in:

```
function! s:AnimalGreeting(animal)
   echo a:animal . 'says hi!'
endfunction
```

```
function! s:AnimalGreeting(animal)
  return a:animal . ' says hello!'
endfunction
```

This will make sure that `s:AnimalGreeting` overwrites itself when sourcing the file again. But be careful not to overwrite somebody else's function.

Classes

While Vim doesn't explicitly contain classes, dictionaries support having methods on them, supporting the object-oriented programming paradigm. There are two ways to define a method on a dictionary.

Given an existing dictionary, `animal_names`:

```
let animal_names = {
  \ 'cat': 'Miss Cattington',
  \ 'dog': 'Mr Dogson',
  \ 'parrot': 'Polly'
  \ }
```

You could do the following to add a method to it:

```
function animal_names.GetGreeting(animal)
  return self[a:animal] . ' says hello'
endfunction
```

You can now execute the function:

```
:echo animal_names.GetGreeting('cat')
Miss Cattington says hello
```

You can use `self` (just like in Python!) to refer to dictionary keys.

In the previous example, `GetGreeting` becomes a callable dictionary key. Effectively, `animal_names` becomes this:

```
{
\ 'cat': 'Miss Cattington',
\ 'dog': 'Mr Dogson',
\ 'parrot': 'Polly',
\ 'GetGreeting': function <...>
\ }
```

For the next example, let's wrap our `animal_names` dictionary in a slightly more generic `animals`. This will make our next example behave slightly more like classes we're used to in other languages (and would help us avoid name collisions):

```
let animals = {
\ 'animal_names' : {
   \ 'cat': 'Miss Cattington',
   \ 'dog': 'Mr Dogson',
   \ 'parrot': 'Polly'
   \ }
\ }
```

You can also define a function before having a dictionary ready, by using `dict` keyword after the function name:

```
function GetGreeting(animal) dict
  return self.animal_names[a:animal] . ' says hello'
endfunction
```

Now, we'll need to assign the function as another dictionary key:

```
let animals['GetGreeting'] = function('GetGreeting')
```

Now, you can call `GetGreeting` in the same manner:

```
:echo animals.GetGreeting('dog')
 Mr Dogson says hello
```

Lambda expressions

Lambdas are anonymous functions that can be really useful when working with somewhat straightforward logic.

Here's how we would define `AnimalGreeting` from the previous example using lambda expressions:

```
let AnimalGreeting = {animal -> animal . ' says hello'}
```

Let's test it:

```
:echo AnimalGreeting('cat')
cat says hello
```

Lambdas provide short and sweet syntax for writing compact functions.

Map and filter

Vimscript supports `map` and `filter`—higher-order functions (aka functions that operate on functions). Both of these functions take either a list or a dictionary as a first argument, and a function as a second.

For instance, if we wanted to filter out every animal name that is not proper, we would write a filter function:

```
function IsProperName(name)
  if a:name =~? '\(Mr\|Miss\) .\+'
    return 1
  endif
  return 0
endfunction
```

`IsProperName` will return 1 (true) if the name starts with `Mr` or `Miss` (which is, as we know, a proper form to address an animal), and 0 (false) otherwise.

Now, given the following dictionary:

```
let animal_names = {
  \ 'cat': 'Miss Cattington',
  \ 'dog': 'Mr Dogson',
  \ 'parrot': 'Polly'
  \ }
```

We will write a filter function that will only leave key or value pairs with proper names:

```
call filter(animal_names, 'IsProperName(v:val)')
```

And we'll do this to see that it worked:

```
:echo animal_names
{'cat': 'Miss Cattington', 'dog': 'Mr Dogson'}
```

If you're coming from other programming languages, this syntax probably feels somewhat awkward. The second argument to the filter function is a string, which gets evaluated for every key value pair of the dictionary. Here, v:val will get expanded to the dictionary value (while v:key could be used to access the key).

The second argument to filter can also be a function reference. Vim lets you reference a function like this:

```
let IsProperName2 = function('IsProperName')
```

Now, you can call IsProperName2 just like you would IsProperName:

```
:echo IsProperName2('Mr Dogson')
1
```

This can be used to pass functions around as arguments to any function:

```
function FunctionCaller(func, arg)
   return a:func(a:arg)
endfunction
```

Try running it:

```
:echo FunctionCaller(IsProperName2, 'Miss Catington')
1
```

Armed with this knowledge, we can also pass a function reference as a second argument to the filter function. However, if we decide to pass a function reference, we have to change our original function to take two arguments: the key and the value for the dictionary (in that order):

```
function IsProperNameKeyValue(key, value)
   if a:value =~? '\(Mr\|Miss\) .\+'
     return 1
   endif
   return 0
endfunction
```

Now, we can execute the filter function as follows:

```
call filter(animal_names, function('IsProperNameKeyValue'))
```

And to validate that it works, let's echo the animal_names dictionary:

```
:echo animal_names
{'cat': 'Miss Cattington', 'dog': 'Mr Dogson'}
```

When operating on lists, v:key refers to a item index, and v:val refers to the item value.

The map function behaves in a similar manner. It lets you modify each list item or dictionary value.

For example, let's make every name *proper* in the following list:

```
let animal_names = ['Miss Cattington', 'Mr Dogson', 'Polly', 'Meowtington']
```

In this exercise, we'll reuse the IsProperName function from the earlier example.

Lambdas come in especially useful with this type of function. Here's how we prefix 'Miss ' to a name if it's not proper:

```
call map(animal_names,
\ {key, val -> IsProperName(val) ? val : 'Miss ' . val})
```

Verify the results are as expected:

```
:echo animal_names
['Miss Cattington', 'Mr Dogson', 'Miss Polly, 'Miss Meowtington']
```

This Lambda is the equivalent of the following:

```
function MakeProperName(name)
  if IsProperName(a:name)
    return a:name
  endif
  return 'Miss ' . a:name
endfunction
call map(animal_names, 'MakeProperName(v:val)')
```

The map function can be called with a function reference the same way a filter is. The mapping function will still take two values (key and value for dictionaries, and index and value for lists).

Interacting with Vim

The `execute` command lets you parse and execute a string as a Vim command. For example, the two following statements will produce equivalent results:

```
echo animal . ' says hello'
execute 'echo ' . animal . ' says hello'
```

You can use `normal` to execute keys just like the user would in normal mode. For instance, if you wanted to search for a word `cat` and delete it, you could do this:

```
normal /cat<cr>dw
```

 `<cr>` here needs to be typed with *Ctrl + v*, followed by the *Enter* key. However, `execute "normal /cat<cr>dw"` would use the literal string `<cr>` to represent *Enter* key press. Just a quirk to be aware of.

Running normal like this will respect the user's mappings, so if you want to ignore custom mappings, you could use `normal!`:

```
normal! /cat<cr>dw
```

Another command can suppress output from other commands (such as `execute`): `silent`. Neither of these will produce any output:

```
silent echo animal . ' says hello'
silent execute 'echo ' . animal . ' says hello'
```

Furthermore, `silent` can suppress the output from external commands and ignore prompts:

```
silent !echo 'this is running in a shell'
```

You can also check if the Vim you're running in has a particular feature enabled:

```
if has('python3')
  echom 'Your Vim was compiled with Python 3 support!'
endif
```

You can view the full list of features via `:help feature-list`, but something worth noting is OS indicators: `win32`/`win64`, `darwin` (macOS), or `unix`. These are extremely helpful if you're planning to build a cross-platform script.

File-related commands

Since Vim is a text editor, much of what you do operates on files. Vim provides a number of file-related functions.

You can manipulate file path information using expand:

```
echom 'Current file extension is ' . expand('%:e')
```

When passed a filename (through %, #, or shortcuts such as <cfile>), expand lets you parse the path using these modifiers:

- :p expand to full path
- :h head (last path component removed)
- :t tail (last path component only)
- :r root (one extension removed)
- :e extension only

See :help expand() for more information about these.

You can check the file exists (aka can be read) by using filereadable:

```
if filereadable(expand('%'))
  echom 'Current file (' . expand('%:t') . ') is readable!'
endif
```

When executed from files.vim, the output would be:

```
Current file (files.vim) is readable!
```

Similarly, you can check you have write permissions to the file using filewritable.

You can perform the rest of the file operations using the execute command. For example, you'd write the following to open the animals.py file:

```
execute 'edit animals.py'
```

Prompts

There are two primary ways to prompt the user for input. You can either use confirm to display a multiple choice dialog (such as **yes/no/cancel**), or input to process a more complex input.

The `confirm` function prompts the user with a dialog and a multiple answers a user can select from. Let's try a simple example:

```
let answer = confirm('Is cat your favorite animal?', "&yes\n&no")
echo answer
```

If you execute the script, you'll get the following prompt:

```
let answer = confirm('Is cat your favorite animal?', "&yes\n&no")
echo answer
~
~
~
~
~
~
~
~
~
~
~
~
~
~
:so %
Is cat your favorite animal?
[y]es, (n)o: █
```

Hitting y or n will select an option. Let's hit y:

```
~
~
~
:so %
Is cat your favorite animal?

1
Press ENTER or type command to continue
```

The result of this is **1**. Now, what if we replay it and choose no?

```
~
~
~
:so %
Is cat your favorite animal?

2
Press ENTER or type command to continue
```

We get a **2**. As you can see, `confirm` returns an integer with the number of the selected choice.

Oh, and if you're running from a GUI, you'll get a dialog window pop up:

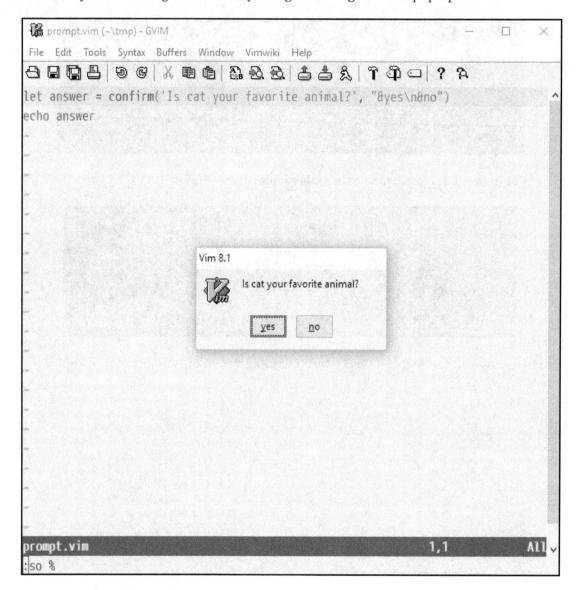

Now, let's get back to our original example:

```
let answer = confirm('Is cat your favorite animal?', "&yes\n&no")
echo answer
```

Here, you can see that confirm takes two arguments: a prompt to be displayed, and a newline-separated (\n) list of options to select from. In the previous example, an option string is non-literal, since we want the newlines to be processed.

A set of ampersand & symbols are used to denote the letters representing each option (in the previous example, y and n become the available options). Here's another example:

```
let answer = confirm(
    \ 'Is cat your favorite animal?', "absolutely &yes\nhell &no")
```

This would display the following prompt:

```
~
~
~
:so %
Is cat your favorite animal?
absolutely [y]es, hell (n)o: 
```

Note that y and n are still the letters a user can press to reply to the prompt.

Lastly, input lets you work with free-form text input. Its use is fairly straightforward:

```
let animal = input('What is your favorite animal? ')
echo "\n"
echo 'What a coincidence! My favorite animal is a ' . animal . ' too!'
```

 echo "\n" prints a newline, as otherwise cat and What a coincidence! will not be separated by a newline.

And this is how the prompt looks when executed:

```
~
~
~
What is your favorite animal? 
```

And this is what it looks like after we enter our string:

```
~
~

~
What is your favorite animal? cat
What a coincidence! My favorite animal is a cat too!
Press ENTER or type command to continue
```

However, a word of warning. If you're using input from inside a mapping, you must prefix it with `inputsave()` and follow it with `inputrestore()`. Otherwise, the rest of the characters in a mapping will be consumed into input. In fact, you should always use `inputsave()` and `inputrestore()` in case your function is ever used in a mapping. Here's an example of how to use them:

```
function AskAnimalName()
  call inputsave()
  let name = input('What is the animal"'s name? ')
  call inputrestore()
  return name
endfunction

nnoremap <leader>a = :let name = AskAnimalName()<cr>:echo name<cr>
```

Using :help

Most of the information about Vimscript is in Vim's `eval.txt`, which you can access by searching `:help eval`. Give it a read if you're ever feeling stuck.

A word about style guides

Consistent style is important. One of the more prominent style guides for Vim is the one published by Google: https://google.github.io/styleguide/vimscriptguide.xml. It highlights some common development practices and outlines common pitfalls.

Here are some excerpts from the Google Vimscript style guide:

- Use two spaces for indents
- Do not use tabs
- Use spaces around operators
- Restrict lines to 80 columns wide
- Indent continued lines by four spaces
- Use `plugin-names-like-this`
- Use `FunctionNamesLikeThis`
- Use `CommandNamesLikeThis`
- Use `augroup_names_like_this`
- Use `variable_names_like_this`
- Always prefix variables with their scope
- When in doubt, apply Python style guide rules

Give the Google Vimscript style guide a read, it's rather useful even if you never plan on doing more than customizing your `.vimrc`. It'll help with self-consistency.

Let's build a plugin

Let's try building a simple plugin; this way, we can learn by the example.

A common task you have to perform when working with code is commenting out chunks of code. Let's build a plugin that does just that. Let's (uninspiringly) name our plugin `vim-commenter`.

Plugin layout

Since the Vim 8 release, there's thankfully only one way of structuring your plugins (which is also compatible with major plugin managers, such as vim-plug, Vundle, or Pathogen). The plugins are expected to have the following directory structure:

- `autoload/` lets you lazy load bits of your plugin (more on that later)
- `colors/` color schemes
- `compiler/` (language-specific) compiler-related functionality
- `doc/` documentation
- `ftdetect/` (filetype-specific) filetype detection settings

- `ftplugin/` (filetype-specific) filetype-related plugin code
- `indent/` (filetype-specific) indentation-related settings
- `plugin/` the core functionality of your plugin
- `syntax/` (language-specific) defines language syntax group

As we develop our plugin, let's use Vim 8's new plugin functionality and place our plugin directory into `.vim/pack/plugins/start`. Since we decided to name our plugin commenter, we'll plop it into `.vim/pack/plugins/start/vim-commenter`.

> Remember, the `plugins/` directory can have any name. See Chapter 3, *Follow the Leader - Plugin Management* for more info. The `start/` directory means that the plugin will be loaded on Vim startup.

Let's create a directory for it now:

```
$ mkdir -p ~/.vim/pack/plugins/start/vim-commenter
```

The basics

Let's start simple: let's get our plugin to add a key binding that comments out the current line by prefixing it with a Python-style comment (#).

Let's start in `~/.vim/pack/plugins/start/vim-commenter/plugin/commenter.vim`:

```
" Comment out the current line in Python.
function! g:commenter#Comment()
  let l:line = getline('.')
  call setline('.', '# ' . l:line)
endfunction

nnoremap gc :call g:commenter#Comment()<cr>
```

In the previous example, we've created a function that inserts # in front of the current line (`.`) and maps it to `gc`. As you might remember, `g`, while having some mappings assigned to it (see `:help g`), is effectively a free namespace for the user to fill, and `c` stands for "comment".

> Another popular prefix for custom mappings is the comma (`,`), which is a rarely used command.

Save the file and load it (either using :source, or by restarting Vim). Let's open a Python file and navigate to some line we'd like to comment:

```
class Animal:

    def __init__(self, kind, name):
        self.kind = kind
        self.name = name
```

Now, try running gc:

```
class Animal:

    def __init__(self, kind, name):
#        self.kind = kind
        self.name = name
```

Success! Well, kind of. First, the comment begins at the beginning of the line and not at the current indentation level, as the user might want. Also, the cursor hasn't moved from the current position, which might be a little annoying for the user. Let's fix these two issues.

You can get the indentation level of the line (in spaces) using the indent function:

```
" Comment out the current line in Python.
function! g:commenter#Comment()
  let l:i = indent('.') " Number of spaces.
  let l:line = getline('.')
  call setline('.', l:line[:l:i - 1] . '# ' . l:line[l:i:])
endfunction


nnoremap gc :call g:Comment()<cr>
let s:comment_string = '# '

" Comment out the current line in Python.
function! g:Comment()
  let l:i = indent('.') " Number of spaces.
  let l:line = getline('.')
  let l:cur_row = getcurpos()[1]
  let l:cur_col = getcurpos()[2]
  call setline('.', l:line[:l:i - 1] . s:comment_string . l:line[l:i:])
  call cursor(l:cur_row, l:cur_col + len(s:comment_string))
```

```
endfunction

nnoremap gc :call g:Comment()<cr>
```

Let's go back to our file:

```
class Animal:

    def __init__(self, kind, name):
        self.kind = kind
        self.name = name
```

Now, run gc to comment out an indented line:

```
class Animal:

    def __init__(self, kind, name):
        # self.kind = kind
        self.name = name
```

Wonderful! But now, we'll probably need a way to uncomment the line as well! Let's change our function to g:ToggleComment():

```
let s:comment_string = '# '

" Comment out the current line in Python.
function! g:ToggleComment()
  let l:i = indent('.')   " Number of spaces.
  let l:line = getline('.')
  let l:cur_row = getcurpos()[1]
  let l:cur_col = getcurpos()[2]
  if l:line[l:i:l:i + len(s:comment_string) - 1] == s:comment_string
    call setline('.', l:line[:l:i - 1] .
    \ l:line[l:i + len(s:comment_string):])
    let l:cur_offset = -len(s:comment_string)
  else
    call setline('.', l:line[:l:i - 1] . s:comment_string . l:line[l:i:])
    \ let l:cur_offset = len(s:comment_string)
  endif
  call cursor(l:cur_row, l:cur_col + l:cur_offset)
endfunction

nnoremap gc :call g:ToggleComment()<cr>
```

Let's give it a shot! Reload the script, and go back to our file:

```
class Animal:

    def __init__(self, kind, name):
        self.kind = kind
        self.name = name
```

Hit `gc` to comment the line:

```
class Animal:

    def __init__(self, kind, name):
        # self.kind = kind
        self.name = name
```

And hit `gc` again to uncomment it:

```
class Animal:

    def __init__(self, kind, name):
        self.kind = kind
        self.name = name
```

Let's make sure we covered corner cases! Let's try to comment out the line without indentation. Move your cursor to an un-indented line:

```
class Animal:

    def __init__(self, kind, name):
        self.kind = kind
        self.name = name
```

Hit `gc` to run our function:

```
class Animal:# class Animal:

    def __init__(self, kind, name):
        self.kind = kind
        self.name = name
```

Oh no! Looks like our script is not working well for when there's no indentation. Let's fix it:

```
let s:comment_string = '# '

" Comment out the current line in Python.
function! g:ToggleComment()
  let l:i = indent('.') " Number of spaces.
  let l:line = getline('.')
  let l:cur_row = getcurpos()[1]
  let l:cur_col = getcurpos()[2]
  let l:prefix = l:i > 0 ? l:line[:l:i - 1] : '' " Handle 0 indent cases.
  if l:line[l:i:l:i + len(s:comment_string) - 1] == s:comment_string
    call setline('.', l:prefix . l:line[l:i + len(s:comment_string):])
    let l:cur_offset = -len(s:comment_string)
  else
    call setline('.', l:prefix . s:comment_string . l:line[l:i:])
    let l:cur_offset = len(s:comment_string)
  endif
  call cursor(l:cur_row, l:cur_col + l:cur_offset)
endfunction

nnoremap gc :call g:ToggleComment()<cr>
```

Let's save, reload, and run the script using `gc`:

```
# class Animal:

    def __init__(self, kind, name):
        self.kind = kind
        self.name = name
```

And run `gc` again to test uncommenting:

```
class Animal:

    def __init__(self, kind, name):
        self.kind = kind
        self.name = name
```

Wonderful! The very basic version of our plugin is complete!

Housekeeping

So far, we've had our plugin all within one file. Let's see how we can break it down into multiple files to keep our newly created project organized! Give a look at the list in *Plugin layout* section of this chapter.

First, you can see that the `ftplugin/` directory contains filetype-specific plugin configuration. Right now, most of our plugin is actually pretty independent from working with Python, except for the `s:comment_string` variable. Let's move it out to `<...>/vim-commenter/ftplugin/python.vim`:

```
" String representing inline Python comments.
let g:commenter#comment_str = '# '
```

We've changed the scope from `s:` to `g:` (since the variable is now used in different scripts), and added the `commenter#` namespace to avoid namespace collision.

The name should also be updated in `<...>/vim-commenter/plugin/commenter.vim`. Now might be a good time to test those substitution commands you learned earlier in this book:

```
:%s/\<s:comment_string\>/g:commenter#comment_str/g
```

Another directory of interest is `autoload/`. Currently, whenever Vim starts, it will parse and load `g:commenter#ToggleComment`. That's not very fast. Instead, we can choose to move the function to the `autoload/` directory. The name of the file needs to correspond to its namespace; in this case, it's `commenter`. Let's create `<...>/vim-commenter/autoload/commenter.vim`:

```
" Comment out the current line in Python.
function! g:commenter#ToggleComment()
```

```
    let l:i = indent('.') " Number of spaces.
    let l:line = getline('.')
    let l:cur_row = getcurpos()[1]
    let l:cur_col = getcurpos()[2]
    let l:prefix = l:i > 0 ? l:line[:l:i - 1] : '' " Handle 0 indent cases.
  if l:line[l:i:l:i + len(g:commenter#comment_str) - 1] ==
    \ g:commenter#comment_str
  call setline('.', l:prefix .
      \ l:line[l:i + len(g:commenter#comment_str):])
    let l:cur_offset = -len(g:commenter#comment_str)
  else
    call setline('.', l:prefix . g:commenter#comment_str . l:line[l:i:])
    let l:cur_offset = len(g:commenter#comment_str)
  endif
  call cursor(l:cur_row, l:cur_col + l:cur_offset)
endfunction
```

At this point, the only thing left in `<...>/vim-commenter/plugin/commenter.vim` is the mapping:

```
nnoremap gc :call g:commenter#ToggleComment()<cr>
```

Here's how our plugin will get loaded when a user is working with Vim:

- User opens Vim, and `<...>/vim-commenter/plugin/commenter.vim` is loaded. Our `gc` mapping is now registered.
- User opens a Python file, and `<...>/vim-commenter/ftplugin/python.vim` is loaded. `g:commenter#comment_str` is initialized.
- User runs `gc`, which loads and executes `g:commenter#ToggleComment` within `<...>/vim-commenter/autoload/commenter.vim`.

One directory we haven't given much love to yet is `doc/`. Vim is known for having extensive documentation, and we have a recommendation to uphold this. Let's add `<...>/vim-commenter/doc/commenter.txt`:

```
*commenter.txt* Our first commenting plugin.
*commenter*


===============================================================================
CONTENTS                                                    *commenter-contents*

  1. Intro...............................................|commenter-intro|
  2. Usage...............................................|commenter-usage|


===============================================================================
1. Intro                                                       *commenter-intro*
```

```
Have you ever wanted to comment out a line with only three presses of a
button? Now you can! A new and wonderful vim-commenter lets you comment
out a single line in Python quickly!

2. Usage                                          *commenter-usage*

This wonderful plugin supports the following key bindings:

  gc: toggle comment on a current line

That's it for now. Thanks for reading!

  vim:tw=78:ts=2:sts=2:sw=2:ft=help:norl:
```

Vim help has its own format, but here are some highlights:

- `*help-tag*` is used to denote a help tag. Whenever you run :help help-tag, Vim takes you to a file containing `*help-tag*`, and places the cursor right at the tag.
- `Text...|help-tag|` is used for navigation within a help file. It lets the reader jump to the desired tags from this section.
- All the `===` lines are just for pretty looks. They don't actually mean anything.
- A line like `vim:tw=78:ts=2:sts=2:sw=2:ft=help:norl:` lets you tell Vim how to display a file when editing it (all of these are options you can set using the `set` keyword). This becomes really useful for files without clearly identifiable filetypes (such as `.txt` files).

You can learn more about Vim's help format by reading `:help help-writing`. The easiest thing though is to find some popular plugins and copy what they do.

After you finished writing the doc, you'll need to tell Vim to generate its help tags in order for the entries to be indexed by the `:help` command. Run the following:

```
:helptags ~/.vim/pack/plugins/start/vim-commenter/doc
```

Now, you'll be able to visit entries you added to the help file:

```
:help commenter-intro
```

Here's a screenshot of Vim help taking you to the requested section:

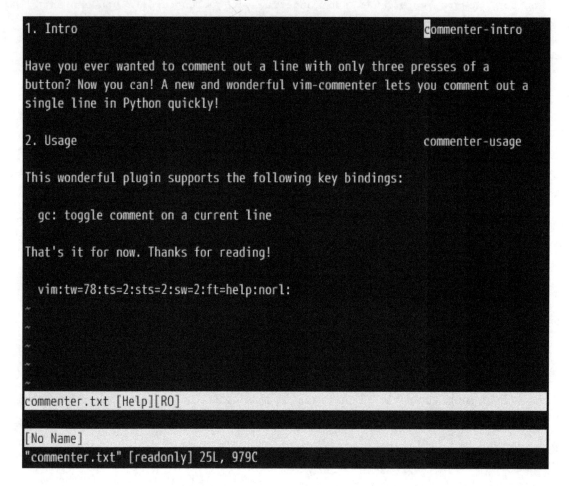

```
1. Intro                                              commenter-intro

Have you ever wanted to comment out a line with only three presses of a
button? Now you can! A new and wonderful vim-commenter lets you comment out a
single line in Python quickly!

2. Usage                                              commenter-usage

This wonderful plugin supports the following key bindings:

  gc: toggle comment on a current line

That's it for now. Thanks for reading!

  vim:tw=78:ts=2:sts=2:sw=2:ft=help:norl:




commenter.txt [Help][RO]

[No Name]
"commenter.txt" [readonly] 25L, 979C
```

Improving our plugin

There are many paths we can take our plugin in, but let's focus on two main issues we have right now:

- Our plugin fails with spectacular errors when we try to execute it in any other language
- The plugin does not provide a way to operate on multiple lines at once

Let's start with the first problem: making the plugin work across different languages. Right now, if you try to execute the plugin in, for example, a `.vim` file, you'll get the following volley of errors:

```
~
~
~
Error detected while processing function commenter#ToggleComment:
line    6:
E121: Undefined variable: g:commenter#comment_str
E116: Invalid arguments for function len(g:commenter#comment_str) - 1] ==  g:com
menter#comment_str
E15: Invalid expression: l:line[l:i:l:i + len(g:commenter#comment_str) - 1] ==
g:commenter#comment_str
line   14:
E121: Undefined variable: l:cur_offset
E116: Invalid arguments for function cursor
Press ENTER or type command to continue
```

That's because we define `g:commenter#comment_str` in `<...>/vim-commenter/ftplugin/python.vim`, and the variable is only defined when we're working with a Python file.

Vim syntax files define what the comments look like for each language, but they're not very consistent, and the logic to parse those and all the corner cases is outside of the scope of this book.

However, we can at least get rid of the nasty error, and make our own!

The canonical way of checking a variable exists is with `exists`. Let's add a new function to `<...>/vim-commenter/autoload/commenter.vim`, which would throw a custom error if `g:commenter#comment_str` is not set:

```
" Returns 1 if g:commenter#comment_str exists.
function! g:commenter#HasCommentStr()
  if exists('g:commenter#comment_str')
    return 1
  endif
  echom "vim-commenter doesn't work for filetype " . &ft . " yet"
  return 0
endfunction
```

```
" Comment out the current line in Python.
function! g:commenter#ToggleComment()
  if !g:commenter#HasCommentStr()
    return
  endif
  let l:i = indent('.') " Number of spaces.
  let l:line = getline('.')
  let l:cur_row = getcurpos()[1]
  let l:cur_col = getcurpos()[2]
  let l:prefix = l:i > 0 ? l:line[:l:i - 1] : '' " Handle 0 indent cases.
  if l:line[l:i:l:i + len(g:commenter#comment_str) - 1] ==#
      \ g:commenter#comment_str
    call setline('.', l:prefix .
      \ l:line[l:i + len(g:commenter#comment_str):])
    let l:cur_offset = -len(g:commenter#comment_str)
  else
    call setline('.', l:prefix . g:commenter#comment_str . l:line[l:i:])
    let l:cur_offset = len(g:commenter#comment_str)
  endif
  call cursor(l:cur_row, l:cur_col + l:cur_offset)
endfunction
```

Now, we get a message when we try to comment out a line in a non-Python file:

```
vim-commenter doesn't work for this filetype yet
```

A much better user experience if you ask me.

And now, let's add a way for our plugin to be invoked on multiple lines. The easiest thing to do would be to allow the user to prefix our `gc` command with a number, and we'll do just that.

Vim lets you access a number that prefixes a mapping by using `v:count`. Even better, there's a `v:count1`, which defaults to 1 if no count was given (this way, we can reuse more of our code).

Let's update our mapping in `<...>/vim-commenter/plugin/commenter.vim`:

```
nnoremap gc :<c-u>call g:commenter#ToggleComment(v:count1)<cr>
```

`<c-u>` is required to be used with `v:count` and `v:count1`. You can check `:help v:count` or `:help v:count1` for an explanation.

In fact, we can also add a visual mode mapping to support visual selection:

```
vnoremap gc :<cu>call g:commenter#ToggleComment(
  \ line("'>") - line("'<") + 1)<cr>
```

 `line("'>")` gets the line number of the end of the selection, while `line("'<")` gets the line number of the beginning of the selection. Subtract the beginning line number from the end, add one, and we have ourselves a line count!

Now, let's update `<...>/vim-commenter/autoload/commenter.vim` with a few new methods:

```
" Returns 1 if g:commenter#comment_str exists.
function! g:commenter#HasCommentStr()
  if exists('g:commenter#comment_str')
    return 1
  endif
  echom "vim-commenter doesn't work for filetype " . &ft . " yet"
  return 0
endfunction

" Detect smallest indentation for a range of lines.
function! g:commenter#DetectMinIndent(start, end)
  let l:min_indent = -1
  let l:i = a:start
  while l:i <= a:end
    if l:min_indent == -1 || indent(l:i) < l:min_indent
      let l:min_indent = indent(l:i)
    endif
    let l:i += 1
  endwhile
  return l:min_indent
endfunction

function! g:commenter#InsertOrRemoveComment(lnum, line, indent, is_insert)
  " Handle 0 indent cases.
  let l:prefix = a:indent > 0 ? a:line[:a:indent - 1] : ''
  if a:is_insert
    call setline(a:lnum, l:prefix . g:commenter#comment_str .
      \ a:line[a:indent:])
  else
    call setline(
      \ a:lnum, l:prefix . a:line[a:indent +
len(g:commenter#comment_str):]
  endif
endfunction
```

```
" Comment out the current line in Python.
function! g:commenter#ToggleComment(count)
  if !g:commenter#HasCommentStr()
    return
  endif
  let l:start = line('.')
  let l:end = l:start + a:count - 1
  if l:end > line('$') " Stop at the end of file.
    let l:end = line('$')
  endif           \
  let l:indent = g:commenter#DetectMinIndent(l:start, l:end)
  let l:lines = l:start == l:end ?
  \ [getline(l:start)] : getline(l:start, l:end)
  let l:cur_row = getcurpos()[1]
  let l:cur_col = getcurpos()[2]
  let l:lnum = l:start
  if l:lines[0][l:indent:l:indent + len(g:commenter#comment_str) - 1] ==#
      \ g:commenter#comment_str
    let l:is_insert = 0
    let l:cur_offset = -len(g:commenter#comment_str)
  else
    let l:is_insert = 1
    let l:cur_offset = len(g:commenter#comment_str)
  endif
  for l:line in l:lines
    call g:commenter#InsertOrRemoveComment(
        \ l:lnum, l:line, l:indent, l:is_insert)
    let l:lnum += 1
  endfor
  call cursor(l:cur_row, l:cur_col + l:cur_offset)
endfunction
```

This script is now much bigger, but it's not as scary as it looks! Here, we've added two new functions:

- `g:commenter#DetectMinIndent` finds the smallest indent within a given range. This way, we make sure to indent the outermost section of code.
- `g:commenter#InsertOrRemoveComment` either inserts or removes a comment within a given line and at a given indentation level.

Let's test run our plugin. Let's, say, run it with `11gc`:

```
import util


# class Animal:
#
#     def __init__(self, kind, name):
#         self.kind = kind
#         self.name = name
#
#     def introduce(self):
#         print('This is', self.name, 'and it\'s a', self.kind)
#
#     def act(self, verb, target):
#         print(self.name, verb, 'at', target)


class Dog(Animal):

    def __init__(self, name):
        super().__init__(self, 'dog', name)


class Dogfish(Animal):
:call g:commenter#ToggleComment(v:count1)
```

Ta-da! Now, our little plugin can comment out multiple lines! Give it a go with a few more tries to make sure we covered corner cases such as commenting in the visual mode going past the end of the file, commenting and uncommenting a single line, and so on.

Distributing the plugin

Effectively, we're all set up to distribute the plugin. Just a few things left.

Update the documentation, and add a README.md file to let people know what your plugin does (this can be copied from the intro of your plugin). You'll also want to add a LICENSE file, indicating the license under which you're distributing the plugin. You can distribute the plugin under the same license as Vim (:help license), or choose your own (GitHub has a helpful https://choosealicense.org for this purpose).

Now, you'll just have to turn $HOME/.vim/pack/plugins/vim-commenter into a Git repository, and upload it somewhere.

At the time of writing this book, GitHub is the go-to bastion of freedom for storing code (however, as SourceForge proved around 2015, times change).

Let's give it a shot:

```
$ cd $HOME/.vim/pack/plugins/start/vim-commenter
$ git init
$ git add .
$ git commit -m "First version of the plugin is ready!"
$ git remote add origin <repository URL>
$ git push origin master
```

Done! You're now ready to distribute the plugin, and plugin managers such as vim-plug can now pick up your plugin!

Where to take the plugin from here

There's a lot more room for improvement, but we'll take a break here. You're welcome to continue working on this plugin on your own—you can add visual selection support, make it work with additional languages, or do whatever it is you would like with it.

Further reading

Vimscript is a long and complex topic, and this chapter only brushes it. If you want to learn more, there are a few options.

You can read :help eval, which contains most of the information about Vimscript.

You can also choose to follow a tutorial online, or pick up a book. A lot of people recommend 'Learn Vimscript the Hard Way' by Steve Losh, and it is indeed rather good. It's available online at http://learnvimscriptthehardway.stevelosh.com/ (you can buy a paper copy from the website as well).

Summary

That was quite a bit of work! Let's do a quick recap!

We've learned that Vimscript lets us take Vim anywhere we want, limiting your productivity only by your imagination. We've covered setting and manipulating variables, working with lists and dictionaries, surfacing output, and control flows using `if`, `for`, and `while` statements. We've also covered functions, lambda expressions, the Vimscript equivalent of classes, as well as some more functional approaches using map and filter functions. We've also looked at Vim-specific commands and functions.

We've also built our first plugin, vim-commenter. The plugin lets you comment and uncomment lines in a Python file at the press of a button (well, two). We've learned how to structure our plugins, and how to use Vimscript to accomplish our goals. We've even brushed distributing the plugin!

Lastly, we covered a few possible directions you can take for learning Vimscript, including digging into `:help eval` or picking a book up off the (possibly virtual) shelf.

In the next chapter, we'll take a look at Neovim, a developer effort which tries to build and improve upon Vim.

9
Neovim

In this chapter, we'll take a look at a branch of Vim that became a phenomenon of its own, known as **Neovim**. Neovim aims to make Vim easier to maintain for its core developers, as well as make plugin development and various integrations easier. We'll look at the following:

- Why does Neovim matter?
- How to install and configure Neovim
- Synchronizing Vim and Neovim configuration
- Neovim-specific plugins

Technical requirements

In this chapter, you will create a Neovim configuration using your existing `.vimrc`. You can create your own, or grab an existing configuration from `https://github.com/PacktPublishing/Mastering-Vim/tree/master/Chapter09`

A detailed explanation is available in the `README.md` file in the `Chapter09/` directory.

Why make another Vim?

Neovim is a fork of Vim, that branched out into its own thing in 2014. Neovim aims to address a few core issues about Vim:

- Working with a 30-year-old code base while maintaining backward compatibility is hard.
- It's very difficult to write certain kinds of plugins, asynchronous operations being a huge culprit (asynchronous support has been added to Vim in version 8.0, some time after Neovim was forked).

- In fact, writing plugins is difficult overall, and requires the developer to be comfortable in Vimscript.
- Vim is difficult to use on modern systems without tinkering with `.vimrc`.

Neovim aims to solve these problems with the following methods:

- Large-scale refactoring of the Vim code base, including choosing a single style guide, increasing test coverage
- Removing support for legacy systems
- Shipping Neovim with modern defaults
- Providing a rich API for plugins and external programs to talk to, including Python and Lua plugin support

Vim is installed on a vast number of machines, which makes backward compatibility and rare corner cases important. By branching out, Neovim is able to move faster, experiment, make mistakes, and make Vim even better than it currently is.

Neovim matters because it makes it easier to add new features, as time goes on, and develop plugins. Hopefully, it'll attract more developers, and bring more perspectives and fresh ideas to the table as time goes on.

Installing and configuring Neovim

Neovim and its installation instructions are available from GitHub at `https://github.com/neovim/neovim`. You can either download the binary, or install it through one of the package managers. The installation instructions are rather detailed, and may change rather quickly, so you should give them a read at `https://github.com/neovim/neovim/wiki/Installing-Neovim`.
If you are working on Debian based Linux distribution, you can install Neovim by running: `$ sudo apt-get install neovim` and `$ Python3 -m pip install neovim` to add Python3 to support neovim.

Once you install Neovim, it's available through the `nvim` command:

```
$ nvim
```

You're greeted by a screen similar to a vanilla Vim intro screen:

```
                    NVIM v0.3.2-610-g6e146d413


             Nvim is open source and freely distributable
                     https://neovim.io/community


             type  :help nvim<Enter>        if you are new!
             type  :checkhealth<Enter>      to optimize Nvim
             type  :q<Enter>                to exit
             type  :help<Enter>             for help


                    Help poor children in Uganda!
             type  :help iccf<Enter>        for information
```

```
[No Name]                                          0,0-1              All
```

All of the commands familiar to you from Vim will work, and Neovim uses the same configuration format as Vim. However, your `.vimrc` is not picked up automatically.

Neovim adheres to the XDG base directory specification, which suggests placing all of your configuration files into the `~/.config` directory. Neovim configuration is stored inside the `~/.config/nvim` directory:

- `~/.vimrc` becomes `~/.config/nvim/init.vim`
- `~/.vim/` becomes `~/.config/nvim/`

Most likely, you'll want to symlink your Neovim configuration to your Vim configuration:

```
$ mkdir -p $HOME/.config
$ ln -s $HOME/.vim $HOME/.config/nvim
$ ln -s $HOME/.vimrc $HOME/.config/nvim/init.vim
```

All done! Neovim will now read your `.vimrc`!

Under Windows, Neovim configuration is likely located in
`C:\Users\%USERNAME%\AppData\Local\nvim`.

You can configure Windows symlinks as follows:

```
$ mklink /D %USERPROFILE%\AppData\Local\nvim %USERPROFILE%\vimfiles
$ mklink %USERPROFILE%\AppData\Local\nvim\init.vim %USERPROFILE%\_vimrc
```

Checking health

The intro screen suggests you run `:checkhealth`; let's give it a shot:

```
:checkhealth
```

You will be greeted by a screen that may look something like this:

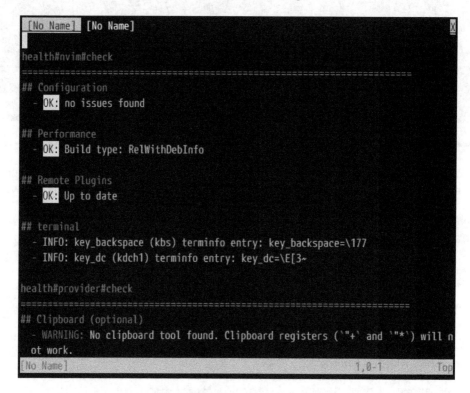

Neovim health checks will outline everything wrong with your Neovim setup, and suggest
ways to fix those issues. You should go through the list and fix the errors relevant to you.

For instance, my installation required a `neovim` library for Python support:

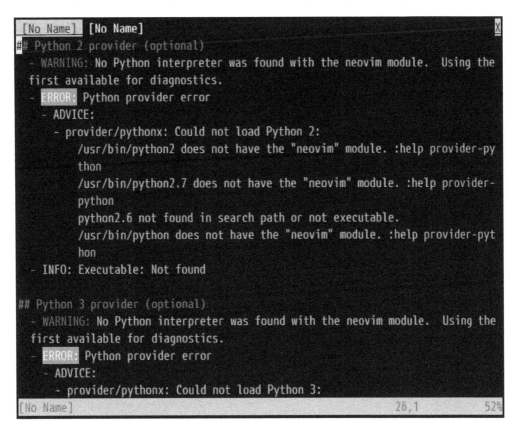

And here's how to install the missing Python provider:

```
$ pip install neovim  # Python 2
$ python3 -m pip install neovim  # Python 3
```

One of the really nice things about Neovim is the fact that you don't have to recompile it to enable certain options. For instance, Python support will work as soon as you install the `neovim` Python package and restart Neovim.

Sane defaults

Neovim comes with a number of different defaults than Vim. The defaults are meant to be more applicable to working with a text editor in the modern world. Compared to using Vim with an empty `.vimrc`, some of the more noticeable defaults include enabled syntax highlighting, sensible indentation settings, `wildmenu`, highlighted search results, and search-as-you-type.

You can check `:help nvim-defaults` from within Neovim to learn more about the defaults.

If you wanted to synchronize your settings between Vim and Neovim, you could add the following to your `~/.vimrc` (which is hopefully symlinked to `~/.config/nvim/init.vim`):

```
if !has('nvim')
  set nocompatible                      " not compatible with Vi
  filetype plugin indent on             " mandatory for modern plugins
  syntax on                             " enable syntax highlighting
  set autoindent                        " copy indent from the previous line
  set autoread                          " reload from disk
  set backspace=indent,eol,start        " modern backspace behavior
  set belloff=all                       " disable the bell
  set cscopeverbose                     " verbose cscope output
  set complete-=i                       " don't scan current on included
                                        " files for completion
  set display=lastline,msgsep           " display more message text
  set encoding=utf-8                    " set default encoding
  set fillchars=vert:|,fold:            " separator characters
  set formatoptions=tcqj                " more intuitive autoformatting
  set fsync                             " call fsync() for robust file saving
  set history=10000                     " longest possible command history
  set hlsearch                          " highlight search results
  set incsearch                         " move cursor as you type when searching
  set langnoremap                       " helps avoid mappings breaking
  set laststatus=2                      " always display a status line
  set listchars=tab:>\ ,trail:-,nbsp:+  " chars for :list
  set nrformats=bin,hex                 " <c-a> and <c-x> support
  set ruler                             " display current line # in a corner
  set sessionoptions-=options           " do not carry options across sessions
  set shortmess=F                       " less verbose file info
  set showcmd                           " show last command in the status line
  set sidescroll=1                      " smoother sideways scrolling
  set smarttab                          " tab setting aware <Tab> key
  set tabpagemax=50                     " maximum number of tabs open by -p flag
  set tags=./tags;,tags                 " filenames to look for the tag command
```

```
    set ttimeoutlen=50             " ms to wait for next key in a sequence
    set ttyfast                    " indicates that our connection is fast
    set viminfo+=!                 " save global variables across sessions
    set wildmenu                   " enhanced command line completion
endif
```

I've left some short comments, attempting to briefly describe each one of these settings, and you can learn more about them by checking the corresponding :help entry.

Oni

Oni (https://github.com/onivim/oni) is a cross-platform GUI editor on top of Neovim, that brings IDE-like features into Neovim, including an embedded browser, built-in autocompletion and fuzzy search, a command palette, a set of tutorials, and a lot more quality-of-life features. All of this while respecting Neovim configuration and key bindings. It looks rather nice:

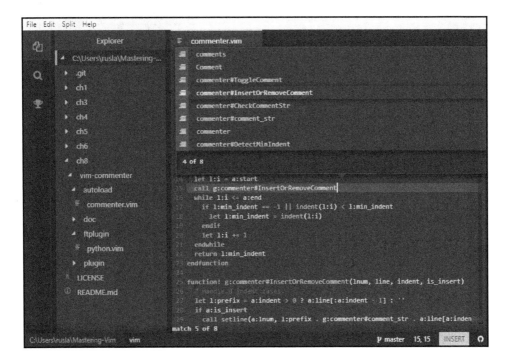

For instance, here's how its embedded browser looks (open the command palette with *Ctrl + Shift + p* and type `Browser`):

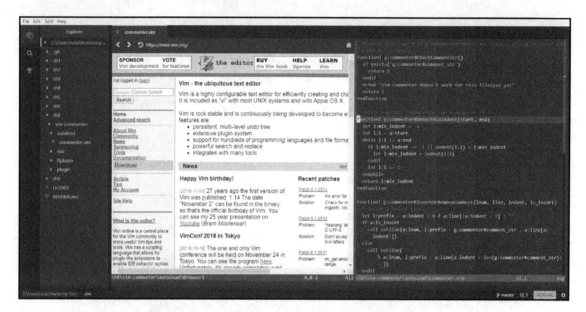

In the true spirit of Vim, it supports mouse-free navigation (press *Ctrl + g* followed by a key combination on screen to click on an element):

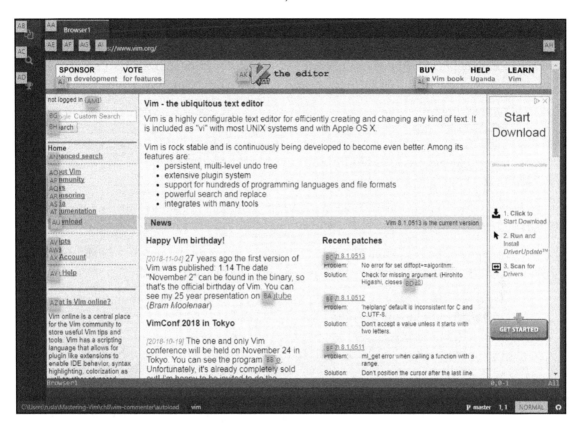

The vast list of features is easy to get lost in, and it's worth trying out Oni.

Neovim plugin highlights

Neovim is mostly backward compatible with Vim, and supports a huge number of Vim plugins (in fact, Neovim supports every plugin listed in this book except for Powerline).

However, since Neovim natively supports the implementation of asynchronous plugins and adds other developer-friendly features, there's a number of plugins that are only possible due to Neovim. It's worth mentioning that Vim added some of the features unique to Neovim in 8.0 (asynchronous plugin support) and 8.1 (Terminal mode) a few years after Neovim was created.

All of the following plugins (except for NyaoVim) were backported to Vim, but it's worth giving the Neovim community credit for the crea

tion of the plugins. The list is not in any way extensive, and might get out of date pretty quickly. The plugins are rated by popularity as of the time of writing of this book:

- Dein (`https://github.com/Shougo/dein.vim`) is an asynchronous plugin manager, similar to vim-plug.
- Denite (`https://github.com/Shougo/denite.nvim`) is a fuzzy search plugin for everything, including buffers, lines in the current files, or even color schemes (effectively a CtrlP for everything). For instance, here's how a fuzzy completion for lines of code within a current file looks:

```
import sys
zoo.py                                                          1,1         Top
  7:       animal_name = argv[2]
 10:           animal = animals.Cat(animal_name)
 12:           animal = animals.Dog(animal_name)
 14:           animal = animals.Dogfish(animal_name)
 16:           animal = animals.Animal(animal_name, animal_kind)
 27: if __name__ == '__main__':
~
~
-- INSERT --  line(6/28)                    [/home/ruslan/hands_on_vim/zoo] 1/6
# name
```

- NyaoVim (`https://github.com/rhysd/NyaoVim`) is a cross-platform web component-based GUI for Neovim. Its primary selling point is ease of extensibility and adding new UI plugins as web components.
- Neomake (`https://github.com/neomake/neomake`) is an asynchronous linter and compiler, that adds a file-type-aware asynchronous `:Neomake` command.
- Neoterm (`https://github.com/kassio/neoterm`) extends Vim/Neovim Terminal functionality, making it easier to reuse a single existing Terminal for running commands.
- NCM2 (`https://github.com/ncm2/ncm2`) is a robust and extensible code completion framework for Vim and Neovim.
- gen_tags (`https://github.com/jsfaint/gen_tags.vim`) is an asynchronous `ctags` and `gtags` generator. For reference, `gtags` is slightly more powerful than `ctags`, but limited to a smaller number of languages.

Summary

In this chapter, we've covered Neovim, a Vim fork aimed at making the Vim code base more maintainable, making it easier to add new features and develop plugins, and encouraging integration with external applications.

We've touched on installation instructions and learned how to port existing Vim configuration to work with Neovim. We've also looked at backporting Neovim defaults to Vim to synchronize the editing experience between the two.

Finally, we've taken a brief look at some of the plugins the Neovim community have built.

Next chapter will point at a few more Vim-related resources and communities, as well as leave the reader with a few ideas and further exploration avenues.

10
Where to Go from Here

Welcome to the last chapter of mastering Vim. You have now begun your journey into the wonderful world of Vim.

This book concludes with a few final thoughts:

- Healthy text editing habits, pulled from Bram Moolenaar's presentation
- Taking modal interfaces outside of Vim and into other IDEs, web browsers, and everywhere else
- Some of the Vim communities and recommended reading

Seven habits of effective text editing

This section is a condensed version of Bram Moolenaar's article from 2000, and a subsequent presentation from 2007. It's rather good, give it a read on Bram's website: `https://moolenaar.net/habits.html`. In case you decide to skip reading the whole thing, here follows a very high-level summary.

Since developers spend so much time reading and editing code, Bram highlights an important cycle when it comes to improving your text-editing experience:

1. Detect inefficiency
2. Find a quicker way
3. Make it a habit

Those three steps are augmented with numerous examples. Here's one of the examples for each:

1. **Detect inefficiency**: Moving around takes a lot of time.
2. **Find a quicker way**: Often, you're looking for something that's already there. You can search for a piece of text to move faster. Or you can take a step or two further:

   - Use `*` to search for a word under the cursor
   - Use `:set incsearch` to search as you type
   - Use `:set hlsearch` to highlight every instance of a search pattern on the screen

3. **Make it a habit**: Use what you've learned! Set `incsearch` and `hlsearch` in your `.vimrc`. Use `*` every time you catch yourself using the `/` command to search for a pattern near your cursor.

Modal interfaces everywhere

You've read through this book, and now, hopefully, you think that modal interfaces are pretty great. How can you get more of that?

Many applications support some sort of modal interactions with them, particularly Vi-friendly ones.

Many mature text editors and IDEs provide Vi-like key bindings for moving around and manipulating text. Here are a few of them (with the corresponding URLs):

- Evil is a Vi layer for Emacs: `https://github.com/emacs-evil/evil`.
- IdeaVim is a Vim emulator for IDEA-based IDEs (IntelliJ IDEA, PyCharm, CLion, PhpStorm, WebStorm, RubyMine, AppCode, DataGrip, GoLand, Cursive, and Android Studio):
  `https://github.com/JetBrains/ideavim`.
- Eclim lets you access Eclipse features from Vim: `http://eclim.org`.
- Vrapper adds Vi-like key bindings to Eclipse:
  `http://vrapper.sourceforge.net/home`.
- Atom has a vim-mode-plus plugin:
  `https://github.com/t9md/atom-vim-mode-plus`.

There are many others, so if other editors accomplish your tasks better than Vim (because you might be locked into a particular IDE), but you enjoy using Vim key bindings, then this might be an approach for you.

A Vim-like web browsing experience

Modern developer workflow is very web-heavy, and I have my browser open most of the time when I'm working on code. Sometimes, I feel like switching my focus from keyboard-driven workflow in Vim to mouse-driven web browsing, which detracts from my productivity. To avoid that, I use add-ons that enable Vi-like key bindings in the browser.

It's hard to predict the future landscape when it comes to web browsers, but this section is based on the most popular browsers as of the moment of writing.

Vimium and Vimium-FF

Vimium is a Chrome extension that enhances web browsing by allowing you to use Vim-friendly key bindings to navigate pages. It has also been ported to Firefox under the name Vimium-FF.

Vimium is available from the Chrome Web Store or at `https://vimium.github.io`. Vimium-FF is available from `https://addons.mozilla.org/en-US/firefox/addon/vimium-ff`.

For instance, if you hit f, Vimium will highlight every link on a page with a letter or a combination of letters (similar to the way EasyMotion works in Vim). This is shown in the following screenshot:

Pressing the right combination of letters will open a link, or place your cursor in a text box. Vimium supports visual selection to copy text without using a mouse: hitting v once enters a caret mode (where you can move the cursor around the page), and hitting v again enters a visual selection mode. Most movement keys familiar to you from Vim work in these modes, as shown in the following screenshot:

Once you select the text in a visual mode, press y to copy (yank) it.

Vimium also provides an omnibar for switching between tabs (T), opening URLs/history entries (o/O), and bookmarks (b/B), as shown in the following screenshot:

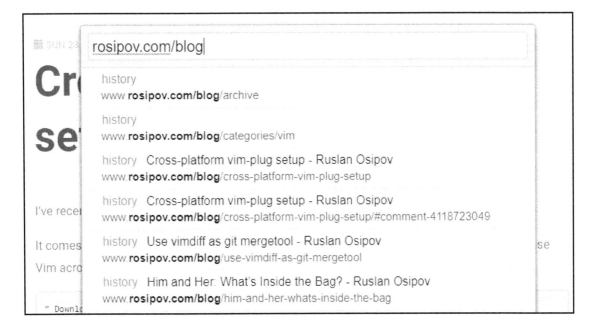

Finally, help is available at the press of a button. Press **?** to open a help page and learn more about Vimium features, as shown in the following screenshot:

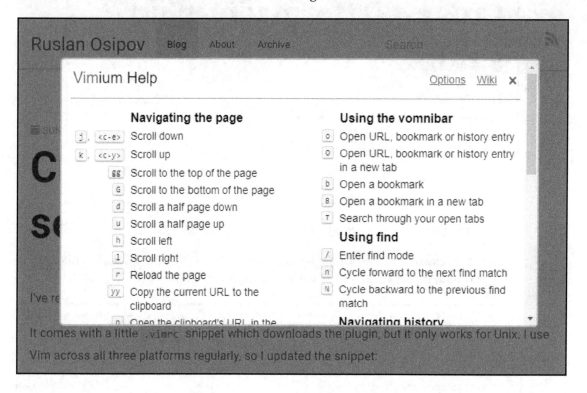

Alternatives

Vimium and Vimium-FF are possibly the most popular extensions as of the moment of writing (based on the number of users on Chrome Web Store and on the Firefox Add-Ons website). There are many more available, and most mature browsers have Vi-like plugins. Here are a few more examples:

- Google Chrome also has extensions including cVim or Vrome, that perform a similar function to Vimium, each providing slightly different functionality. Extensions such as `wasavi` focus on using Vim emulators to edit text areas.
- Safari supports `Vimari`, a port of Vimium.
- Mozilla Firefox has more add-ons similar to Vimium-FF: `Vim Vixen` and `Tridactyl` to name a few.
- Opera supports installation of Chrome extensions.

Vim everywhere else

There are solutions for editing text in Vim in every text field on your system! In particular, there is vim-anywhere on Linux and macOS, and Text Editor Anywhere on Windows.

vim-anywhere for Linux and macOS

vim-anywhere lets you invoke `gVim` to edit any text on your Linux or macOS machine. The vim-anywhere is available from `https://github.com/cknadler/vim-anywhere`. Once installed, place your cursor in a text field, and press *Ctrl + Cmd + v* on macOS or *Ctrl + Alt + v* on Linux. Depending on your platform, vim-anywhere will open either `MacVim` or `gVim`, as shown in the following screenshot:

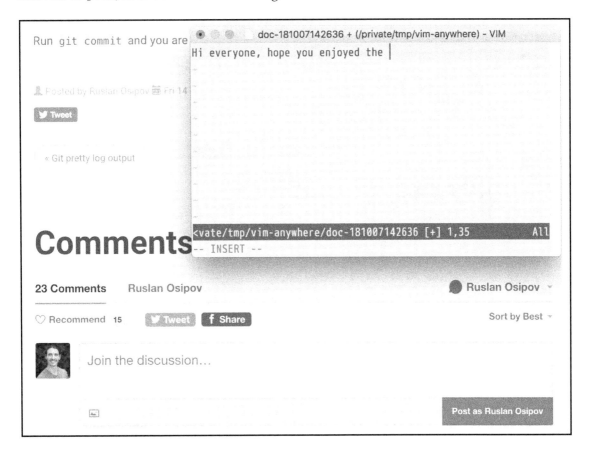

Save the buffer, exit `MacVim` or `gVim`, and vim-anywhere will insert the buffer contents into the original text field.

Text Editor Anywhere for Windows

Text Editor Anywhere allows you to select any text, open it in an editor of your choice, and insert the modified text back once you're done editing. Text Editor Anywhere is available for download from `https://www.listary.com/text-editor-anywhere`.

I use Text Editor Anywhere whenever I work with Windows, having it configured to open `gVim` on a selected text when *Alt* + *a* is pressed.

The following screenshot shows what it looks like:

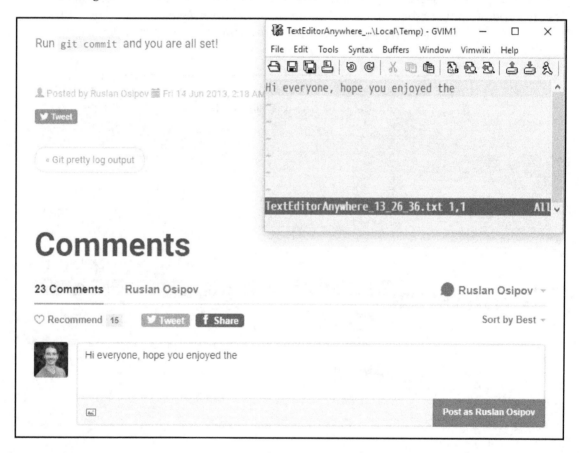

When I'm done writing, I save the buffer and quit `gVim`. Text Editor Anywhere populates the text area with the saved buffer contents.

Recommended reading and communities

This book doesn't aim to be a complete source of information about Vim, so there's a lot more to learn and explore. Depending on your preferred learning style, you might want to comb through the Vim manual by running `:help usr_toc.txt` (which can be read from beginning to the end), head to the community chat groups or mailing lists, or dive deeper into educational materials.

This section covers some possible routes you can take.

Mailing lists

Vim has a few primary mailing lists that you can browse or subscribe to. Details for each mailing list are listed at `https://www.vim.org/maillist.php`, but here are a few primary ones:

- `vim-announce@vim.org` is an official announcement channel; the archive is available at `https://groups.google.com/forum/#!forum/vim_announce`.
- `vim@vim.org` is the primary user support mailing list; the archive is available at `https://groups.google.com/forum/#!forum/vim_use`.
- `vim-dev@vim.org` is the mailing list used by Vim developers; the archive is available at `https://groups.google.com/forum/#!forum/vim_dev`.

IRC

In case you're not familiar, **IRC** stands for **Internet Relay Chat**, which is a protocol for exchanging messages. IRC is mainly used for group discussions.

A number of Vim core developers and users frequent the Vim IRC channel. At the moment of writing the #vim IRC channel on freenode.net averaged at a 1,000 users a day (not all active at once of course, as IRC has many idlers). The Vim channel is a great place to ask questions and get a general feeling for the Vim community.

You can log in through the Freenode's Web client at `https://webchat.freenode.net` or through an IRC client of your choice. Personally, I prefer using the irssi command-line client, but it takes quite a lot of tinkering to get the settings just right.

Other communities – learning resources

There are a lot more active communities on the web. Here are a few highlights:

- An active Reddit community can be found at `https://reddit.com/r/vim`
- A Vim Q&A site available at `https://vi.stackexchange.com/`
- Neovim has a very active chat on Gitter available at `https://gitter.im/neovim/neovim`
- Learning resources

Everyone learns differently, and it's very hard to recommend a resource that will work for everyone. Here are a few resources I found helpful:

- Vim Tips Wiki is a huge repository of bite-sized Vim tips: `https://vim.wikia.com`
- Vim screencasts: `http://vimcasts.org`
- Learn Vimscript the Hard Way, a fantastic in-depth Vimscript tutorial: `http://learnvimscriptthehardway.stevelosh.com`

Bram Moolenaar, the original creator of Vim, also has a personal website with a few Vim-related notes: `https://moolenaar.net`. Bram is also actively involved in a non-profit making organisation helping kids in Uganda, and you can head over to his homepage to learn more about it.

Finally, I sometimes post Vim-related snippets on my blog at `https://www.rosipov.com`. It's usually filled with unrelated articles, but you can filter to only display Vim-related posts: `https://www.rosipov.com/blog/categories/vim`.

Summary

In the final chapter of this book, we've looked at *Seven habits of effective text editing*—Bram Moolenaar's article, which primes you to detect inefficiencies in your workflow, correct them, and turn them into a habit.

We've also exposed some ways in which you can continue using Vi-like editing experience in other IDEs and text editors, web browsers (through the likes of Vimium), and everywhere else (through vim-anywhere or Text Editor Anywhere).

We've also covered some of the ways to get in touch with Vim users and developers: through mailing lists, IRC channels, Reddit, and other mediums. We've also touched on some some learning resources, including Vim Tips Wiki and Learn Vimscript the Hard Way.

Happy Vimming!

Other Books You May Enjoy

If you enjoyed this book, you may be interested in these other books by Packt:

Clean Code in Python

Mariano Anaya

ISBN: 9781788835831

- Set up tools to effectively work in a development environment
- Explore how the magic methods of Python can help us write better code
- Examine the traits of Python to create advanced object-oriented design
- Understand removal of duplicated code using decorators and descriptors
- Effectively refactor code with the help of unit tests
- Learn to implement the SOLID principles in Python

Functional Python Programming - Second Edition
Steven F. Lott

ISBN: 9781788627061

- Use Python's generator functions and generator expressions to work with collections in a non-strict (or lazy) manner
- Utilize Python library modules including itertools, functools, multiprocessing, and concurrent features to ensure efficient functional programs
- Use Python strings with object-oriented suffix notation and prefix notation
- Avoid stateful classes with families of tuples
- Design and implement decorators to create composite functions
- Use functions such as max(), min(), map(), filter(), and sorted()
- Write higher-order functions

Leave a review - let other readers know what you think

Please share your thoughts on this book with others by leaving a review on the site that you bought it from. If you purchased the book from Amazon, please leave us an honest review on this book's Amazon page. This is vital so that other potential readers can see and use your unbiased opinion to make purchasing decisions, we can understand what our customers think about our products, and our authors can see your feedback on the title that they have worked with Packt to create. It will only take a few minutes of your time, but is valuable to other potential customers, our authors, and Packt. Thank you!

Index

.

.vimrc
  used, for Vim configuring 27

A

ack
  installation link 86
arglist
  used, for performing operations across files 196
Asynchronous Lint Engine (ALE)
  about 187
  reference 187

B

buffers 52, 54
built-in autocomplete 128
built-in registers
  * register 94
  + register 94

C

classes 255
Clipboard selection 95
cmake
  download link 129
code autocomplete
  about 127
  built-in autocomplete 128
  YouCompleteMe 129
code base
  navigating, with tags 134
code testing
  about 182
  vim-test 182
color schemes, Vim UI
  about 222

  browsing 224
  issues 224
  reference 224
command-line mode 112
commands
  remapping 119
communities
  references 306
conditional statements 244
configuration files
  keeping track 230
Ctags
  reference 135
CtrlP
  reference 77
customization habits
  .vimrc, organizing 232, 234
  about 231
  workflow, organizing 231
Cygwin
  installation link 16
  using 18

D

dictionaries 249

E

EasyMotion
  about 91
  reference 89
ex mod 113

F

file trees
  CtrlP 77
  navigating 70

NERDTree 73
Netrw 70
set wildmenu option 72
Vinegar 75
file-related commands 261
files
swap files 34
filter function 257, 259
folds
about 66
types 69
freenode IRC
reference 305
functions 253

G

Git
branches, creating 152, 153
branches, merging 152, 153
files, adding 149, 151
files, committing 149, 151
files, pushing 150, 152
integrating, with Vim (vim-fugitive) 154, 157, 158
reference 146
working with 149
graphical user interface (GUI) 26
graphical version of Vim (gVim)
about 15
Visual Vim, using with 21
Gundo 139, 142

H

help command
used, for reading Vim manual 44, 46, 48
Homebrew
installation link 9

I

insert mode
about 114
simple edits, performing 40, 43
Internet Relay Chat (IRC) 305

L

Lambda expressions 256
leader key 121
linters
used, for syntax checking code 183
using, with Vim 183
Linux
Vim installation, setting up 7
lists 246, 248
llvm
reference 130
location list 180
loops 250, 253

M

MacOS
Vim installation, setting up 9
macros
editing 214, 215
executing, across multiple files 218
playing 207, 208, 211, 213
recording 207, 208, 211, 213
recursive macros 215
magic mode 201
mailing lists
references 305
map function 257, 259
modal interfaces 6, 298
modes
command-line mode 112
ex modes 112
exploring 112
insert mode 114
normal mode 112
remappingccommands 120
replace mode 116
select mode 114
terminal mode 117
virtual replace mode 116
visual mode 114

N

Neovim
checkhealth, executing 288, 289

configuring 286, 288
installing 286, 288
plugin highlights 294, 295
sane defaults 290
NERDTree
  about 73, 75
  reference 50, 73
Netrw 70, 72
no magic mode 201
normal mode 112

O

Oni
  about 291, 294
  reference link 291, 294
output
  surfacing 243

P

papercolor-theme
  reference 223
Pathogen
  about 106
  reference 106
PEP8
  reference 183
persistent repeat 43
persistent undo
  performing 43
plugins
  basics 268, 271, 273
  building 267
  configuring 122, 126
  distributing 281
  housekeeping 273, 275
  improving 276, 278, 281
  installing 50
  layout 267
  managing 98
  Pathogen 106
  plugin management alternatives 102
  profiling 106
  solution, implementing 104
  specific actions, profiling 108, 111
  startup, profiling 106

used, for performing job 218
vim-plug 98
visual selection support, adding 282
Vundle 102
prompts 261, 265, 266
Python code
  folding 67, 68

Q

quickfix list
  using 177, 179

R

regex
  alternation and grouping 199
  basics 198
  quantifiers or multis 200
  special characters 198
registers
  origin 93
  used, for copying text 91
  used, for pasting text 91
regular expressions
  class, renaming 202, 204
  files operations, using arglist 196
  function arguments, reordering 204, 206
  method, renaming 202, 204
  used, for replacing 192, 195
  used, for searching 191, 193, 195
  using 202
  variable, renaming 202

S

screen 167, 174
select mode 114, 115
status line, Vim UI
  airline 228
  powerline 226
style guides
  about 266
  reference 266
Syntastic
  about 185
  reference 185
syntax

learning 241

T

tabs 65
tags
    automatic updation 139
    used, for code navigation 134
terminal mode 167, 174, 176, 177
text editing
    best practices 297
    reference 297
Text Editor Anywhere
    reference 304
    using, for Windows 304
text navigation
    about 78, 81
    ack option, using 86
    EasyMotion 89
    insert mode, entering into 82
    searching, across files 84
    searching, with / and ? option 82
    text objects, utilizing 87
tmux
    and Vim splits 172
    multiple panes 168
    reference 167
    sessions, creating 172
    windows, as tabs 171

U

undo tree
    about 139, 142
    reference 139
unimpaired
    reference 54

V

Vanilla Vim
    versus gVim 26
variables
    setting 241
Version Control Systems (VCS) 146
version control
    commits 147
    existing repository, cloning 149

implementing 146
    new project, setting up 147
    working with 146
very magic mode 202
Vi improved 9
Vim installation
    about 7
    setting up, on MacOS 9
    setting, up on Linux 7
    troubleshooting 24
    verifying 24
Vim UI
    color schemes 222
    gVim-specific configuration 229
    playing 221
    status line 225
Vim, installation on MacOS
    .dmg image 15
    .dmg image, downloading 13
    about 9
    Homebrew, using 9, 12
Vim, installation on Windows
    ggVim, installing 15
Vim, setting up on Windows
    Cygwin, using 15
    using, with gVim 21
vim-anywhere
    alternatives 302
    using 303
    using, for Linux 303
    using, for macOS 303
vim-dispatch plugin
    about 181
    reference 181
vim-fugitive
    reference 154
Vim-like web browsing experience 299
vim-mode-plus plugin
    reference 298
vim-plug
    about 98, 101
    reference 99
vim-test plugin
    reference 182
vim-tmux-navigator plugin

reference 173
vim-unimpaired
  working with 55
Vim
  building 177
  code, building 180
  configuring, with .vimrc 27
  content, navigating 36, 38
  customization habits 231
  existing, operations 29
  files, closing 33
  files, opening 29
  files, saving 33
  interacting with 260
  manual, reading with help command 44, 47
  need for 285
  references 305
  testing 177
  text, changing 31
vimdiff
  git config 163
  merge conflict, creating 163
  merge conflict, resolving 164, 166
  used, for comparing two files 158, 161, 162
  used, for resolving conflicts 158
  using, as Git merge tool 162
Vimscript
  about 238, 282
  executing 238, 239, 241
  Help. using 266
  reference 282, 306

Vinegar
  about 75
  reference 76
visual mode 114
Vrapper
  reference 298
Vundle
  about 102
  reference 102

W

windows
  creating 55, 58
  deleting 55, 58
  moving 58, 62, 63
  navigating 55, 58
  resizing 64
workspace
  buffers 52, 54
  folds 66
  organizing 51
  tabs 65
  unimpaired 54
  windows 55

Y

YouCompleteMe
  about 129
  installation 129
  using 131, 133

CPSIA information can be obtained
at www.ICGtesting.com
Printed in the USA
LVHW100033010819
626119LV00004B/78/P